Indian Armed Forces

Socio-Legal Perspective

Indian Armed Forces Socio-Legal Perspective

Wg Cdr U C Jha (Retd)

(Established 1870)

Published in association with
United Service Institution of India
New Delhi

Vij Books India Pvt Ltd
21 Ansari Road, Daryaganj, New Delhi

Published by

Vij Books India Pvt Ltd
(Publishers, Distributors & Importers)
4675-A, 21 Ansari Road
New Delhi - 110002
Phones: 91-11-43596460, 91-11- 65449971
Fax: 91-11-30126465
e-mail : vijbooks@rediffmail.com

ISBN: 978-93-80177-22-9

Contents

Foreword

The United Service Institution of India (USI) was established in 1870. A special feature of the Institution is that it organises talks/discussions on the subjects of varied military interest on a regular basis. This book contains updated texts of eight talks delivered by Wg Cdr UC Jha (Retd) at the USI. In addition the texts of presentations made before the Parliamentary Standing Committee on Defence and other academic institutions have also been included in the book.

The subjects with which the author has grappled with in the book are varied and cover a wide spectrum of legal issues affecting the Armed Forces in India. There is a continued need of good governance in the Armed Forces. Although an imprecise concept, the principles of good governance include rule of law, transparency, participation, responsiveness and accountability, besides others. Good governance requires fair legal framework that are impartially enforced and that the human rights are given full protection. We must constantly adjust our focus and refine our applications of legal rules, especially with the changing international and constitutional norms.

In India, literature on the socio-legal aspects of military is limited and little research has been done. Wg Cdr Jha has critically examined these issues and has made various suggestions for bringing reforms in the system. This book is a scholarly work of merit and would make a distinctive contribution to our knowledge of military legal system. It should prove to be useful to the policy makers of the Armed Forces, unit officers, formation commanders, legal professionals and the public in general.

New Delhi
31 Mar 2010

Lt Gen Milan L Naidu
PVSM, AVSM, YSM (Retd)
Member Armed Forces
Tribunal, Delhi and former
Vice Chief of Army Staff

Preface

A large number of Indians, serving as well as retired members of the three Services, have a stake in the social and legal aspects of the military. Notwithstanding the importance, critical studies on military matters are rare in India. This book containing 12 chapters, is an attempt to collate various socio-legal issues affecting the armed forces in India. The first chapter on military criminal law is introductory, and makes a critical analysis of the military legal system in India. The chapter is an updated version of a talk delivered at the United Service Institution (USI) of India, on 18 January 2006. A shorter version of the text was published in the USI Journal Vol. CXXXVI, No. 564, April-June 2006.

In India, the rights of Armed Forces personnel are restricted by Article 33 of the Constitution. While curtailing some of their civil liberties, the State has given Armed Forces personnel the right to make complaints in order to seek the redress of their grievances. However, at times the unjust processing of grievance petitions damages the effectiveness of their statutory right. Chapter II deals with the system of redress of grievance in the armed forces, its shortcomings and various measures that can be taken to make the system more effective. The text of the chapter is based on a talk delivered at USI on 27 January 2009.

Until August 2009, there was no independent adjudicatory forum for hearing complaints of Armed Forces personnel relating to service matters and appeals against the judgments of courts-martial. This prompted a large number of Armed Forces personnel to go to the higher courts for relief under their writ jurisdiction. The Ministry of Defence, therefore, proposed to enact a new legislation by constituting an Armed Forces Tribunal for members of the three Services. The Armed Forces Tribunal Bill, 2005 was introduced in Parliament on 20 December 2005. The Speaker referred the bill to the Parliamentary Standing Committee on 23 December 2005 for examination and report. The author was invited by the Standing Committee on 13 April 20006 to express his view on the Bill. A talk on the subject was also delivered at the USI on 02 April 2008. Chapter III of this book is devoted to a detailed discussion on Amed Forces Tribunal. A shorter version of the text was published in the USI Journal Vol. CXXXVIII, No. 572, April-June 2008.

The Parliamentary Standing Committee had recommended in its Tenth Report that an expert committee be constituted to thoroughly review the three Service Acts and modify them in accordance with the norms being followed in other democratic countries. The Committee also recommended that a common disciplinary code be framed for the three Services. The author submitted a paper titled "Modernization and Unification of the Military Justice System in India" to the Standing Committee on 12 April 2006. Chapter VI of the book is an updated version of the paper. A talk on the subject was also delivered at the USI on 17 August 2006. A shorter version titled "Unification of the Army, the Navy and the Air Force Act" was published in the Journal of the USI, Vol. CXVII, No. 568, April-June 2007.

If the participants in an armed conflict violate the laws of war, they cannot obtain immunity on the grounds of acting in pursuance of orders of the State if the state in authorizing such action outside its competence under international law. The principles of command responsibility are ageless, but the international legal mechanism is new. Chapter V of the book deals with the issue of command responsibility in an armed conflict. It is based on the talk delivered at the USI on 8 August 2007. A shorter version of the text was published in the USI Journal Vol. CXXXVII, No. 570, October-December 2007.

The St. Petersburg Declaration of 1868 states that "the only legitimate object which States endeavour to accomplish during war is to weaken the military forces of the enemy". "This object", it continues, "would be exceeded by the employment of arms which uselessly aggravate the sufferings of disabled men, or render their death inevitable" and that the use of such arms would "be contrary to the laws of humanity". Chapter VI deals with the laws of weaponry, including prohibited weapons. The law relating to the development of new weapons and the need to review it has also been discussed. The text of the chapter is based on a paper presented at the workshop on International Law on 8 January 2005, held at the Amy Institute of Law, Mohali.

The International Criminal Court (ICC) was established in 2002, as a permanent tribunal to prosecute individuals for genocide, crimes against humanity, war crimes and crimes of aggression. The court came into existence on 1 July 2002 — the date its founding treaty, the Rome Statute of the International Criminal Court, came into force — and it can only prosecute crimes committed on or after that date. It may be debatable whether its creation was with bona fide motives, but the fact is that as of January 2010, only 110 States are members of the Court. However, a number of States, including the United States, India and China are critical of the Court and have not joined. Chapter VII of the book discusses the Rome Statute and the need to make the Indian military justice system compatible with the provisions of the Rome Statute. The text is based on a talk given at a seminar organized by the International Committee of the Red Cross in New Delhi on 13 January 2007.

The issue of military discipline amongst UN peacekeepers is inextricably linked with the question of uniformity in military discipline (within the UN peacekeepers) and command responsibility. Following a large number of cases of sexual exploitation by the peacekeepers in the late 1990s and early part of this decade, the UN Department of Peacekeeping Operations has made various reforms. Chapter VIII of the book discusses the legal principles governing UN intervention, divergence of disciplinary and penal practices and the system of ensuring disciplinary amongst the military troops involved in peacekeeping operations. The Chapter is based on a talk delivered at the USI on 22 May 2009.

War has always had adverse effects on the environment. Some battlefields of the First and Second World War remain unfit for cultivation or dangerous for population because of the unexploded devices (especially mines) and projectiles still embedded in the soil. The Gulf War of 1991 was perhaps the first explicitly environmental war of the modern era. Spilling of an estimated total of eight million barrels of oil and wanton explosion of 732 oil wells created a disaster that affected the entire region. Chapter IX deals with the protection of the environment during armed conflicts. It is based on the text of talk delivered at the USI on 20 January 2010. The existing legal regime for the protection of the environment—both during internal and international conflicts and need for future reforms have been discussed in this chapter.

The primary role of the Armed Forces is to defend the State and its citizens against internal and external threats. They are also bound to protect and uphold human rights and fundamental freedoms on which democratic societies are based. Chapter X deals with the subject of human rights in the context of the Armed Forces. It argues that only when the human rights and fundamental freedoms of the members of the armed forces are protected (within their institutions), will they be inclined to uphold these while carrying out their duties. The chapter is based on a talk delivered at the USI on 14 March 2007.

Sumit Ganguly, in his book *India and Counterinsurgency: Lessons Learned* (2009), writes "India has fought counterinsurgency campaigns from the mountains of its northeast provinces to the vale of Kashmir to the jungles of Sri Lanka; it has confronted insurgencies inspired by tribal desires for independence, fueled by religious zealotry, driven by Maoist extremism, and manipulated by foreign powers seeking to weaken India." Armed Forces personnel engaged in anti-insurgency operations in J&K and North-East get enhanced powers under the Armed Forces (Special Powers) Act (AFSPA). The demand for the populace affected by the AFSPA either to completely withdraw or substantively review the Act is matched by the demand for its retention by the Armed Forces. Chapter XI of the book discusses various provisions of AFSPA, the judicial interpretations of the Act, and the necessity for its continuation. It is based on a talk delivered on 14 October 2009 at North-East India Studies Programme, at Jawaharlal Nehru University.

Concerned over as many as 635 cases of suicide and 67 cases of fratricidal killings in the Armed Forces during 2003-2007, the Parliamentary Standing Committee on Defence had examined the issue of stress in the Armed Forces. The author was invited on 19 May 2008, by the Standing Committee to express his views on stress management in the Armed Forces. The text of Chapter XII is based on the presentation made before the Standing Committee.

I am grateful to Lt Gen P K Singh PVSM, AVSM (Retd), Director, United Service Institution of India, for his encouragement and consent for taking out this book as a USI publication. My sincere thanks to Ms Chandana Banerjee and Ms Medha Dubey for editorial assistance.

CHAPTER 1

MILITARY CRIMINAL LAW: AN INTRODUCTION[1]

Introduction

The British military justice system is the progenitor of the Indian military legal system. Only a few minor changes were made before the British laws were adopted by independent India. Today, the Army Act, 1950, the Air Force Act, 1950, and the Navy Act, 1957 govern the three services in India. There are a few minor differences between these three Acts. However, in this discussion the general term 'Army Act' has been used.

The object of military law is to provide for the maintenance of good order and discipline among members of the armed forces and, in certain circumstances among, others who work in a military environment. Such a provision is necessary in order to maintain the operational efficiency of an armed force. Military law also regulates certain aspects of administration—aspects which affect individual rights in spheres such as enrolment, commission, terms of service, promotion and forfeiture of and deduction from pay. Most often in practice, however, the term 'military legal system' is used with regard to disciplinary provisions rather than administrative ones.

The Army Act, 1950

The Army Act consists of ten chapters. Chapter I is preliminary, Chapter II deals with special provisions for the application of the Act, and Chapter II relates to commission, appointments and enrolment. The conditions of service are described in Chapter IV, while Chapter V lists out service

---

1 This chapter is an updated version of a talk delivered at the United Services Institution (USI) of India, New Delhi, on 18 Jan 2006.

privileges. Chapter VI sets out the various offences and Chapter VII the punishments. Chapters X, XI and XII deal with the court-martial, its procedure, and confirmation and revision of sentence respectively. Chapter VIII deals with penal deductions and Chapter IX describes arrests and related proceedings before trial. Chapter XIII relates to execution of sentences, Chapter XIV pardons, remissions and suspensions, while Chapter XV, deals with rule-making powers, under which the Army Rules, 1954, and Regulations for the Army, 1987 (revised) have been made.

The Role of Commanding Officer

In the system of military law, a commander occupies an important position. Unlike a superior in a civilian government organization, a military commander exercises discretion in deciding whether an offence should be charged and how an offender should be punished. On of the most difficult decisions facing a commander concerns the manner in which to dispose of a case. Administrative or disciplinary action may be taken against a service person who fails to meet or uphold the service's standard of conduct. The fundamental purpose of administrative or disciplinary processes is to foster and promote discipline and the type of behaviour required for the maintenance of operational effectiveness. **The commander has a number of options for the resolution of disciplinary problems. He may: (i) take no action, (ii) take administrative action, (iii) award minor punishment summarily, or (iv) recommend a court-martial.**

The commander may choose to take no action. The circumstances surrounding an event may warrant that no adverse action be taken. The preliminary inquiry might indicate that the accused is innocent, that the only evidence is inadmissible, or the commander may decide that other valid reasons exist for not prosecuting the alleged accused. The commander may initiate administrative action against a military offender. He might decide that the best disposition for the offence and offender is to take administrative rather than punitive action.

The commander may dispose of the offence summarily with a minor punishment. The trial is conducted by the commanding officer or a superior officer depending upon the rank of the accused. The maximum punishment depends on the rank of the commander imposing punishment and the rank of the service member being punished. The military accused does not have a right to appeal against the commander's decision to the next higher commander.

The commander may dispose of the case with the help of a court-martial. If he decides that the offence is serious enough to warrant trial by court-martial, he may exercise the fourth option of preferring and forwarding charges. He may choose from four potential levels of court-martial: summary, district, summary-general, or general. These courts-martial differ in the procedures, rights, and possible punishment that can be adjudged.

Administrative Action

Administrative actions include measures ranging from reproof or reprimand to dismissal from the service. Administrative action is not punitive in character; instead, it is meant to be corrective and rehabilitative. Warning, or a minor censure, may take the form of reproof and be administered verbally or in writing to the service personnel by the commanding officer or by an officer superior in command to the commanding officer. A warning is not recorded in the service documents of the person concerned.

As per customs of service, censure can be awarded to officers and junior commissioned officers (JCO) by a superior officer for an act, conduct, omission or offence of a minor nature. Censure is not awarded to a warrant officer or other ranks. The award of severe displeasure may be 'recordable' or 'non-recordable'. The authority awarding censure needs to examine the evidence of the inquiry and ensure that a prima facie case exists for issuing of a show cause notice. Reasonable opportunity must be given to the affected person whose character or military reputation is affected to reply to the show cause notice. Officers and JCOs who consider that they have been wronged by the award of censure may submit a grievance application which is processed in accordance with paragraph 364 of the Regulations for the Army.

In the armed forces, occasions may arise when it is considered risky to retain a person in service. The 'doctrine of pleasure' under Section 18 of the Army Act may be invoked when the risk apprehended may be too great. It provides that "Every person subject to this Act shall hold office during the pleasure of the President." Under Section 19 of the Army Act, the Central Government may dismiss or remove from the service any person subject to the Army Act. Dismissal or removal under Section 19 could be for reasons of serious misconduct, failure to qualify at an examination, inefficiency or physical disability. The Chief of the Army Staff (COAS), under Section 20 of the Army Act, may dismiss or remove from the service any person subject to the Army Act other than an officer. A brigade commander or equivalent commander may dismiss or remove from the service any person serving under his command, other than an officer or a junior commissioned officer. The procedure for dismissal or removal is contained in Army Rule 17. An officer, JCO or other rank who deems himself wronged by an administrative action may seek redress by submitting a statutory complaint under Sections 26 and 27 of the Army Act.

Minor Summary Punishments

Though every service offence may be dealt with by a court-martial, certain offences are deemed appropriate for summary disposal. Ordinary offences committed by junior officer, JCOs or other ranks may be disposed of in summary trials either by the commanding officer or subordinate commander of the accused. The commanding officer holds a formal investigation into the case. The accused is informed of the offence and the witnesses present depose to facts within their knowledge in support of the charge. A charge means an accusation contained in a charge-sheet. Each charge contains a statement of the offence and particulars of the act, neglect or omission constituting the offence. The charge-sheet is signed by the commanding officer of the accused.

Under the Army Act, an area commander or equivalent officer may proceed against an officer below the rank of Lieutenant Colonel, a Junior Commissioned Officer or a Warrant Officer, and award punishments of forfeiture of seniority, reprimand, stoppage or forfeiture of pay and allowances. In case an accused is awarded the punishment of forfeiture of seniority or service, he will have the right to elect to be tried by a court-martial. Similarly an officer commanding a brigade may proceed against an officer below the rank of field officer, a junior commissioned officer or a warrant officer and award reprimand and or stoppage of pay and allowances. A commanding officer can proceed against a junior commissioned officer and award him sentence of reprimand and/or stoppage of pay and allowances. However, if the commanding officer is below the rank of Colonel, he cannot award the punishment of reprimand. A commanding officer or his designated subordinate commander may proceed against a person other than an officer, junior commissioned officer or warrant officer who is charged with an offence under the Act and can award certain minor punishments.

The accused is present throughout the investigation and is at liberty to cross-examine the witnesses, call witnesses to his defence and make any statement in his defence. The commanding officer can dismiss the charge if evidence does not disclose any offence or if he considers it inexpedient to proceed with the case. The commanding officer can dispose of the charge summarily within the limits of his power. The Army Act does not specifically provide for any right of appeal against summary punishments awarded under the Act. However, if any punishment awarded in a summary trial appears to a superior officer to be illegal, unjust or excessive, he may cancel, vary or remit the punishment or make such other direction as may be appropriate in the circumstances of the case.

Court-Martial

In cases of serious offences by soldiers, or offences committed by officers or warrant officers, the commanding officer can (a) refer the case to a superior military authority, or (b) adjourn the case for the purpose of having the evidence reduced to writing, or (c) if the accused is below the rank of warrant officer, order his trial by a summary court-martial. If the commanding officer remands the case for trial by court-martial, the case is adjourned for recording a 'summary of evidence', against the accused. A 'summary of evidence' is a written statement of the evidence similar to depositions taken at a magistrate's court. Its chief purpose is to give the commanding officer, the convening officer and the accused, particulars of evidence in respect of the charge or charges. The accused is not entitled to be represented at the recording of the summary of evidence but he can cross-examine all witnesses who depose against him.

When the summary of evidence has been completed, it is considered again by the commanding officer, who can take any of the following actions. He may (a) remand the accused for trial by a court-martial, (b) refer the case to a proper superior military authority, or (c) rehear the case and either dismiss the charges or dispose of it summarily. If the accused is remanded for trial by a court-martial, the commanding officer either assembles a summary court-martial or applies to the proper military authority to convene a court-martial.

The Army and Air Force Acts provide for three common types of courts-martial: general, district, and summary general court-martial. In addition to these, the Army has a summary court-martial. The Navy Act provides for only one type of court-martial. It also caters for a disciplinary court to try offences committed during war or on active service. Only a court-martial that is properly convened and composed is authorized to render valid judgments.

A general court-martial (GCM) may be convened by the Central Government or the Chief of the Army Staff (COAS), or by any other officer empowered to do so through a warrant issued by him. A district court-martial (DCM) may be convened by an officer who has the power to convene a general court-martial, or by any officer empowered by a warrant issued by such an officer. A summary general court-martial (SGCM) can be convened by (a) an officer empowered for this purpose by an order of the Central Government or the COAS, or (b) an officer on active service, the officer commanding of the forces in the field, or any officer empowered by him in this regard; or (c) an officer commanding any detachment of the regular army on active service, when in his opinion it is not practicable, with due regard to discipline and the exigencies of the service, for a GCM to try an offence. A summary court-martial (SCM) may be held by the commanding officer of any corps, department or detachment of the regular Army to which the accused belongs. The commanding officer alone constitutes the court; however, the proceedings are attended by two other persons who may be officers, JCOs or one of either. The SCM is peculiar to the India Army.

A GCM consists of not less than five officers, each of whom has held a commission for not less than three years. The members of the court-martial must not be of a rank lower than that of the officer being tried. It is desirable that every court should consist of an uneven number of officers. A DCM consists of not less than three officers, each of whom has held a commission for not less than two years. An SGCM consists of not less than three officers.

A GCM is the highest court-martial in military law. It has the power to try any person subject to the Army Act for any offence punishable therein and award a sentence up to death. A DCM has the power to try any person subject to the Army Act other than an officer or a junior commissioned officer, for any offence made punishable therein, and to pass any sentence authorized by the Act, other than the sentences of death, transportation or imprisonment for a term exceeding two years. An SGCM has the same power as a GCM. It can try any person subject to the Army Act for any offence punishable therein, and award any sentence thereby authorized. An SCM may try any person subject to the Army Act and under the command of the officer holding the court, except an officer, JCO or a warrant officer. An SCM may pass any sentence under the Army Act except the sentence of death or imprisonment for a term exceeding one year in case the officer holding the trial is of or higher than the rank of Lieutenant Colonel, and three months, if the officer is below that rank.

The position in the Indian Air Force is similar to that in the Army, except that the provision of SCM does not exist in the Air Force. The position in the Navy is different. The Navy has only one type of court-martial in addition to the wartime disciplinary court. A court-martial in the Navy consists of not less than five and not more than nine officers. Unlike in the Army and the Air Force, where the senior-most officer of the court-martial becomes the presiding officer, in the Navy, the Presiding Officer of a court-martial always belongs to the executive branch of the Navy and is nominated by the convening authority.

The convening officer, upon receipt of application for trial by court-martial from the commanding officer, appoints the officers to form the court. He also details the prosecuting officer. A civilian can also be allowed to appear on behalf of the prosecution at a general or district court-martial, if the COAS or the convening officer declares that it is expedient. An accused may be represented at any general or district court-martial by any officer subject to the Act, and such an officer is called the 'defending officer'. An accused can also procure the services of any person of his choice. The person is called the 'friend of the accused'. The Act also permits the accused to be represented by a counsel at his own expense.

The Act provides that every general court-martial shall, and every district or summary general court-martial may be attended by a judge-advocate who either belongs to the Judge-Advocate General department or an officer approved by the Judge-Advocate General or his deputies. The Act authorizes the appointment of a judge-advocate without specifying whether he shall be a military person. In the Indian Army and the Air Force, judge-advocates have always been service officers whereas in the Navy, they have either been service officers or civilian lawyers working in the department of the Judge- Advocate General.

In a court, the finding is reached by a majority vote. A death sentence, however, cannot be passed by a general court-martial without the concurrence of at least two-thirds of the members of the court. A sentence of death cannot be passed by a summary general court-martial without the concurrence of all the members. The members of a court-martial may not be qualified in law. They discharge double functions of jury and judge and decide two distinct and separate matters. As jury they consider whether according to the evidence, the accused is 'guilty' or 'not guilty' of the charge(s). They also consider the sentence to be awarded for such an offence. The findings of the court are subject to confirmation. The finding or sentence of a general, district or summary general court-martial is not valid unless confirmed.

Punishments

The punishments authorized under the military legal system are more severe than those under the prevailing civilian criminal justice system. The basic jurisdiction for punishment is prescribed by the Act as an integral part of each offence. Though the maximum punishment is prescribed, the court-martial has the discretionary power to award punishment according to the degree of guilt of the accused. Those convicted of offences in relation to the enemy, mutiny or desertion on active service could be awarded the punishment of death or such less extreme punishment as is prescribed in the Act. All other offences are punishable either with imprisonment or cashiering, or dismissal from service or lower punishment. Cashiering is not defined in statutes, but is a form of dishonourable dismissal of officers where a person is stripped of his ranks and medals. The table of punishment includes death; transportation for life; imprisonment (rigorous or simple) up to 14 years; cashiering; dismissal from service; reduction to the ranks; forfeiture of seniority or service; reprimand; and forfeiture or stoppage of pay and allowances.

Appeal/ Review of Court-Martial Decisions

Until August 2009, there was no provision under the Army Act, for appeal against the findings and sentence of a court-martial. Article 136(2) of the Constitution provides that the Supreme Court cannot give special leave to appeal against any judgement, determination or sentence of a military court or tribunal. Similarly, Article 227 (4), debars the High Courts from entertaining appeals from the decisions of military tribunals. The absence of even one appeal with power to review the findings and punishment by a civilian court was a glaring lacuna in military law in India. The military tribunals are not, however, exempt from the Supreme Court's writ jurisdiction under Art 32 and the High Court's writ jurisdiction under Art 226.

Role of the Convening Officer

The convening officer holds an authoritative position. He is responsible for (i) making the decision to prosecute; (ii) deciding the charges against the accused; (iii) detailing the prosecutor and the court-members; (iv) appointing a judge advocate for trial (the judge advocate, the prosecutor and the court members come under his authority in the chain of command); (v) reviewing the sentence awarded by the court-martial and referring the proceedings back to the court for reconsideration (enhancing the punishment) even if an accused is acquitted by the court; (vi) considering the pre-confirmation petition of the accused; (vii) confirming or not confirming the sentence awarded by the court-martial; and (viii) considering the post-confirmation petition of the convicted person. He can also deny the service of a defence counsel on the ground of expediency.

Deficiency in the Legal System

The Army Act reflects the old system with all its inherent defects. Some of these defects are as follows:-

- **Right to Bail.** There is no provision of bail for a military person arrested on a charge. It is entirely a matter of the discretion of the commanding officer, or the superior military authority.

- **Trial in Summary Court Martial (SCM).** Trial by the SCM does not come up to the recognized standard of justice because there is no prosecutor and the court itself performs some of the functions of the prosecutor. The accused is not entitled to defend himself with the help of a counsel, or defending officer. This is in direct conflict with the safeguards provided in Article 22 of the Constitution. It also violates Article 21, as the procedure prescribed for the SCM cannot pass the test of just and fair trial. The Supreme Court and high courts have criticized the decisions of a number of SCMs as being biased, awarding excessive punishment and being violative of Article 14 of the Constitution.

- **Legal aid to Accused.** The insufficiency of legal aid to the accused during a court martial is another serious defect of the present system. The most significant is the absence of the services of an experienced legal officer as counsel for the accused. Military rules permit an accused to engage a civilian lawyer at his own expense or to be defended by a military officer known as the defending officer. In reality, very few of the accused can engage a civilian lawyer at their own expense and service officers normally detailed for the duty are inexperienced and unwilling to undertake this commitment. The infrastructure required to meet this obligation of legal aid has not been developed in the armed forces. Consequently, cases before the court martial are not adequately defended, which is in violation of the provisions of Article 22 of the Constitution.

- **Members of Court-Martial.** The court-martial is subject to considerable influence of the convening officer. A court-martial constituted under military law determines both findings and sentence. The members are neither legally qualified nor trained in the administration of justice. They are exposed to varying degrees of 'command influence' and cannot be completely independent in exercising their judgment in a trial. Invariably, the members are detailed from the command whose commander-in-chief orders the court-martial. He appoints the principal functionaries of the court martial and controls their service career. Even if he does not wish to influence the functionaries directly, they function under the 'command influence'.

- **Functioning of Judge Advocate General (JAG) Department.** The JA performs no functions, either as an advocate or as a judge. The Judge Advocate is not a judge as one in a trial by jury except in the sense that he has to maintain an entirely impartial position and his address cannot be styled as or in the nature of a direction. The department of JAG is placed under the administrative and functional control of the same executive who orders a trial by court-martial and reviews the proceedings. The officers of the JAG department are, therefore, not independent and cannot be expected to give a fair and just opinion.

- **Double Jeopardy.** The constitutional protection against double jeopardy enshrined in Article 20(2), whilst available before a court martial is not available to prevent a second trial on the same offence before a civil court. A person subject to the Air Force Act, who has once been tried and convicted or acquitted before a court-martial can be tried again on the same charge by a civil court.

- **Denial of Right to Appeal.** Until the Armed Forces Tribunal and its Benches were established in August 2009, there was no provision of appeal against the finding and sentence of a court martial. The pre-confirmation and post-confirmation remedy available under the Army Act, was an exercise on paper and took place in closed rooms where the accused had no right of personal representation. Thus, in reality, there was no right to appeal against the order of the court-martial.

The existing system of military justice is un-Indian having come to us by inheritance and some of its provisions are fundamentally intolerable. It is archaic, belonging to an age when the army was a band of mercenaries. The system was regulated by the mere power of military command rather than by the rule of law. Having undergone very little change in the last fifty years, the system remains under the control of the military commander, who exercises an almost unrestrained and unlimited discretion at every stage of a trial. It is generally said that under the Indian military justice system a soldier goes before a court-martial, not for trial but to receive punishment.

Article 33 of the Constitution

Part III of the Indian Constitution guarantees that every person (limited to citizens in some cases) shall be entitled to certain fundamental rights irrespective of race, caste, creed, sex or place of birth. These fundamental rights are rooted in the recognition of the dignity of the individual as well as the rights of groups and the rights of the society. These rights are enforceable in a court of law. In fact, the remedial right of obtaining the enforcement of these is also a guaranteed constitutional right. The executive, legislature and judiciary have been entrusted with the job of balancing the rights of the individual and the interest of the society. However, if fundamental rights are to be restricted or abrogated, keeping in mind the good of the society as a whole, it has to be done by the Constitution itself. Article 33 is an exception to the general provisions contained in Part III of the Constitution. It gives Parliament the power to modify the rights conferred by Part III in their application to armed forces personnel. Article 33 reads as:-

> 33. Parliament may, by law, determine to what extent any of the rights conferred by this Part shall, in their application to—
>
> (a) the members of the armed forces; or
>
> (b) the members of the forces charged with the maintenance of public order; or
>
> (c) persons employed in any bureau or other organization established by the State for purposes of intelligence or counter intelligence; or
>
> (d) person employed in, or in connection with the telecommunication systems set up for the purposes of any force, bureau or organization referred to in clauses (a) to (c),
>
> be restricted or abrogated so as to ensure the proper discharge of their duties and maintenance of discipline among them.

A reading of Article 33 suggests that Parliament can make a law abrogating or restricting the fundamental rights of members of the armed forces or the forces charged with the maintenance of public order only for two reasons: (i) for ensuring the proper discharge of their duties, and (ii) for the maintenance of discipline among them. However, Article 13 cl. (2) states, "The state shall not make any law which takes away or abridges the rights conferred by this part (Part III of the Constitution) and any law made in contravention of this clause shall, to the extent of the contravention, be void."

Article 33 is thus an exception to the provisions of Article 13 (2) of the Constitution. While recognizing the immutability of the fundamental rights, the Constitution has, under Article 33, provided for the suspension or modification of the fundamental rights under specific circumstances. The article applies not only to the armed forces but also to other forces such as the police and intelligence bureau. The article has given the power to abridge or abrogate the rights of the personnel covered by its provision only to the Parliament and not to the state legislature or the executive.

In pursuance of the provisions under Article 33 of the Constitution, Section 21 of the Army Act, 1950 states:-

> 21. Power to Modify certain fundamental rights in their application to persons subject to this Act. Subject to the provisions of any law for the time being in force relating to the regular army or to any branch thereof, the central government may, by notification, make rules restricting to such extent and in such manner as may be necessary the right of any person subject to this Act:
>
> (a) to be a member of, or to be associated in any way with, any trade union, or any society, institution or association or any class of societies, institutions or associations;
>
> (b) to attend or address any meeting or to take part in any demonstration organized by any body of person for any political or other purposes;
>
> (c) to communicate with the press or to publish or cause to be published any book, letter or document.

Section 21 of the Army Act, 1950 has been enacted under the authority of Article 33 of the Constitution. The restrictions imposed by the government under this rulemaking power are found in Rules 19, 20 and 21 of the Army Rules, 1954, and relate to trade union activities, joining organizations, involvement in political and non-military activities and communications to the press, publication of books, and delivery of lectures, etc.

The armed forces, entrusted with the defence of a country, need to be highly disciplined and efficient. The government has to make every effort to ensure that its armed forces are capable of guarding the frontiers of the country. The constitution makers therefore placed the need for maintaining discipline among the members of the armed forces above their fundamental rights. Article 33 does not make it obligatory for Parliament to specially adumbrate each fundamental right enshrined in Part III and specify in the law the degree to which each right is restricted or the rights that are abrogated.

Fundamental Rights: Armed Forces Personnel

The military plays an important role in nation-building and national security. Its primary role of defending the territorial integrity of the country and secondary role of aid to civil power make it a major pillar of society. However, its insulated existence in the isolation of the garrison and cantonment has screened it from the rest of the society and prevented society from acknowledging the basic rights of its personnel. There is a need for more authentic projection of the military, its traditions and style of working in independent India. There is a need also to redefine the rights and duties of military personnel in our nation since the military can no longer be looked upon as an instrument of colonial power.

An individual joining the armed forces in the 'ranks' cannot be considered to be uneducated, uncultured and indisciplined as he was by his colonial masters. The military law which was drafted after the mutiny of 1857 is no longer required to 'discipline' the troops. An Indian joining the forces is a loyal and patriotic person who is not required to be tried through an unfair and arbitrary justice system denying him the basic human rights.

Judiciary and the Armed Forces

Section 21 of the Army Act, 1950 and the rules related to it, place certain restrictions on the fundamental rights of military personnel. The high courts and the apex court are yet to agree with this simple and literal interpretation of Article 33. The only way to remove the gap between military governance under the Army Act and a reasonable interpretation of Article 33 seems to be to make suitable amendments to the Act itself. Surely it could never have been in the minds of our Constitution-makers to subject military personnel to an orthodox and colonial military justice system, which is what the Army Act is in reality. It is not up to the courts always to decide disputed questions of fact. It is up to the legislature to remove the ambiguity prevailing in this regard. As Dr. Rajendra Prasad once said, "After all, a Constitution like a machine is a lifeless thing. It acquires life because of the men who control it and operate it." The Supreme Court has, in various cases relating to military justice, described the trials as biased, arbitrary and fanciful and said that such trials by courts-martial cannot be called reasonable, fair or just. However, it has not yet declared that the military justice system is against the provisions of Article 21.

Though judicial activism in the sphere of human rights has generally steered clear of the conditions of service of military personnel as well as to the justice delivered by the courts-martial, courts-martial are regarded in legal and lay circles as the archetype of summary and arbitrary proceedings. There are glaring deficiencies in the safeguards accorded to the accused and in the attitude of those administering the military justice delivery system. For example, in the supposed interest of furthering military discipline, the convening officer may, at times, express his personal views on the guilt of the accused or the sentence that should be awarded. He sees no incompatibility between his conduct and the judicial doctrine of impartiality in the administration of criminal justice. Apart from this, an accused does not even know what principles of law the court members actually considered in determining his guilt or innocence. The justice delivery system in the armed forces is considered a part of the executive department and is, in fact, simply an instrument of the executive power for enforcing discipline.

Military Justice System in Other Democracies

The world has moved forward in the last twenty-five years, and there have been major changes in the military justice systems of other democracies.

In fact, a number of democracies have abolished military tribunals during peacetime (Austria, Finland, Norway, and Switzerland). Protection to armed forces personnel from the unrestrained and unlimited powers of the commander has been strengthened by the United Kingdom and the United States of America. The United Kingdom, after the decision of the European Court of Human Rights in the case of *Findlay* (1997) has made a number of reforms in its military justice system bringing it at par with the civilian criminal justice system. Reforms in the military justice system of some democracies are discussed herewith.

United Kingdom

Under the recent reforms in the British military justice system, the duties of the commander have been distributed among three separate bodies. An independent prosecuting authority decides whether to take a case to court-martial, an administration officer selects the court-martial panel members, and a reviewing officer justifies the decision. The UK's Armed Forces Discipline Act 2000 has also established a summary appeal court for the purpose of hearing appeals against the findings and punishments awarded by commanding officers while dealing summarily with charges. The order of trial in a Summary Appeal Court follows very closely that of the Crown Court.

The 2003 European Court of Human Rights decision *Grieves v. The United Kingdom* led to further reforms in the British military justice system. The Court remarked that Naval Judge Advocates are serving naval officers appointed by the Chief Naval Judge Advocate, who is also a naval officer. It found that the nature of a Judge Advocate's appointment and his position within a chain of command was not a strong guarantee of independence. Following the *Grieves* decision, the British Government amended the procedure for appointing Naval Judge Advocates.

The British Government has also passed the tri-service Armed Forces Act, 2006, replacing separate systems for each service by a uniform system applicable to all the services.

Canada

The Canadian military justice was reformed following challenges in the Supreme Court. The Supreme Court in *R v. Généreux* [1992] 1 S.C.R 259 concluded that the court-martial system violated the constitutional guarantee of an independent and impartial trial. The Court held that actual lack of independence need not be established. The test should be whether an informed and reasonable person would perceive the tribunal to be independent—in other words, "the legal framework governing the status of the tribunal as opposed to the actual good faith of the adjudicator".

Canadian military courts are now required to have a greater degree of institutional independence from the command structure of the armed forces. The commander has no authority to appoint judges or panel members. In cases where the accused is a non-commissioned officer, Warrant Officers are authorized to sit as members of the court-martial panel. A director of military prosecutions determines whether to pursue a case, and court members are chosen under a modified random selection process based on rank. There is a right to appeal to the Supreme Court of Canada on questions of law.

The United States

In the United States, the modern military justice system is based on the Constitution, which gives Congress the authority to "provide for the common defence", "to raise and support armies", and "to make rules for the government and regulation of the land and naval forces", and designates the President as Commander in Chief of the armed forces. It was established with a foundation resting on four authorities: the Uniform Code of Military Justice (UCMJ); the Manual for Court-Martial (MCM); a Presidential Executive Order that includes the rules for trial by court-martial; and the body of case laws developed from the courts that review military justice cases. Military members do not forfeit their constitutional rights. Like all American citizens, service members enjoy the fundamental protections of the Constitution.

The UCMJ represents a masterpiece of legislation that balances the need for good order and discipline with the constitutional rights afforded to all citizens. It provides for a single criminal code applicable to all the services and a criminal justice system containing safeguards for the soldier that go beyond the rights enjoyed by civilians. The military justice system provides checks and balances to ensure that an accused's procedural and substantive rights are protected. The military judges base their rulings on constitutional provisions, common law, Rules for the Court-Martial, and Military Rules of Evidence. These rules and procedures ensure that an accused's rights are maintained throughout the trial. The military justice system also offers the accused extraordinary access to the appeals process through a series of appellate forums: the Court of Criminal Appeals (one for each service), the Court of Appeals for the Armed Forces, and the United States Supreme Court.

The military justice system gives service members virtually all the rights and privileges afforded to citizens who face prosecution in civilian courts. In many areas, such as, the right to counsel, pre-trial investigations, discovery, sentence, post-trial process, and appeals, the military justice system offers benefits that are more favourable to the accused than those available in the civilian system.

Switzerland

Swiss military justice (MJ) is mainly governed by the 1928 Military Penal Code and the 1979 Code of Military Penal Procedure (CMPP) as amended from time to time. There are eight permanent military tribunals of first instance. Three for the French region, four in the German region, and one in Italian. There are three Military Appeal Tribunals (MAT), one per linguistic region. Each of these has a committee. The MAT decides on appeals against first instance judgements, whereas the committees decide on objections concerning disciplinary measures. At the highest level there is the Military Supreme Court (MSC). This has the same authority as the Swiss Federal Tribunal. The system is headed by the Military Attorney General (*Oberauditor*), a Brigadier who, together with the other members of the court, are appointed by the Swiss Federal Council. He holds a four-year mandate and reports to the Swiss Department of Defence. His tasks are the supervision of the correct functioning of the system and the performance of a prosecutorial role in military court proceedings.

Switzerland has ratified both the European Convention on Human Rights (ECHR) and the International Covenant on Civil and Political Rights (ICCPR) and abides by them. In keeping with Article 14 ICCPR and Articles 5-7 ECHR, and Articles 29-32 of the Swiss Constitution, several procedural rights apply in the military justice system. The principal ones are (i) the presumption of innocence; (ii) the principle of double jeopardy; (iii) the independence and impartiality of judges; (iv) the principle of legality; and (v) the right to be tried without undue delay. These rights are also reflected in the Swiss Constitution and the CMPP. An important aspect of the system is that an accused undergoes disciplinary sanctions in military prisons, so that he does not have to mix with ordinary criminals.

The Swiss military and ordinary penal codes are under revision. The aim of this revision is to reconsider the repartition of competencies of the civil and military tribunals for trying suspects of violation of international law, and to draft more specific provisions for international crimes, in order to fully implement the statute for the International Criminal Court (ICC).

Australia

In Australia, the Senate Committee evaluated the effectiveness of the military justice system and submitted a report in June 2005. Of the 40 recommendations made by the Committee, 32 were accepted. The government has created three new statutory appointments (i) Director of Military Prosecutions, a specialist prosecutor independent of the military chain of command, (ii) Registrar of Military justice, and (iii) Inspector General of Australian Defence Force (IGADF). The IGADF is to conduct internal audit and review of the military justice system independent of the ordinary chain of command; and examine and expose the failures and flaws so as to remedy the causes of any injustice.

In a significant milestone for military justice the Australian Military Court (AMC) was established in October 2007. The AMC replaces the system of individually convened trials by Court Martial or Defence Force Magistrate. The court will be a 'service tribunal' under the Defence Force Discipline Act 1982. It provides members of the Australian Defence Force with an even more transparent and impartial military justice system reflecting world's best practice. Key features of the AMC include (i) statutory appointment of legally qualified military judges, (ii) security of tenure (10 year fixed terms), (iii) remuneration set by the Commonwealth Remuneration Tribunal, (iv) mid-point promotion during tenure, (v) the necessary para-legal support to be self administering, (vi) judges to sit alone or with a jury in the case of more serious offences (military judge presiding), and (vi) appeals on conviction or punishment to the Defence Force Discipline Appeals Tribunal.

International Law

The right to a fair trial is a norm of international human rights law designed to protect individuals from the unlawful and arbitrary curtailment or deprivation of their basic rights and freedoms, the most prominent of which are the right to life and liberty. It is guaranteed under Article 14 of the ICCPR, which provides that "everyone shall be entitled to a fair and public hearing by a competent, independent and impartial tribunal established by law." Article 14 of the ICCPR, which provides for equality before the courts and for the right to a fair and public hearing contains a catalogue of "minimum procedural guarantees" for an individual undergoing a trial for criminal charges.

Rule of Law

The rule of law is the basis for any liberal political system that is characterized by a system of checks and balances and which recognizes individual rights protected by an independent judiciary. It presupposes the existence of a set of rules, drawn up in advance to determine the powers of institutions and the government, which must apply to all organs of society and every citizen. The rule of law implies that the functions of the government should be exercised in such a manner as to create conditions in which the dignity of man as an individual is upheld. It means that no man can be punished or be lawfully made to suffer in body or goods except for a distinct breach of law established in the ordinary legal manner before the ordinary courts of law. The rule of law is a part of the 'basic structure', which cannot be abrogated in the exercise of the amending power of Parliament under Article 368 of the Constitution.

The Indian military legal system falls short of the international legal standards in that it is not free from command pressure and there are chances of its being applied with discretion. An individual cannot be governed by regulations that depart from known rules or be tried by a judiciary under the influence of a higher command or have no forum to appeal against the decision of quasi-judicial authorities.

Conclusion

In conclusion, we may say that the human rights principles recognize the inherent dignity and fundamental freedoms of all members of the human family. They form the foundation of all basic freedoms, justice and peace in the world. Under Article 14 of the ICCPR, the right to a fair trial and equality before the court have been regarded as fundamental rules of law. The recognition of these principles have brought about changes in the military justice systems of the US, Canada, Australia and the UK. Even countries like China, Indonesia, New Zealand, Russia, and Thailand have procedural safeguards and appellate courts which entertain appeals against the decisions of the court-martial. But in India there are glaring deficiencies in the safeguards provided to the accused and in the attitude of those administering the military justice system. The system is considered a part of the executive department and is an instrument in the hands of the executive to enforce discipline. This, despite the fact that the Constitution of India makes a declaration that justice shall be secured for *every* citizen.

The Indian military legal system is antiquated and weighed heavily against the accused. It is a hangover from a time when the battlefield was so far removed from the normal world that the armed force needed to be self-contained. No legal system can or should operate in a vacuum, disregarding the changing norms of society. The military justice system has become outdated and the mere creation of the Armed Forces Tribunal has not made it dynamic. It requires the incorporation of fundamental protections based on international legal norms and the experiences of other democracies in the world. There is an urgent need to review the entire system in view of the reforms made in the civilian criminal justice system and the changes made by other democracies in their military justice systems. The functioning of the military justice delivery system and the need for reforms must be viewed in this context. If reforms have to be made, the new system must ensure: (i) a uniform code for all members; (ii) that the tribunal exercising military jurisdiction must be a part of the overall legal structure of the country's legal system; (iii) no control or interference by the military executive; (iv) a system that is updated at regular intervals based on the prevailing international standards; and (vi) that the acts of executives, including the award of non-judicial punishments be subject to judicial review. If the government succeeds in making military law more humane and dynamic, it will serve to reassure military personnel that they are overseen by a fair, just and impartial justice delivery system under the Indian Constitution.

CHAPTER 2

REDRESS OF GRIEVANCE[1]

Introduction

In India, the fundamental rights of armed forces personnel are restricted by Article 33 of the Constitution to ensure the proper discharge of duties and maintenance of discipline among them. They are denied the right to be members of trade unions or associations, to attend political meetings and to communicate with the press. The State has, however, bestowed on them the right to make complaints seeking the redress of their grievances. This statutory right has been accorded exclusively to armed forces personnel and is not available to the members of the para-military forces. The provision for the redress of grievances is contained in the Army Act, 1950, the Air Forces Act, 1950 and the Navy Act, 1957. The Regulations of the three services provide different procedures for the processing of complaints.

Procedure for Redress of Grievances

Chapter V of the Army Act, which deals with service privileges, makes provision for the redress of the grievances of army personnel. Section 26 of the Army Act provides that any person below the officer rank (PBOR) who deems himself wronged by any superior or other officer may complain to the commanding officer (CO) for the redress of his grievance. When the officer complained against is the officer to whom the complaint should be preferred, the aggrieved person may complain to the officer who is next in superiority to such officer. Section 27 of the Army Act provides that any

---

1 The text of this chapter is based on a talk delivered before the Parliamentary Standing Committee on Defence on 19 May 2008 and at the USI on 07 Jan 2009.

officer who deems himself wronged by his CO or any superior officer, and who on due application made to his CO does not receive the redress to which he considers himself entitled, may complain to the Central Government. Redress applications by the officers are to be addressed to the Central Government and by the PBORs to the Chief of the Army Staff (COAS).

Processing of Complaints. The Regulations for the Army, Paragraph 364, provide that the complaints may be of two kinds: statutory and non-statutory. Statutory complaints may be made under the provisions of Sections 26 and 27 of the Army Act by the following:-

(a) Any person subject to the Army Act other than an officer who deems himself wronged by any superior or other officer.

(b) Any officer who deems himself wronged by his commanding officer or any other superior officer.

(c) Any person subject to the Army Act against the decision of an authority disposing of a case under Sections 80, 83, 84 or 85, as the case may be.

(d) An officer or a JCO who deems himself wronged by the award of censure (recordable or non-recordable).

An officer has the right to complain to the Central Government, while a JCO, WO and OR can complain only to the COAS and not the Central Government. This right can be exercised only once. A second complaint to these authorities will be allowed only if fresh facts and circumstances have come to light necessitating reconsideration of the case.

Procedure for Submission and Channel to be Followed. Statutory complaints by officers are to be addressed to the Central Government, and those by JCOs, WOs and OR will be addressed to the COAS. The following channel is to be followed while forwarding a statutory complaint:

(a) Company commander or other immediate superior.

(b) Commanding officer.

(c) Brigade commander or the Sub-Area Commander.

(d) Divisional Commander or Area Commander.

(e) GOC Corps, where applicable.

(f) GOC-in-C Command.

(g) COAS.

(h) Central Government.

In order to make it easier for all intermediary formations and the Army Headquarters to closely monitor the progress of a statutory complaint, the commanding officer of the complainant shall forward an advance copy of the complaint to all the intermediary formation headquarters and the concerned branches or directorates and Complaint and Advisory Board (CAB) (in respect of officers only) at the Army Headquarters. An advance copy of complaints on discipline and vigilance ((DV) matters will not be endorsed to the CAB but only to the Army Headquarters.

The complainant must desist from writing directly to the Army Headquarters or the Central Government with regard to the progress of the case. However, if the final decision on the statutory complaint, with or without an accusation against any superior officer, is not taken within a period of 12 months or 9 months, respectively, from the date such a complaint is submitted, the complainant will have the right to represent directly to the Army Headquarters or the Central Government. The complainant needs to inform his commanding officer about his action.

Statutory complaints by officers of the Army Medical Corps (AMC) and Army Dental Corps (ADC) and by all JCOs, WOs and OR which pertain to matters relating to promotion, posting, release and discharge are processed through departmental channels. Where no departmental channel exists, the complaints will be processed through the respective staff channel.

Layout of Complaint. The format for the submission of a complaint is laid down by the Army Headquarters from time to time. Accordingly, all complaints will be submitted in a standard format prescribed by the Army Headquarters. The complainant is to ensure that the complaint is couched in respectful and proper language. A complaint containing a false statement or a false accusation would render the complainant liable for disciplinary action under the Army Act. If a complaint contains an accusation, the complainant is required to render a certificate, which will be annexed to the complaint, stating, "I undertake that any false statement or false accusation made by me in this complaint will render me liable for disciplinary action."

If the complaint contains a serious accusation against any superior officer pertaining to moral turpitude, maturity or professional competence, the next superior authority to the one against whom such an accusation has been made will take the necessary steps to conduct an investigation, as considered necessary.

Action by the Intermediary Authorities. The immediate superior authority in chain will offer his detailed paragraph-wise comments on the complaint. He will also ensure that if the conditions mentioned below are not satisfied, he will withhold the complaint to inform the next superior authority and will inform the complainant of the reasons for withholding the complaint:

(a) That the complaint is complete in all respects and is in the correct form,

(b) That the complaint is not couched in discourteous, disrespectful or improper language,

(c) That the complaint does not contain official documents and correspondence, access to which has not been sanctioned by any formal authority.

Where the complaint is withheld on any of the grounds mentioned in sub-paragraphs (a), (b) and (c) above, the date of submission of the complaint will be counted from the date of the revised complaint, if any. An intermediary authority will examine the complaint and may take any of the following actions:-

(a) Where the intermediary authorities arrive at a view, after due examination, that only a partial redress will meet the ends of justice, the same may be granted. In such cases, the intermediary authority granting such redress will further call upon the complainant to express whether he desires to withdraw the complaint, in view of the partial redress granted, within 90 days, and if he concurs it will be communicated to all concerned and the complaint proceeds.

(b) Where the intermediary authority decides to grant full redress, the complainant shall be suitably informed. The next higher authority to the authority granting such relief will be kept informed of the redress sought. Such cases will not be forwarded to the authority to whom the complaint is addressed.

(c) Where the redress prayed for is not given at all, the intermediary authority will forward the complaint, along with his comments and recommendations, through the normal channels to the authority to whom the complaint is addressed for final disposal.

Before forwarding the complaint to the next higher authority, the immediate superior authority of the aggrieved individual will endeavour to interview the complainant, if required, and make such investigations as he considers necessary. He will then forward the complaint, along with his detailed paragraph-wise comments and recommendations, to the next superior intermediary authority. While forwarding the statutory complaint to the next higher authority, the concerned formation headquarters will invariably inform the Army Headquarters about the progress of the case and also inform the complainant through his commanding officer. The paragraph-wise comments are not communicated to the complainant.

Time-Frame for Processing of Complaints. All complaints are required to be dealt with expeditiously at all levels. Where the complaint does not contain any accusation requiring investigation, it is required to reach the Army Headquarters within 135 days, including the transactions period.

Where the complaint contains an accusation requiring investigation, it must reach the Army Headquarters within 180 days

With a view to enable all intermediary formations and the Army Headquarters to closely monitor the progress of statutory complaints, all intermediary and higher authorities are to be kept informed. The statutory complaints must be accompanied by a delay report, which will be duly filled and initialled, before the complaint is forwarded to the next higher authority. Whenever a complaint is delayed for any period exceeding the stipulated time-frame, the reasons for the delay will be annexed to the delay report on a separate sheet of paper. The monitoring of statutory complaints through suitable monitoring schedules and standard operating procedures (SOPs) will be strictly enforced at all levels of the chain of command. The delay apprehended will be projected in time to ensure timely processing and finalization of the complaint. The intermediate formations and headquarters will maintain a record and watch the progress of complaints scrupulously. This includes ensuring accountability for delays and taking action against the defaulting officers.

The orders of the authority disposing of the complaint will be communicated to the complainant through normal channels. However, a copy of the orders will also be endorsed directly to the complainant by the disposing officer. This will be acknowledged by the individual directly to the authority disposing of the complaint. In addition, the formation/unit concerned will also inform the branch concerned at the Army Headquarters, in writing, that a copy of the order has been handed over to the individual. The orders of the authority need not be reasoned.

Procedure for Processing Statutory Complaints at Army Headquarters. All statutory complaints in respect of JCOs, WOs and OR are to be put up to the COAS for a final decision by the directorates concerned through the respective Principal Staff Officer (PSO) dealing with the subject on which the complaint has been made. In case the subject pertains to more than one branch, the views of the PSOs of those branches should be obtained while projecting the case to the COAS. Cases involving disciplinary matters need to be routed through the Adjutant General.

The PBOR's statutory right is exhausted after his application has been considered and a decision taken by the COAS. The Central Government is empowered to revise the decision of the COAS, but a PBOR has no statutory right to petition the government for such a revision. While relief to the petitioner may be given by the lower authority, the final rejection of the application can only be at the level of the COAS. The COAS cannot delegate this power to a subordinate authority. In the case of officers, the decision of the Central Government is final.

The statutory complaints of officers will be put up to the COAS by the respective directorate/branches at the Army Headquarters. The COAS may grant full redress to the complainant. In cases where the COAS grants partial redress and in cases where no redress has been granted, the complaint will be forwarded to the Central Government with the recommendations of the COAS. The Regulations do not provide any time-frame within which the Army Headquarters and the Central Government are bound to give the final order.

Non-Statutory Complaints. These can be made under the authority of the Army Order on subjects where the complainant considers himself wronged by an authority other than his superior officer or commanding officer and is subjects that are not covered under the Army Act, Sections 26 and 27. Non-statutory complaints will only be addressed only to the immediate superior, company commander or commanding officer, as the case may be. Such complaints will not be addressed directly to higher authorities other than those mentioned in this paragraph, nor will copies be endorsed to such authorities. These complaints are also required to be dealt with expeditiously. The provisions relating to the layout of the complaint, its language and timely processing are the same as in the case of statutory complaints.

Air Force

In the Air Force, two conditions must be satisfied before a person can complain under Section 26 or 27 of the Air Force Act. Firstly, he must deem himself to be wronged by any superior or other officer (in case of officers, by the commanding officer or any other superior officer). Secondly, the wrong must relate to his treatment as such person subject to the Air Force Act, by his superior in a matter pertaining to the service. In other words, the complainant must show that he has been denied or deprived of something to which he has the right under the air force law or procedure. For example, an NCO who has been refused compassionate leave has no right to complain under this Section unless he can produce some evidence of improper motive for the refusal of leave. Similarly, non-acceptance of an officer's request for premature retirement does not constitute a service wrong under Section 27 of the Air Force Act.

Complaints under Section 26 and 27 can be made by an individual only. A combined complaint by several persons is not permissible. Any person can complain only once in respect of any service matter. Repetitive complaints may be summarily rejected unless the applicant has brought out some new events that occurred subsequently or which came to the knowledge of the complainant subsequently.

A complaint cannot legitimately be preferred to a superior officer except in the regular course specified in paragraphs 621 and 622 of the Regulations. It is only where the immediate superior officer refuses to give a legitimate redress or unnecessarily delays forwarding the complaint that direct application can be made to a higher authority.

A person making a false accusation or false statement in a complaint under Section 26 or 27 is punishable under Section 56 (b) of the Air Force Act, but the mere fact that a complaint appears to be baseless, or even frivolous, does not render the maker liable to punishment. A person submitting a complaint in disrespectful language may be held liable for action under Section 65 of the Air Force Act.

Remedy for Aggrieved Airmen

An airman who deems himself wronged by any superior or other officer may complain to the officer under whose command or orders he is serving. When the officer complained against is the officer to whom any complaint should be preferred, the aggrieved airman may complain to such officer's next superior officer. If the airman thinks himself wronged by such superior officer, he may complain to the Chief of the Air Staff (CAS). The complaints are to be preferred in the prescribed manner, under Section 26 of the Air Force Act, as specified. Joint or collective or anonymous petitions of any kind are forbidden. Collective petitions or representations include separate petitions or representations prepared by separate airmen in consultation with each other. No notice will be taken of a representation on service matters submitted by the relatives of airmen.

Scope of the Complaint. Complaints must show that a service wrong has been done to the complainant, in that he has been deprived of a service right or privilege. An airman who has been administratively dismissed/ removed/ reduced under Section 20 of the Air Force Act has the statutory right to submit a petition under Section 26 if he considers himself aggrieved by such order. An airman may make a complaint on matters not arising from the service, but such complaints will not be deemed to have been made under Section 26 of the Air Force Act.

An application for redress, be it for a service wrong or a personal matter affecting morale and welfare, must, in the first instance, be addressed by the airman to his commanding officer and be submitted through proper channels, as given below.

(i) Section Commander.

(ii) Unit/Detachment Commander.

(iii) Station Commander.

(iv) Group Headquarters, where applicable.

(v) Command Headquarters.

(vi) Air Headquarters.

The application may be addressed to the higher authorities in cases where the officer complained against is a superior officer. The practice of bypassing the normal service channels and making direct representations to the higher authorities, except as provided, is prohibited. Advance copies of the application will not be sent to any higher authority. Airmen will render themselves liable to severe disciplinary/administrative action for any violation of these regulations.

Procedure for Processing of Complaints. Every officer receiving a complaint must make as complete an investigation into it as may be possible for giving full redress to the complainant, or when necessary, refer the complaint to a superior authority. On receipt of the application, the section commander is to investigate the case, and if possible, redress the grievance of the airman. If, however, he is unable to do so, the application, together with a report from him on the points raised in the application, will be forwarded to the unit/detachment commander and the airman concerned will be informed of the fact in writing. The application will continue to be forwarded to the next higher authority in the chain mentioned, until such time as the grievance of the airman is redressed or a final decision on the case is given by the Air Headquarters.

Complaints/ applications for redress of grievances may be addressed directly to the next higher authorities only when the commanding officer or intermediate authority refuses to give legitimate redress or there are unnecessarily delays in forwarding the complaint to the higher authorities. Under such circumstances, the complainant will inform the intermediate authority of his action.

If an aggrieved airman feels that his application has not received due consideration in a reasonable period of time, he may seek an interview with the station commander or an inspecting officer, i.e., the CAS or Air Officer Commanding-in-Chief. It is entirely at the discretion of the inspecting officer to grant or refuse the interview.

It is of the utmost importance that the applications are dealt with expeditiously, so that they to reach the authority competent to redress the grievance not later than 45 days from the date of submission. No intermediate authority will hold up the application for more than 10 days. In the event of a longer delay, a report indicating the reasons will be made to the next higher authority.

An airman's statutory right is exhausted after his application has been considered and a decision given by the CAS. The Central Government may revise any decision by the CAS under this rule but subject thereto, the decision of the CAS shall be final. The rejection of a complaint under Section 26 of the Air Force Act need not be by a speaking order, and the applicant has no right to demand that a speaking order be issued in the event of rejection of his application.

Remedy for Aggrieved Air Force Officers

An officer who deems himself wronged by his commanding officer or any superior officer and who, on due application made to his commanding officer, does not receive the redress to which he considers himself entitled, may complain to the Central Government in such manner as specified by the proper authority. Complaints made under Section 27 of the Air Force Act must show that a service wrong has been done to the complainant, in that he has been deprived of a service right or privilege. An officer may make a complaint on matters not arising from the service, but such complaints will not be deemed to have been made under Section 27 of the Act. In applications for redress of grievances, criticism of superiors should be avoided.

Channel for Processing. An officer's application is to be addressed to his commanding officer and copies of the application are not to be forwarded to the higher authorities. Complaints/ applications for the redress of a grievance may be addressed to the next higher authorities only when the commanding officer/intermediate authority refuses to give a legitimate redress or there are unnecessarily delays in forwarding the complaint to the higher authorities. Under such circumstances, the complainant will inform the intermediate authority of his action.

Processing of Complaints. On receipt of the application, the commanding officer will investigate the case and if possible, redress the grievance of the officer locally. If the commanding officer redresses the grievance, he will inform the applicant and obtain from him in writing a statement to the effect that his grievance has been redressed. If, however, the commanding officer is not in a position to redress the grievance, the application, together with a report from the command officer, will be forwarded to the next higher formation in the chain of command, and the officer concerned informed of this fact in writing.

On the receipt of the application at a higher formation, action similar to that mentioned above will be taken and the application will continue to be forwarded to the higher authority until it reaches the Air Headquarters, unless the grievance is redressed. The applicant is to be informed of the fact that his application has been forwarded to the next higher authority. After due consideration at the Air Headquarters, the officer will be informed through the normal channels as to what action has been taken on his grievance. If the officer is not satisfied with the redress granted by the Air Headquarters, his application will be forwarded to the Central Government for a decision.

If an aggrieved officer feels that his application has not received due consideration in a reasonable period of time, he may seek an interview with an inspecting officer, i.e., the CAS, Air Officer Commanding-in-Chief or Air Officer Commanding, as the case may be. It is entirely at the discretion of the inspecting officer to grant or refuse an interview.

An officer's statutory right is exhausted after his application has been considered and a decision has been given by the Central Government. The Regulations do not provide any time-frame within which the CAS and Central Government are bound to give the final order.

Redress of Grievances in the Navy

The Navy Act, 1957, provides that if an officer or sailor thinks that he has suffered personal oppression, injustice or other ill treatment at the hands of any superior officer, he may make a complaint in accordance with paragraphs 235-240 of the Regulations for the Navy, Part II. The complaint is to be forwarded to the Central Government if the complainant is not satisfied with the decision on his complaint.

Addressing of Complaint. If the complainant is a commanding officer of an Indian naval ship, his complaint shall be in writing and addressed to his immediate superior. If the complainant is an officer serving in an Indian naval ship, his complaint shall be made orally to the commanding officer, in accordance with the service custom whereby a complainant is to make an oral request to see the commanding officer for that purpose. If the complainant is an officer below the rank of Captain, such request shall be made through the Executive Officer, and if the complainant is not the Head of Department, the request shall be made in the first place to the Head of Department.

If the complainant is serving in a naval establishment not commissioned as a ship and not under the command of a commanding officer of an Indian naval ship, the complaint shall be made orally to his immediate superior. If the complainant is an officer who is not serving in a naval establishment, he shall submit his complaint to his immediate superior, either orally or in writing, as may be practicable.

If the complainant is a sailor, his complaint shall be made orally to the Commanding Officer. A request to see the Commanding Officer shall be made to the Executive Officer through the complainant's Divisional Officer and Head of Department. A sailor detached from his ship or establishment shall make his complaint to the officer under whose command he may be at the time.

Assistance to Complainant. A unique feature under the Regulations for the Navy is that if the complainant is an officer of junior rank or a sailor, he may request any officer to advise and assist him in the statement of his case at all stages. If no such request is made, it shall be the duty of the Divisional Officer, or such other officer as the Commanding Officer may detail, to give his assistance. Such officer shall inform the complainant of the rules to be observed while making a complaint.

Rules to be observed by the Complainant. The complainant shall confine himself to a statement of the facts complained of and to the alleged consequences to the complainant himself. Joint complaints by two or more persons are not allowed; each individual shall make his own complaint. It shall be an offence against good order and naval discipline to make a complaint, either oral or written, which includes a statement of fact that is untrue to the knowledge of the complainant. It shall also be an offence against good order and naval discipline to make a complaint which uses language or includes comments that are disrespectful, insubordinate or subversive of discipline, except in so far as such language or comments are necessary for an adequate statement of the facts.

Processing of Complaint. On the receipt of a complaint, the Commanding Officer or other officer is to satisfy himself that the complaint is made in accordance with the Regulations. He shall then deal with it as he deems right, and have the complainant informed of his decision. If the Commanding Officer or other officer receiving the complaint refuses or is unable to remedy the complaint, the complainant may respectfully ask that he be allowed to make his complaint in writing. On receiving such a request, the Commanding Officer or other officer shall give the complainant 24 hours to reconsider the matter. The complainant, while still having the assistance of the officer, may then address his complaint to the Commanding Officer or other officer in writing. The latter shall then forward the complaint, together with his own remarks thereon, to his next superior officer.

If the complainant is not satisfied with the decision on his complaint, or if he does not get the redress asked for within one month of the date of submission of his complaint or the date of its despatch to the next superior authority, as the case may be, he may request that his complaint be forwarded to the next superior authority and so on to the Chief of the Naval Staff, and finally to the Central Government, and all such requests shall be complied with.

In the Navy, a complainant shall be justified in appealing directly to the next superior authority if he does not receive the final reply within six months of the date of submission of his complaint. No officer or sailor can be penalized for having made a complaint in accordance with the Regulations.

Except as specifically permitted in the Navy Regulations, no officer or sailor shall make remarks on or pass criticism of the conduct or orders of his superiors which may tend to bring them into contempt. No officer shall say or do anything which, if heard or seen by or reported to those under him, might discourage them or render them dissatisfied with their condition or with the service in which they are or may be employed.

The Navy Regulations do not provide any time-frame within which the Chief of the Naval Staff and the Central Government are bound to give the final order.

Representation Affecting Conditions of Service. A sailor who wishes to make a representation affecting his welfare or who has any suggestion concerning the service is required to bring the subject to the notice of his Divisional Officer through his Divisional Petty Officer. If the representation is one with which the Divisional Officer cannot himself deal, he shall bring it to the notice of the Executive Officer (through the departmental officer, where applicable) and subsequently, if necessary, through him to the Commanding Officer, and so on to the higher authority, as the circumstances may require. It shall be the duty of every Chief Petty Officer, Petty Officer or leading sailor to keep himself informed of any cause of complaint or dissatisfaction among the sailors and to inform his Divisional Officer, so that the matter may be investigated.

The Problem

The unscrupulous processing of a grievance petition damages the effectiveness of a statutory right. Undue delays in the processing and disposal of complaints are another source of trouble. The Regulations for the Army provide that whenever the disposal of a complaint is delayed for any period exceeding the stipulated time-frame, the reasons for the delay need to be annexed. Often, the delay is justified under the pretext that the military chain of command is engaged in making investigations. There is also no fixed time-frame for the Army Headquarters or the Central

Government to give its final decision in the matter. In addition, during the processing of a complaint, the complainant is not informed about the comments of the section commander/CO and intermediate authorities on his grievance application.

All levels of the military hierarchy are entitled to seek legal advice on a complaint. However, the aggrieved person is not provided any legal help for preferring his complaint. If the grievance is against the CO or higher military authorities, the affected individual or his family may also face social seclusion and harassment. There have been allegations that those lodging complaints against their military superiors have been transferred to far-flung places, causing harassment to them and their family members.

The decision on an application is not required to be a "reasoned" order and it could be conveyed in a brief sentence, such as: "Your application has been rejected by the competent authority as being devoid of merit." Stereotyped rejection orders reinforce the doubt that complaints are treated arbitrarily and against the principles of natural justice. The Supreme Court has recently held that the failure to give reasons amounts to denial of justice. It held, "reasons are live links between the minds of the decision taker to the controversy in question and the decision or conclusion arrived at." Reasons substitute subjectivity with objectivity.

The need to give reasons for a legal decision is closely linked to the character of law. A judgement which does not give reasons may not be, but certainly appears to be, arbitrary. In case the individual affected by the decision desires to go for appeal, he must have the opportunity to study the reasons on which the original judgement was based, so as to be able to present his counter-arguments in appeal. A reasoned decision would also highlight that the authority has examined the arguments. The rejection of a grievance, in the absence of any reasoning, indicates either that the authority did not listen or that it took an arbitrary decision. A decision is arbitrary if it is not based on reasons and as such amounts to an interference with the principles of justice. The Supreme Court, in *Arunima Baruah v. Union of India* (2007) 6 SCC 120, held that access to justice is a human right. For a person who has a grievance against the state, a forum must be provided for redress. The right to a reasoned decision, therefore, may be viewed in terms of the human rights concept of access to justice.

The impersonal approach to handling grievance cases, inordinate delay in processing and harassment may cause stress and dissatisfaction among military personnel. There have been a large number of cases of suicide and fratricide in the armed forces in recent years. The core of the problem in these cases could have been an unresolved grievance. Frustration and harassment can also lead to alcohol dependence and stress-related mental disorders. In the year 2006 alone, over 550 personnel were discharged from service due to these reasons. The indirect cost of stress is very difficult to estimate. It includes such things as impaired motivation, poor maintenance of equipment, poor decision-making, poor quality of work and loss of creativity.

There has been an unusual increase in the filing of writ petitions and civil suits by military personnel, which demonstrates a gradual erosion of faith in the system of governance in the armed forces. The large number of cases that have come up before the superior civil courts in recent years shows that the grievance redress system of the defence forces has not only been moving at a very slow pace, but has also not been able to satisfy the aspirations of men in uniform. In 2005, there were more than 100,000 petitions pending in various subordinate courts and defended by the Ministry of Defence. Besides, more than 12,000 cases were pending in the high courts and the Supreme Court. The recent judgements of the high courts and the Supreme Court have found the existing system of governance 'antiquated' and 'not in consonance with the liberal spirit of the Indian Constitution'.

The Impact of the Armed Forces Tribunal

The Armed Forces Tribunal and its benches have started functioning since August 2009. The Tribunal has a wide jurisdiction in service matters, like promotions, pay and allowance, pension and other retirement benefits, tenure, including commission enrolments, confirmation, penal deductions, premature retirement and superannuation. Once the Tribunal and its benches become fully operational, cases pending before the different high courts and lower courts shall be transferred to the Tribunal. The following flawed provisions of grievance redress, could come under the scrutiny of the Tribunal.

1. Comments of Intermediate Authorities.

The complainant is not informed about the comments of the intermediate authorities on his grievance application. Recently, in the case of *Union of India v. Maj Gen Arun Roye* 2008 CWN 528, the Calcutta High Court opined: "...non-furnishing of comments of the intermediate authorities to the complainant who lodged the statutory complaint is tantamount to violation of the principles of natural justice." The Court held, "This is because the comments that are furnished by the intermediate authorities to the Central Government are essential to the complainant, so as to enable that person to know what has been commented against him/her by the said military authority while forwarding the complaint to the Government." The authorities, therefore, must convey the comments of the intermediate authorities to the complainant.

2. Timely Disposal of Grievance Applications.

There may be unnecessary delay in processing of a complaint. There is also no fixed time-frame for the services headquarters or the government to give its final decision in the matter. There have been cases where the final decision on a grievance relating to promotions has been delayed until the complainant retires.The delay in the finalization of a complaint often frustrates the complainant, leading to dissatisfaction and demoralization. The Delhi High Court in the case of *AVM MS Brar v. Union of India* CWP 2600/2002 decided in July 2002 has observed that while disposing of representation by the Air Force authorities, the petitioner has been deprived of his valuable rights, as he was not given a reasonable opportunity of hearing. The decision on the application for extension of service was given after the retirement of the petitioner. The Court imposed a penalty of Rs 50,000 on the government.

Section 21 of the Tribunal Act specifies the condition for not admitting an application unless other available remedies are exhausted under the Act/ Regulations. Applications are required to be made to the Tribunal within six months of the final order of the competent authority. An aggrieved person can approach the Tribunal if no order has been made by the competent authority within six months of the date of petition. The Regulations of the three services, therefore, need to be amended to ensure redress in less than six months.

3. Reasoned Order.

The Supreme Court, in *State of Himachal Pradesh v Manoj Kumar* 2008 (13) SCALE 82, has held that failure to give reasons amounts to denial of justice. It held,

> Reasons substitute subjectivity by objectivity. The emphasis on recording reasons is that if the decision reveals the "inscrutable face of the sphinx", it can, by its silence, render it virtually impossible for the Courts to perform their appellate function or exercise the power of judicial review in adjudging the validity of the decision. Right to reason is an indispensable part of a sound judicial system, reasons at least sufficient to indicate an application of mind to the matter before Court. Another rationale is that the affected party can know why the decision has gone against him. One of the salutary requirements of natural justice is spelling out reasons for the order made, in other words, a speaking out. The "inscrutable face of a sphinx" is ordinarily incongruous with a judicial or quasi-judicial performance.

The need of a reasoned decision could be justified on the following grounds:-

(a) In case the individual affected by the decision desires to go for appeal, he must have the opportunity to study the reasons on which the original judgement was based, so as to be able to present his counter-arguments in appeal.

(b) The need to give reasons for a legal decision is closely linked to the character of law. A judgement which does not give reasons may not be, but certainly appears to be, arbitrary.

(c) A judgement will normally have an adverse result for one of the parties. In order to make such a result acceptable, it is necessary to give convincing reasons. Without reasoning, a judgement is not justifiable.

(d) For reasons of transparency, a judgement must assure that appropriate care has been taken while determining the result, and that the outcome is not the result of improper motives.

(e) A reasoned decision would provide the necessary feedback on the views of the authority on his arguments. It would also highlight that the authority has examined the arguments.

The reason given for a judgement plays a significant role in demonstrating that the person concerned has actually been heard. The Madras High Court in *Brigadier L. Venkatachalam v. Union of India* (WP No. 3913/86, order dated 16 July 1987), has held that statutory complaint must be disposed of by a speaking order. It also held that Army Headquarters should not return the second complaint stating that it does not contain any fresh material. The High Court was of the view that the Army Headquarters is only a channel and is duty bound to forward the same for consideration of the Government. The rejection of a grievance, in the absence of any reasoning, indicates either that the authority did not listen or that it took an arbitrary decision. A decision is arbitrary if it is not based on reasons and as such, amounts to an interference with the principles of justice. The effect of a failure to provide proper reason is that the decision is unlawful.

4. Deletion of Coercive Provision.

In the Army, if a complainant has made an accusation, he/she is required to render a certificate stating, "I undertake that any false statement or false accusation made by me in this complaint will render me liable for disciplinary action." In cases of the use of abusive language, misbehaviour and sexual harassment, which may take place in private, it may not be possible for a victim to support his/her accusation with any documentary proof or witness.

Then the victim would be liable to disciplinary action based on the certificate rendered with his/her petition. This often deters the victim from seeking redress and makes the statutory right meaningless.

5. Legal Help.

All levels of the military hierarchy are entitled to seek legal advice on a complaint. However, the aggrieved person is not provided any legal help for preferring his complaint. The persons objected to may participate in disposing of the objection. It is, therefore, necessary that the affected person is provided legal help by the service for preferring his complaint.

6. Social Security.

If the grievance is against the CO or higher military authorities, the affected individual or his family may also face social seclusion and harassment. There have been allegations that those lodging complaints against their military superiors have been transferred to far-flung places, causing harassment to them and their family members. The impersonal approach in handling grievance cases, inordinate delay in processing and harassment may cause stress and dissatisfaction among the military personnel.

In the armed forces there have been 553 cases of suicides and fratricide between 2003 and 2006. Frustration and harassment due to an unresolved grievance could also lead to alcohol dependence and stress-related mental disorders. In the year 2006 alone, over 550 personnel were discharged from service due to these reasons. The indirect cost of stress is very difficult to estimate. It includes such things as impaired motivation, poor maintenance of equipment, poor decision-making, poor quality of work, and loss of creativity. The three services, therefore, must assure their personnel that the organization would not harm them for exercising their statuary right.

7. Transparency.

The Tribunal's power includes summoning the attendance of witnesses, production of documents and public records, and acceptance of evidence on affidavit. The Tribunal shall take decisions both on questions of law and the facts raised before it. It has the power to examine the decision of the service authorities on service matters from the standpoint of their justifiability and reasonableness. The service headquarters and the government must make the grievance redress system more transparent.

Grievance Redress in other Democracies

The United States

In the United States, military persons have the right to complain and request redress of grievances against (i) mistreatment by a superior; (ii) failure to act on a request (such as a request for medical attention or a request for hardship discharge); (iii) unlawful restriction of a military person's rights; (iv) violation of justice rights; (v) unlawful discrimination or sexual harassment; (vi) damage to, or improper seizure of, personal property.

There are several formal methods for requesting redress of grievances, including (i) complaints through the chain of command; (ii) correspondence with a member of Congress, (iii) an Inspector General (IG) complaint for instances of fraud, waste and abuse, (iv) an Equal Opportunity complaint for instances of discrimination or sexual harassment, (v) article 138, Uniform Code of Military Justice (UCMJ) complaint, for instances of specific abuse, discriminatory practices of a superior officer, or where the command is not following regulations; (vi) article 139, UCMJ complaint, where personal property is taken or destroyed, (vii) petitioning the Board for correction of military records to change adverse entries. Complaints made to members of Congress and the Inspector General, including Equal Opportunity complaints, are "protected communications" under the Whistleblower Protection Act. The complainant is protected to some extent from adverse actions deemed to be taken in "reprisal" for his complaint.

A complainant who desires to submit a grievance may consult a military lawyer for advice and assistance in drafting. If the commander refuses to redress the grievance, the soldier may submit the complaint, along with the commander's response, to the next superior officer, who is mandated to forward the complaint to the General Court-Martial Convening Authority (GCMCA). The superior officer may attach additional documentary evidence and comment on witnesses or evidence, but may not comment on the merits of the complaint. The GCMCA is to examine the complaint. Specific findings are to be made as to whether the act or omission complained of was in violation of law or regulation; beyond the legitimate authority of the respondent; arbitrary, capricious, or an abuse of discretion; or materially unfair. The GCMCA is required to notify the complainant of the action taken on the complaint.

Canada

Canada was the first country to establish a grievance redress system that includes an external review, separate and independent from the chain of command in the Canadian Forces. The Canadian Forces Grievance Board (CFGB) was created under the National Defence Act in 2000. Canada's military personnel are entitled to file grievances on almost any matter affecting them, including financial benefits, personnel evaluation reports, postings, medical issues, harassment or release from the Canadian Forces (CF). The complainant is required to first submit the grievance to his CO. If he is satisfied with the CO's decision, the grievance process ends there. If the complainant is not satisfied, the CO is to forward the grievance to the Grievance Board. The CFGB is mandated to review all military grievances, and submits its findings and recommendations to the Chief of Defence Staff, and also to the complainant. The CFGB consists of civilians and former military personnel who, alone or in panel, are responsible for reviewing grievances. The Board has quasi-judicial powers and can summon witnesses and compel them to give oral or written evidence. The Board can hold a public hearing to benefit the participants and serve public interest.

The United Kingdom

In the UK, a person in service, or one who has ceased to be subject to service law but thinks himself wronged in any matter relating to his service, may make a complaint under Section 334 of the Armed Forces Act 2006.

The Armed Forces (Redress of Individual Grievances) Regulations, 2007 provides three modes for redress: (i) a complaint may be lodged with the service complaint commissioner (civilian), (ii) a grievance application can be forwarded to the CO, and (iii) where a complaint has been considered by a Service Board, an officer has the right that a report on his service complaint be referred to the Sovereign.

Australia

The right to 'due process' or procedural fairness is not constitutionally guaranteed in Australia. However, at the federal level, the Administrative Decisions (Judicial Review) Act, 1977 requires that administrators observe the principle of natural justice. The administrative system also provides for an Australian Defence Forces (ADF) member to make a complaint about administrative procedures or decisions through the redress of grievance process. It is a formal procedure available only to a member of the ADF, allowing complaints to be investigated and reviewed and for wrongs to be corrected where necessary. It is accepted as a legitimate and important means of ensuring that decisions affecting members' rights, working conditions and careers are made fairly, impartially and according to law. The no bias rule requires the decision-maker to be neutral. He must act impartially, honestly and without prejudice, and be above the suspicion that he has an interest in the outcome of the matter or has prejudged it. The Australian government has recently created a statutory independent organization, called the ADF Administrative Review Board (ADFARB). The chairperson of the Board is a senior lawyer with appropriate administrative law/policy experience. The ADFARB's model of dealing with redress of grievances is similar to that of the Canadian Grievance Board.

Denmark and Germany

> In Denmark, complaints can be brought before the civil courts, as Article 63 of the Constitution guarantees the right to take any administrative question to court. In France, there is a right to complain to the Inspector General regarding personal matters, service conditions, or life in the military community. In Germany, a

soldier is entitled to complain if he thinks he has been treated unjustly by a superior. He has four options for legal remedy:-

(i) the right to complain under the Law on Complaints of Soldiers;

(ii) the right to an informal complaint;

(iii) the right to parliamentary petition; and

(iv) the right of petition to the Ombudsperson.

Need for Reform

Roskill (1964), in *The Art of Leadership*, has assigned the duties of a commander towards his subordinates. He writes: It is my belief that the Commanders should encourage their juniors to come to them with their ideas and their problems, and even with their grievances and complaints. If grievances are bottled up, discipline will suffer—probably through irresponsible talk among junior officers already condemned. Merely to be given an opportunity to state a grievance goes a long way towards eliminating it; since no responsible man will nurse a grievance after he has been brought face to face with the cause of it. Nor should the senior officer hesitate to admit error, or even to make an apology, if he feels there is justice in a complaint against himself."

The 2nd Administrative Reforms Commission Report, 2005 describes nine qualities of good governance. These are participation, rule of law, transparency, consensus orientation, equity, responsiveness, effective and efficient process, accountability and strategic vision of the leaders. The armed forces have to revamp their grievance redress process, keeping in view the principles of good governance and system of grievance redress followed in the other democracies. The recommendations are:-

1. The three services must follow a uniform policy frame-work and timeframe for the redress of grievances. The final order must be made within six months of the submission of a grievance.

2. The coercive provision contained in the Regulations for the

Army (1987), Part I, Para 364.8 needs deletion.

3. The service headquarters may consider appointing an independent body outside the military chain of command for managing complaints and grievances. This body may have former officers and other ranks as members. It can function in addition to the CO's power to redress a grievance to ensure that the processing channel is pruned.

4. The final order for the redress of grievance petition must be a reasoned one, and in case an individual desires to appeal to the tribunal, he/she must have the opportunity to study the reasons so as to be able to present counter-arguments in appeal.

5. The redress system must be made more transparent and the authorities must be held accountable for undue delay.

6. The Regulations for the Army (1987) and the Regulations for the Air Force (1964) need revision. The revised Regulations must be laid before Parliament, as required under Section 193A of the Army Act, 1950 and Section 191A of the Air Force Act, 1950.

As the armed forces constitute the most powerful weapon of the executive, their internal management and other functional systems are required to be efficient, modern and in tune with the times. Military organizations and their management have undergone a sea change the world over. It is the fundamental obligation of the State to create an efficient administrative and legal system for the armed forces that is worthy of respect and embodies the notions of justice. The existing grievance redress system needs to be strengthened further to ensure that the decisions can withstand judicial scrutiny by the Armed Forces Tribunal and the Supreme Court. The hostile environment in which the armed forces operate today demands better protection of the rights of the personnel than what was available to them two decades ago.

CHAPTER 3

ARMED FORCES TRIBUNAL[1]

Introduction

The system of administration of justice in the Armed Forces provides for submission of statutory complaints against grievances relating to service matters and pre- and post-confirmation petitions to various authorities against the findings and sentences of courts-martial. However, until August 2009, there was no independent adjudicatory forum for hearing complaints of defence personnel relating to the service matters and appeals against the judgments of courts-martial. The Supreme Court of India, while hearing the case of *Lt Col P P Singh Bedi* (1982), had emphasized the necessity for an independent appellate forum for the armed forces.

In 1983, the service headquarters were asked to examine the need for the constitution of a Court-Martial Appeals Court. The issue remained dormant and the Government did not take any action for almost two decades. The Standing Committee on Defence (20th Report) recommended to the Lok Sabha on 19 August 2003 that a special court of appeal, on the lines of those in France, Germany, Russia, Sweden and the United Kingdom, be constituted for the redress of the grievances of service personnel. The need was re-emphasized by the Law Commission in its 169th Report. Finally, on 29 September 2005, the Cabinet approved the proposal of the Ministry of Defence (the Ministry) for setting up an Armed Forces Tribunal for adjudicating service matters and appeals against the verdicts of courts-martial. The Armed Forces Tribunal Bill, 2005 (the Bill) was introduced in

---

1 The text of this chapter is based on the presentation made before the Parliamentary Standing Committee on 13 April 20006 and a talk delivered at the USI on 02 April 2008.

the Rajya Sabha/Lok Sabha on 20 December 2005 and was subsequently examined by the Parliamentary Standing Committee on Defence (the Committee). The Committee, after analysing the Bill extensively, submitted its Tenth Report on 23 May 2006.

Armed Forces Tribunal

The Armed Forces Tribunal Bill, passed by the Parliament, received the assent of the President on 25 December 2007. The Tribunal and its benches have started functioning since mid-2009. The Tribunal's Principle Bench is situated in New Delhi, while its Benches have been set up at Chandigarh, Chennai, Guwahati, Jaipur, Kochi, Kotkata, Lucknow and Mumbai. If at any time the vice-chairperson of a bench is satisfied that circumstances exist which render it necessary to have a sitting of the said bench at any place falling within its territorial jurisdiction other than the place or places at which it ordinarily sits, he may, with the previous consent of the chairperson, direct that the additional bench shall hold its sittings at any such appropriate place.

Composition. The Principal Bench of the Tribunal is headed by the Chairperson, and has judicial and administrative members. Only a former judge of the Supreme Court or a former Chief Justice of a High Court can be its chairperson. While judicial members will be serving or retired high court judges, the administrative members, drawn from the forces, would have served as Judge Advocate General for at least a year or be of rank not below Major General or equivalent. A Bench of the tribunal shall consist of one judicial and one administrative member. When a serving person is appointed as an administrative member, he shall have retired from service prior to assuming such appointment.

A. Original Jurisdiction: The Armed Forces Tribunal will have original jurisdiction over service matters. The term 'service matters' as defined in section 3 of the Act, includes (i) remuneration, allowances, pension and retirement benefits; (ii) tenure, including commission, appointment, enrolment, probation, confirmation, seniority, training, promotion, reversion, premature retirement, superannuation, termination of service and penal deductions; and (iii) summary disposal and trials where the punishment of dismissal is awarded. The punishment of dismissal in a summary trial can only be awarded by a Naval disciplinary court constituted during war or active service under the Navy Act.

The tribunal shall not have jurisdiction in matters relating to (i) order of dismissal invoking the doctrine of Presidential pleasure (ii) transfers and postings, (iii) leave; (iv) summary trials, except where the punishment is of dismissal; and (iv) summary court-martial, except where the punishment is of dismissal or imprisonment for more than three months.

A person aggrieved by an order pertaining to any service matters mentioned above, may make an application to the Tribunal accompanied by prescribed the fee and necessary documents. The Tribunal shall not admit his application unless it is satisfied that the applicant had availed himself of the remedies available to him under the Army Act, Rules or Regulations. In a case where an individual has made an application and no final order has been made by the Central Government or other authority or/and a period of six months has expired, his application will be admitted by the Tribunal.

An application is to be filed with the registrar of the bench within whose jurisdiction (i) the applicant is posted for the time being, or was last posted or attached; or (ii) where the cause of action, wholly or in part, has arisen. However, with the leave of the chairperson the application may be filed with the registrar of the principal bench and such application shall be heard and disposed of by the bench which has jurisdiction over the matter.

Retired service personnel including their dependents, heirs and successors will be authorized to approach the Tribunal in case of disputes in service matters. A person who has ceased to be in service by reason of retirement, dismissal, discharge, cashiering, release, removal, resignation or termination of service may file an application with the registrar of the bench within whose jurisdiction such a person is ordinarily residing at the time of filing the application.

Power of the Tribunal in Service Matters. The tribunal, while disposing of an application relating to a service matter, may summon and enforce the attendance of any person, require the production of any document, and may receive evidence of affidavit. While adjudicating an application under Section 14 of the Act, it shall be empowered to issue commission for the examination of witnesses or documents, or may requisition any public record or document from any office. However, this power shall be subject to the provisions of Sections 123 and 124 of the Indian Evidence Act, 1872. The tribunal may (i) review its decisions; (ii) dismiss an application for default or decide it *ex parte*; and (iii) set aside any order of dismissal of any application for default or any order passed by it *ex parte.* It shall decide both questions of law and fact. In case the tribunal dismisses an application, it will record reasons in writing.

B. Appellate Jurisdiction: The Tribunal has jurisdiction in relation to appeals against the order, findings or sentence passed by a court-martial. It shall allow an appeal against conviction by a court-martial where (a) the finding of the court-martial is legally not sustainable, or (b) the finding involves a wrong decision on a question of law; or (c) there was a material irregularity in the trial resulting in the miscarriage of justice. The Tribunal shall be empowered to dismiss the appeal where it considers that no miscarriage of justice is likely to be caused or has actually resulted to the applicant. While dismissing an appeal the tribunal shall give reasons in writing. The Tribunal shall not admit an appeal unless it is satisfied that the applicant had availed himself the remedies available under the Army Act.

The Tribunal, while disposing an appeal against the decision of a court-martial, shall be deemed to be a criminal court. It shall be empowered to (a) substitute for the findings of the court-martial, a finding of guilty for any other offence for which the offender could have been lawfully found guilty by the court-martial and pass a fresh sentence; (b) if the sentence is found to be excessive, illegal or unjust, the Tribunal may (i) remit the sentence, (ii) mitigate the punishment awarded, or (iii) commute such punishment to any lesser punishment mentioned in the Army Act; (c) enhance the sentence awarded by a court-martial; (d) release the appellant, if sentenced to imprisonment, on parole with or without conditions; (e) suspend a sentence of imprisonment; or (f) pass any other order as it may think appropriate.

Retrial. The Tribunal shall also have the power to quash a conviction and order a re-trail by court-martial. The appellant shall not be retried for an offence other than the offence for which he was convicted by the original court-martial and in respect of which his appeal is allowed. He can be retried for any offence charged in the alternative in respect of which the court-martial recorded no finding in consequence of convicting him of the first-mentioned offence.

Court of Record. The Tribunal shall be a court of record and shall have power to punish for contempt. It shall not be bound by the procedure laid down in the Code of Civil Procedure, but shall be guided by the principles of natural justice. The tribunal is empowered to grant bail to a military accused. However, an accused shall not be released if he has been charged with an offence punishable with death or imprisonment for life. A person making an application or appeal to the Tribunal may either appear in person or take the assistance of a legal practitioner of his choice to present his case before the Tribunal.

Time-frame. The Armed Forces Tribunal Act does not provide any fixed time-frame for deciding an application or appeal. Section 23 of the Tribunal Act provides that every application shall be decided "as expeditiously as possible". The Act also provides for the transfer of pending cases. Every suit or other proceeding pending before any court including a High Court before the date of establishment of the Tribunal would stand transferred to the Tribunal.

Appeal to Supreme Court. With the leave of the Tribunal, an appeal against the final decision or order of the Tribunal may be filed in the Supreme Court within 90 days of the decision of the Tribunal. However, such leave shall not be granted unless it is certified by the Tribunal that a point of law of general public importance is involved in the decision, or it appears to the Supreme Court that the point is one which ought to be considered by that Court.

Power to Punish for Contempt. The Tribunal has power to punish for its contempt. Any person who is guilty of contempt of the Tribunal by using any insulting or threatening language, or by causing any interruption or disturbance in the proceedings of the tribunal shall, on conviction, be liable to suffer imprisonment for a term which may extend to three years. For the purposes of trying an offence under this section, the provisions of Sections 14, 15, 17, 18 and 20 of the Contempt of courts Act, 1971 (70 of 1971) shall *mutatis mutandis* apply. An appeal shall lie to the Supreme Court as of right from any order or decision of the tribunal in the exercise of its jurisdiction to punish for contempt. The appeal should be filed in the Supreme Court within 60 days from the date of the order appealed against. Pending any appeal the Supreme Court may order that (a) the execution of the punishment or the order appealed against be suspended; or (b) if the appellant is in confinement, he be released on bail.

Rules

The following Rules have been made under Section 41 of the Armed Forces Tribunal Act, 2007:-

1. The Armed Forces Tribunal (Procedure) Rules, 2008.

2. The Armed Forces Tribunal (Procedure for Investigation of Misbehaviour or Incapacity of Chairperson and other Members) Rules, 2008.

3. The Armed Forces Tribunal (Procedure for Appointment of Vice-Chairperson and other Members) Rules, 2008.

4. The Armed Forces Tribunal (Financial and Administrative Powers) Rules, 2008.

5. The Armed Forces Tribunal (Salaries, Allowances and Conditions of Service of Chairperson and Members) Rules, 2009.

6. The Armed Forces Tribunal (Practice) Rules, 2009.

Appellate Forums in Other Democracies

The Indian military justice system differs greatly from the systems followed in the US, Australia, Canada, South Africa and the UK in respect of the process of review and appeal.

The United States

In the United States, the military system relating to the rights of the convicted person is in numerous ways superior to that of the civilian criminal justice system. Depending upon the type of court-martial that decided the case and the nature of the sentence, the appeal process may proceed all the way up to the United States Supreme Court. The first step in the US military's appellate process is review by the convening authority. This initial review by the convening authority is mandatory and cannot be delegated.

The convening authority may order a revision of proceedings to correct an error or omission, or any other irregularity at the trial. He cannot however change an acquittal or increase a sentence. During the initial review by the convening authority, the accused has the best opportunity for relief. If the convening authority in convinced that the evidence establishes the accused's guilt, he may approve the findings and sentence in portion or in entirety. In case he discovers any error, the convening authority may order revision of proceedings or rehearing of the case. In lieu of approving the sentence, the convening authority may suspend or commute it. He has no power to increase the sentence.

The review process may continue into the other appellate forums under the automatic appeal provisions in the UCMJ. Depending upon the type of court-martial and the sentence approved by the convening authority, there are three levels of appellate forum: the Courts of Criminal Appeals (CCA), the United States Court of Appeals for the Armed Forces (USCAAF), and the United States Supreme Court.

All courts-martial receive a post-trial review. Every trial that results in a sentence which includes a punitive discharge or confinement for a year or more is automatically reviewed at the first level of the appellate military court, the service Courts of Criminal Appeals (CCA). The accused is entitled to representation and the appellate defence counsel is provided free of charge. An accused may also hire a civilian lawyer at his or her own expense to operate alongside the military counsel.

The CCA have fact-finding powers and may review both findings of fact and law. The courts may review the record, judge the credibility of the witnesses and determine questions of controversial facts. They may (1) approve the finding and sentence, (2) set aside all or a portion of the findings or sentence and order a rehearing or dismissal, (3) order hearing on specified issues, or (4) reassess the sentence. Review by the CCA is mandatory and automatic in cases where the sentence is death, dismissal, dishonourable or bad-conduct discharge, or imprisonment for one year or more, and the right to appellate review has not been waived or an appeal has not been withdrawn. Decisions of the CCA are subject to review by the United States Court of Appeals for the Armed Forces.

The US Court of Appeals for the Armed Forces (USCAAF) is constituted under Article I of the Constitution. The court consists of five civilian judges appointed by the President, with the advice and consent of the Senate, to serve fifteen-year terms. The USCAAF has jurisdiction over all cases in which the death penalty is imposed, all cases certified by the judge advocate general for review after CCA review, and certain appeals petitioned by the accused that the court agrees to review. The court may only review questions of law. However, in several cases, the Court has treated evidentiary matters as questions of law. The Court may not reassess a sentence because that might involve fact-finding, nor suspend a court-martial sentence. If the Court determines that the lower court erred, it can remand the case for further review, or order a CCA to reassess an improper sentence. If the Court determines that the findings and sentence are not correct in law, it may direct the JAG to order a dismissal of the charges or order a rehearing. The Court's decisions are reviewable by the Supreme Court.

The review of court-martial by the Supreme Court is limited to decisions of the US Court of Appeal for the Armed Forces in: (1) cases reviewed by the USCAAF; (2) cases certified to the USCAAF by the JAG; (3) cases in which the USCAAF grants a petition for review; and (4) cases in which the USCAAF grants extra-ordinary relief on petition. Both the government and the accused may petition the Supreme Court for a writ of *certiorari* to the Supreme Court. The review of military cases by the Supreme Court is entirely discretionary.

The United Kingdom

Under the British military justice system, until it was revised in 2006, an accused found guilty by a court-martial could, within 28 days following the day on which the sentence was announced, present a petition to the defence counsel against the finding or sentence or both. The reviewing authority would review the findings and sentence passed by a court-martial as soon as practicable after the petition had been presented or at the end of the period within which the petition could have been presented. Thus, the effect was that the reviewing authority would review all findings and sentences of a court-martial whether or not a petition had been presented. However, an accused could raise any particular issues with the reviewing authority by submitting a petition drawing the reviewing authority's attention to the points, which he wished to emphasize.

The review process was a paper exercise by the reviewing authority and the accused had no right to personal representation. The reviewing authority, however, obtained legal advice from the JAG before taking any decision in the case. The advice of the JAG and reasons for the reviewer's decision were supplied to the accused in each case. The power of the reviewing authority (a non-judicial authority) to review the punishment awarded by a court-martial (a judicial body), was considered a glaring lacuna in the military justice system. In *Morris v. United Kingdom* (2002) the European Court of Human Rights held that the post-trial review of a court-martial decision impugns the court-martial itself, and there is, accordingly, a breach of Article 6 of the European Convention on Human Rights (ECHR). The Court ruled that the court-martial system was neither impartial nor independent and contravened Article 6 of the ECHR. The power of the reviewing authority to review the court-martial proceedings has been abolished under the Armed Forces Act, 2006.

In the UK, a convicted person may appeal to the Court-Martial Appeal Court (CMAC) against a finding or sentence or both awarded by a court-martial. The CMAC is part of the judiciary and therefore independent of the Government and of the Armed Forces. The court is a superior court of record and has full power to determine any question necessary to be determined for the purpose of doing justice in any case before it. Its decisions are binding on all inferior criminal courts and on all courts-martial. The Judge Advocate General may also refer cases to the CMAC on a point of law of exceptional importance. In addition, the Secretary of State may, upon consideration of matters appearing to him not to have been brought to the notice of the court-martial at the trial, request that these matters be referred to the CMAC. The Armed Forces Act, 2006 has made an additional provision for appeal to the CMAC. The Attorney General may also appeal to the CMAC in cases where unduly lenient sentence has been passed by the court-martial for an offence of criminal conduct.

Following appeal to the CMAC, a further appeal is possible to the House of Lords, but only where leave is given by the CMAC. The House of Lords acts as the final court on points of law for the whole of the United Kingdom.

Australia

The Australian military justice system contains a hierarchy of service tribunals reflecting civilian criminal standards and processes. A chief of staff may appoint officers as reviewing authorities to review disciplinary proceedings in accordance with the Act and Regulations. All service tribunals are required to forward the record of proceedings to a reviewing authority for automatic review upon the conviction of a person for a service offence. The reviewing authority must obtain a report from a legal officer to review the proceedings promptly. A review by a reviewing authority does not prevent a further review of the proceedings by a chief of staff if it appears to the chief of staff that there are sufficient grounds for a further review. For such review, the chief of staff is deemed to be a reviewing authority. However, before commencing the review, the chief of staff needs to obtain a report from the Judge Advocate General. The chief of staff is bound by any opinion on a question of law set out in the report.

Where it appears to a reviewing authority that a conviction (1) is unreasonable; or (2) is not supported by the evidence; or (3) is the result of a wrong decision on a question of law, or of mixed law and fact, and a substantial miscarriage of justice has occurred; or (4) there was an irregularity in the proceedings and that a miscarriage of justice has occurred; or (5) the conviction is unsafe or unsatisfactory; the reviewing authority must quash the conviction. Where a reviewing authority quashes a conviction and does not order a new trial, the person is acquitted.

A right of appeal against conviction by a court-martial or a Defence Force Magistrate lies initially to the Defence Force Discipline Appeal Tribunal (DFDAT), and from there, in certain circumstances, to the Federal Court of Australia, and finally to the High Court of Australia. The High Court of Australia has jurisdiction to hear and determine appeals from judgments of the Federal Court of Australia in military criminal matters. A Full Court of the High Court consisting of not less than three justices exercises the jurisdiction of the High Court to hear and determine an appeal.

South Africa

In the South African military justice system, when a military court has convicted and sentenced an accused, it must inform him of (a) the review authority to whom the record of proceedings will be submitted for review and the accused's right to submit written representations to that authority; and (b) his right to approach Court of Military Appeal for relief. This subsection implies a right to appeal to the Court of Military Appeal (CMA).

The CMA exercises full appeal and review competencies in respect of the proceedings of any case or hearing conducted before a military court. The CMA may, after due consideration of the record of the proceedings and representations submitted to it: (1) uphold the finding or the finding and the sentence; (2) refuse to uphold the finding and set the sentence aside; (3) substitute the finding with any finding which the evidence on record supports beyond a reasonable doubt and which could have been brought on the charge as a competent alternative verdict by the military court, or any other law; or (4) if it has upheld the finding, or substituted a finding, vary the sentence. This competency of the CMA is in line with the Constitution, which states that every accused person has the right to appeal to, or to be reviewed by a higher court. The High Court can exercise a supervisory jurisdiction over the military courts similar to the supervisory power it exercises over the magistrates' courts.

China

In China, the Supreme People's Court is the highest organ in the military legal system, akin to the Indian Supreme Court. The military courts of the individual services (Navy, Army and Air Force) are the highest military courts below the Supreme Court, corresponding to the higher people's courts established for provinces and autonomous regions. The Ministry of Defence names the military judges, and military courts are directly responsible to the Ministry of Defence, although they are also under the supervision of the Supreme People's Court. There is a time limit of 10 days for filing an appeal and appellate decisions are generally rendered in five days.

Canada

In Canada, the Court-Martial Appeal Board was created in 1950. It could hear appeals from courts-martial, against convictions or against the legality of sentences. There was a further possibility of appeal to the Supreme Court of Canada on matters of law, where the members of the Board were unanimous, or as of right where one member dissented. The Minister of National Defence (representing the Crown before the court-martial) had no right of appeal. In 1959, the Board was replaced with the Court-Martial Appeal Court (CMAC). The title of the head of the court was changed to that of Chief Justice of the CMAC by statute in 1984. It added a further right to appeal to the Supreme Court of Canada which could be exercised by either the accused or the Minister of National Defence, provided certain pre-conditions were satisfied. The CMAC is a superior court of record.

Further amendments were made to the National Defence Act in 1991. The Court was given full power to review the severity of sentences and to substitute new sentences. Further, the Crown, as represented by the Minister of National Defence, was given the right to appeal against both sentence and conviction. In the case of either the Crown or the individual, an appeal against sentence could be brought only with the leave of the Court. On questions of law, there is a right to appeal to the Supreme Court of Canada from the CMAC where one of the CMAC judges dissents on that question, and an appeal, with leave, if the CMAC judges are unanimous.

Armed Forces Tribunal: Critical Appraisal

The Armed Forces Tribunal Bill was introduced in the Rajya Sabha/Lok Sabha on 20 December, 2005 and was subsequently examined by the Parliamentary Standing Committee on Defence. The Standing Committee after extensive analysis of the Bill, had recommended 15 amendments. The Committee was of the view that military law should be strict enough to deal with military offences firmly and effectively to enforce discipline, but at the same time it should not be oppressive to the extent of having a demoralizing affect on defence personnel. The government, however, has not accepted most of the recommendations of the Standing Committee. Some of the important issues which may cause hardship to military personnel are as follows.

Service Matters: The Tribunal will not have any jurisdiction in matters relating to (i) transfers and postings; (ii) leave; and (iii) summary court-martial except where the punishment is of dismissal or imprisonment for more than three months. This is a serious lacuna in the Tribunal's original jurisdiction. The term 'leave' was included in the jurisdiction of the Bill. However, the Ministry of Defence approached the Committee with the apprehension that military units may be burdened with excessive litigation arising out of leave, which may affect their operational preparedness and discipline, and recommended that the issue of leave be excluded from the jurisdiction of the Tribunal. The Ministry's view that units may be burdened with excessive litigations arising out of leave is baseless and not supported by any empirical study.

Transfers and postings is another important issue that has been kept out of the purview of the Tribunal. The Committee was of the view that transfers and postings should not be kept in the purview of the Tribunal as it would affect the "operational requirements and discipline" of the forces. However, the Committee had desired that a clear-cut transfer policy should be formulated by the services. It appears that the Standing Committee erred in its conclusion on this issue. Available data reveal that out of 9365 pending cases involving armed forces personnel in various high courts, only 74 cases (0.79 per cent) relate to postings/transfers. An apprehension that armed forces personnel would rush to the Tribunal for remedy against 'transfers and postings' is not true because they have to make use of the existing remedy.

Military commanders at various levels are empowered to award minor punishments summarily to officers and personnel below the officer rank (PBORs). The Tribunal is not empowered to entertain any petition against the award of minor punishments like forfeiture of seniority or severe reprimand to officers or detention/imprisonment up to 42 days to PBOR. In the Bill, 'Summary Disposals and Trials' were kept within the purview of the Tribunal. The Ministry of Defence, however, subsequently proposed that these be kept outside the purview of the Tribunal since the punishments awarded are minor in nature. As punishments awarded under summary disposals and trials by commanding officers invariably affected the career prospects of serving personnel, the Committee recommended that summary disposals and trials must be kept within the purview of the Tribunal.

The apprehension of the Ministry that the inclusion of matters relating to postings and transfers, leave and summary disposal/trial, would lead to a large number of personnel approaching the Tribunal, would suggest the belief that the system of governance within the services in matters of postings and transfers, leave and summary trials is not just and fair. This apprehension in the minds of the military hierarchy as well as the Ministry needs expunction. The denial of the right to appeal to the Tribunal in these matters, when viewed from a different perspective, means empowering the military chain of command with the power and perception that their decisions relating to postings and transfers, leave and minor punishments, even if arbitrary, cannot be questioned. The aggrieved person would then be forced to seek remedy through the writ jurisdiction of the high courts or the Supreme Court. This would be contrary to the aims and objectives of the Tribunal.

Limited Jurisdiction in Administrative Actions. The Tribunal shall not have any jurisdiction in dismissal or removal from service at the pleasure of the President under Section 18 of the Army Act, 1950. As far as other administrative actions like reproof, displeasure, severe displeasure, dismissal, termination, removal and reduction are concerned, only two terms, 'termination of service' and 'reversion', are included in the definition of the term 'service matters' under sub-section 3 of the Act.

There appears no reason as to why other terms like 'displeasure', 'severe displeasure', 'dismissal' or 'removal' should be excluded from the 'original jurisdiction' of the tribunal. These 'administrative actions' are adverse in nature and have an impact on the career of armed forces personnel. They may affect their future appointments and promotions. The terms 'appointment' and 'promotion' are included in the definition of the term 'service matters'. In this connection, Section 33 of the Armed Forces Tribunal Act provides: "Once the Tribunal starts exercising its jurisdiction, powers and authority in relation to 'service matters' under the Act, no civil court shall be entitled to exercise any jurisdiction, power or authority in those service matters."

Section 33 does not bar the jurisdiction of the civil court in the 'service matters' which are not included in its definition under sub-section 3 of the Act. Does this mean that armed forces personnel would be forced to approach the civil courts with respect to administrative actions not included in 'service matters'? This certainly could not have been the intention of the legislators who enacted the Armed Forces Tribunal Act, 2007. Therefore, the Tribunal needs to clarify its jurisdiction in every administrative action under the definition of 'service matters'.

The Summary Court-martial (SCM). Despite being the most extensively used military procedure against personnel below the rank of junior commissioned officers, this has been excluded from the jurisdiction of the Tribunal, unless it awards imprisonment for more than three months, or dismissal. The SCM is peculiar to the Indian Army. During a period of six years, from 1999 to 2004, an average of 995 SCMs were held every year. Trials held under the SCM have been criticized by the high courts and Supreme Court for awarding excessive and harsh punishments, denying procedural rights guaranteed under Article 14 of the Constitution, lack of evidence, arbitrariness, lack of justice, and non-compliance with the Army Rules. Such an arbitrary system of justice is not followed in any other democratic country. There is an urgent need to abolish this arbitrary system of trial carried over from the era of colonial rule.

Enhancing Punishment: Section 15 (6) of the Act, giving power to the Tribunal to enhance the punishment awarded by a court-martial, is against the fundamental principles of natural justice. Such 'coercive' power to 'enhance punishment' is not exercised by the military appellate courts in other democracies. The UK Court-Martial (Appeals) Act, 1968, provides that the sentence awarded during the disposal of an appeal shall not be of greater severity. The Defence Minister's claim in the Rajya Sabha during the discussions that "the Bill is almost at par with the existing redressal machinery of countries such as the UK, France, Canada and Australia", may not be correct.

Bail: The tribunal is empowered to grant bail to a military accused. However, an accused shall not be released if he has been charged with an offence punishable with death or imprisonment for life. The power of the Tribunal in this regards is lower than that bestowed on the High Courts in India. The Committee's recommendation that the Tribunal may have discretion to grant bail to personnel charged with offences punishable with death or imprisonment for life, as is being provided by the High Courts to accused person under section 437 of Cr. PC, has been ignored by the Government. The Tribunal's power in this regard should not be against the guidelines of the Supreme Court.

Legal Aid: The Armed Forces Tribunal Act does not make any provision for legal aid. Insufficiency of legal aid would pose a serious handicap for armed forces personnel approaching the Tribunal. The question of legal aid becomes more pertinent in the context of the armed forces because the fundamental rights of those serving in the forces have been abrogated by the constitution. The democratic provision of equality before law strongly warrants the provision of legal aid for the armed forces personnel, especially below the officer rank.

Time Frame: The Act does not provide any time-frame within which the Tribunal should decide a petition. It makes a vague commitment in Section 23 (2) that every application shall be decided "as expeditiously as possible". The Standing Committee's recommendation that the Tribunal should decide every case within six months has not been accepted by the government. Since all the documentary evidence would be available with the service HQs and appellant/witnesses could be summoned without undue delay, the Tribunal must have a fixed time-frame to decide an appeal.

Judicial delay: The Act also provides for the transfer of pending cases. Every suit or other proceeding pending before any court including a High Court before the date of establishment of the Tribunal would stand transferred to the Tribunal. The pending cases relating to the armed forces in various courts are over 100,000. The Tribunal will inherit this backlog and may take about 10 years to clear it. Besides, it will also cause inconvenience to litigants who may have to travel great distances for attending their cases. An Alternate Dispute Settlement mechanism must be worked out by the Tribunal to finalize the pending cases.

Conclusion

The colonial hangover in the Indian Armed Forces has caused the military justice delivery system to remain out of step with social justice. The bulk of those who serve in the armed forces are from backward social and economic classes. Even when wronged by the decision of a court-martial or unfair administrative action, they are unable to take recourse to a civil remedy due to economic constraints. Thus, in the past, only a few cases have been referred to the superior courts. In many of these, the courts have been highly critical of the military for awarding biased and disproportionate punishments.

More than 1.4 million Indians who volunteer to serve in our armed forces deserve better. During the discussion on the Bill in the Rajya Sabha on 3 December 2007, the Defence Minister had stated: "....... I sincerely feel we are, actually, not fair to the Armed Forces. They need better care from the nation, from the Government, and from all of us." If the government takes any action to make military law more humane and dynamic, it will serve to reassure military personnel that they are overseen by a fair, just and impartial justice delivery system under the Indian Constitution.

CHAPTER 4

COMMON CODE FOR THE ARMED FORCES[1]

Introduction

Indian military law has its origin in the military law of England. In the early years of British dominion over India, a military commander's authority to punish was unfettered. The British military justice system was command-dominated. It was conceived to discipline a 'mercenary' force. The independence of India and the resultant changes necessitated the revision of the British Indian Army Act, 1911. However, no major change was made in the legal system and the Army Act, 1950, the Air Force, 1950 and the Navy Act, 1957 which governed the independent Indian armed forces were a replica of the British Act of 1911.

In 1966, the Government of India had set up a Committee consisting of officials from the Ministry of Defence and Ministry of Law, and the Judge Advocates General and Directors of Personnel of the three services for drafting a uniform code for the three services. The Committee was to analyse the difficulties being faced in operating the then military laws of the three services, and study the military codes of developed democracies. The Committee was tasked to draft a uniform code to rationalize the three service Acts, making special provisions for each service separately with due regard to their particular requirements.

The Committee completed its task of drafting a uniform code in 1977. It was vetted by the Ministry of Law in 1978 and given the shape of a Bill—

1 The text of this chapter is an updated version of paper titles "Modernization and Unification of the Military Justice System in India" submitted to the Parliamentary Standing Committee on 12 April 2006 and a talk delivered at the USI on 17 August 2006.

The Armed Forces Code Bill, 1978. The views of the Directors of Personnel of the three services were considered by the Chiefs of Staff Committee (COSC) in 1979. The COSC was of the view that:-

1. The uniform code for the three services need not be adopted.
2. The three services Acts should be amended to make them more progressive and fall in line with the law of the land and similar acts of other countries.
3. The Army and the Air Force Acts should be amended with regard to the punishments and restrictions on fundamental rights to fall in line with the Navy Act.

It was felt that since the three forces were not unified and the working problems of each was different, amendments as recommended by the Harris Committee Report (1964), be carried out in the existing Acts. The COSC rejected the adoption of a uniform code and instead recommended amendments to the existing Acts to make them more progressive individually. The above recommendations were accepted by the Central Government. The government, however, failed to introduce recommendations of Harris Committee.

Changes in the three services Acts have been made only when the provisions were in striking opposition to the civilian justice system and the military could no longer justify that the continuation of the contested provisions were needed for the maintenance of discipline. There too the changes were made in a piecemeal manner and at snail's pace. For instance few amendments introduced in the Army Act and Army Rules in 1992 and 1993.

Standing Committee's Recommendations

The Parliamentary Standing Committee on Defence, which examined the Armed Forces Tribunal Bill, 2005, had recommended that (i) an 'expert committee' be constituted urgently to thoroughly review the Army Act, 1950, the Air Force Act, 1950, and the Navy Act, 1957, to bring them at par with the norms followed in other democratic countries, and (ii) a common disciplinary code for the three services be created.

Difference in the three Service Acts

The provisions contained in the three service Acts are not similar. Some of the differences are:-

1. **Types of courts-martial:** Under the Air Force Act, only three types of courts-martial, i.e., general court-martial (GCM), district court-martial (DCM) and summary general court-martial (SGCM), have been provided. The Army Act, in addition to the above three types of courts-martial, also has summary court-martial (SCM), which can try personnel below the rank of Junior Commissioned Officer and can award punishments of dismissal and imprisonment of up to one year. However, the Navy has only one type of court-martial during peacetime and a disciplinary tribunal during war.

2. A court-martial under the Navy Act has to have the majority of its members drawn from the 'Executive Branch' of the Navy, but no such stipulation exists under the Army or the Air Force Act. Unlike the Army and Air Force, where the senior-most officer of the court-martial becomes the presiding officer, in the Navy the convening authority always nominates the president of the court-martial.

3. **Judge Advocate General (JAG):** In the Army and the Air Force the presence of a judge advocate in the district and summary general court-martial is not mandatory. In the Navy, every court-martial is required to be attended by a judge advocate. In the Army and the Air Force, the judge advocate remains present when the court deliberates on the findings, whereas in the Navy the judge advocate does not sit with the court when the court is considering the findings.

4. The proceedings of a court-martial or disciplinary court are reviewed by the JAG of the Navy either on his own motion or on application made by an aggrieved person. The JAG is to transmit

the report of the review, together with his recommendation, to the Chief of the Naval Staff (CNS) for his consideration. In the Army and the Air Force, the officers of the Department of the JAG, before confirmation, review the proceedings of courts-martial and may make recommendations. These reviews are advisory and not binding on the chief of the respective service.

5. **Finding and sentence of court-martial:** In the Navy, the findings and sentences of courts-martial do not require the confirmation of the convening authority or any superior authority and become operative the moment they are pronounced, except in the case of a sentence of death, which requires prior confirmation by the Central Government. The verdict of acquittal is final in the case of the Navy and not subject to confirmation or revision, as in the Army and the Air Force.

6. **Power of minor punishment (PBOR):** Unlike the Army and the Air Force, the commanding officer of a ship may summarily try any person belonging to the ship, other than an officer, for an offence not being a capital offence and can award imprisonment or detention of up to three months. This power of summary trial is limited in the Army and the Air Force, where punishment of up to 28 days of imprisonment/detention can be awarded to personnel below the rank of NCO.

7. Unlike the Army and the Air Force Act, the Naval law does not grant reciprocal mutual disciplinary powers to the Army and the Air Force Officers over the Naval personnel who may be, for the time-being, serving under the command of such Army/Air Force officer.

Notwithstanding these differences, the will of the chiefs of the three services, rather than the rule of law, reign supreme in the Indian military justice system.

Need for Unification

The Indian Army Act, the Air Force Act and the Navy Act differ on various safeguards available to military personnel. These Acts are unable to answer the needs of the modern soldier and are quite at odds with the liberal interpretation of the Indian Constitution. The service Acts are required to be unified due to the following reasons:-

1. Following the creation of India's tri-service Strategic Forces Command in 2001 and uniformity in the functioning of the three services at various levels, there is a need for a uniform disciplinary code for the three services. Within joint command and units, the basic principle should be that service personnel are subject to the same systems and the same rights and penalties, except where a special rule applicable only to the member of one service is essential.

2. A uniform code would be more appropriate in view of the fact that the three services are increasingly deployed on joint operations in India and abroad, for which they train together.

3. A modern and fair system of service law is as important to supporting operational effectiveness as having the best-trained and equipped forces as possible. A harmonized approach to service law would enhance operational effectiveness.

4. The law is not static and needs to be amended at regular intervals to keep pace with the changes in the international norms and domestic law of the country. The piecemeal amendments over the years have brought about a few changes, but they have not been helpful in keeping service law in line with developments in civilian law. Due to bureaucratic apathy and lack of priority given to issues of military justice, amendment to the service laws has taken inordinately long. The existence of the separate Acts makes the use, interpretation and amendment of the Acts more complicated. It would be easier to modernize and amend a common code for the services than to do so individually.

5. The Armed Forces Tribunal and its benches have started functioning since 2009. The creation of a common tribunal for the

three services necessitates that the protection of the rights available to a soldier, sailor and airman is similar under the three services. This can only be ensured by subjecting all these personnel to a common code of conduct. An appeal from a common forum to the proposed appellate tribunal would provide equality to all the members of the armed forces.

6. The ineffectiveness of the existing military justice system has led to a critical situation in which more than 12,000 petitions of serving as well as retired personnel are pending for disposal in the higher courts. The uncertainty and potential for delay in the present military justice system and the discontent associated with applying separate systems within such structures leads one to conclude that it is necessary to have a single system of law that would operate equally well in single, bi- or tri-service environments.

Unification in other Democracies

United States

There are large numbers of democracies in the world which are following a common code of discipline/justice for their armed forces. Before the adoption of the Uniform Code of Military Justice (UCMJ) on 31 May 1951, the US Army operated under the Articles of War for about 175 years. The Navy, during this period, operated under the Articles for the Government of the Navy. Under the Articles of War, military justice was a command-dominated system. The system was designed to secure obedience to the commander and to serve the commander's will. Courts-martial were not viewed as independent, but as tools to serve the commander. They did a form of justice, but it was a different justice than that afforded in civilian criminal trials. Military justice had few of the procedures and protections of civilian criminal justice, and protecting the rights of the individual was not a primary purpose of the system.

During World War II, there were over two million courts-martial. Many people from all walks of life were exposed to the military justice system, and many did not like what they saw. The system appeared harsh and arbitrary, with too few protections for the individual and too much power for the commander. There was widespread criticism of the military justice system. By 1948, the US defence infrastructure itself was reorganized with the creation of a separate Air Force, and the establishment of the Department of Defence. This led to a perceived need for greater protections for men and women serving in the armed forces, and to a desire for a common system for all the services. In 1948, the Secretary of Defence appointed a committee to draft a uniform code of military justice. A common code for the armed forces, the Uniform Code of Military Justice (UCMJ), was signed by the President on 5 May 1950.

In passing the UCMJ, Congress gave power to the President of the United States to establish military criminal procedures. The President did this by publishing the Manual for Court-Martial (MCM). The UCMJ marked a distinct, but not complete break from the past. Most significant was its acceptance of the idea that discipline cannot be maintained without justice, and that justice requires, in large measure, the adoption of civilian procedures. The Code was an effort to combine elements of two competing models: the old command-dominated military justice system and the civilian criminal justice system with its heavy emphasis on due process.

The Code underwent two major changes in 1968 and 1983. The Military Justice Act of 1968 substantially increased the independence of courts-martial and the authority of the military judiciary. It provided for military judges to preside in special as well as general courts-martial. The Military Justice Act of 1983 streamlined pre-trial and post-trial processing, and abolished the practice of having the convening authority detail judges and counsel to courts-martial. Pre-trial agreements, the rights of a suspect/accused, independence of military judges, judicial functioning of the JAG branch and appellate court review are hallmarks of the US military justice system. The UCMJ, a common code, has made an essential contribution to military justice and to the effectiveness of the US armed forces.

The United Kingdom

In the UK, the legislation for the services' disciplinary and criminal justice systems is provided in the three Service Discipline Acts; the Naval Discipline Act 1957, the Army Act 1955, and the Air Force Act 1955, collectively know as the Service Discipline Acts (SDAs). Since 1950, the SDAs have been reviewed every five years and amended piecemeal to reflect changes in civil law and the requirements of the services. In 1996 and 2000, there were some significant changes to ensure that the requirements of the European Convention on Human Rights were met.

The 1998 Strategic Defence Review (SDR) presented by the Secretary of State for Defence stated that there would be advantages from combining the three SDAs into a single Act. It stated that the differences that the Services needed to retain for operational reasons would be kept, but reduced to an absolute minimum. The SDR acknowledged the key principle that a system of service law is essential to operational effectiveness. But it concluded that there were be advantages to be gained from combining the three systems into a single Act, while recognizing that this would be a substantial and complex undertaking.

Following initial work, a Tri Service Act Team was set up in September 2001 to conduct a thorough review of the Armed Forces' discipline policies and procedures. The team comprised service and civilian legal and policy staff. The initial focus of the work was on the services' disciplinary systems. This involved a critical review of the operational requirements justifying the retention of current legislative and policy differences between the services. The Defence Select Committee of the House of Commons undertook initial pre-legislative scrutiny of the Bill on the basis of written and oral evidence.

The new legislation, in the form of the Armed Forces Bill, was introduced in Parliament on 30 November 2005. It was given royal assent in November 2006 and passed as the Armed Forces Act, 2006. The provisions came into force by the end of 2008. Some of the key areas that have been changed are:

(a) **Summary Discipline:** The power of the CO to enforce discipline through summary hearing has been retained. The main proposals include a range of harmonized powers to deal with some offences summarily. The accused now has the right to elect trial by the court-martial and appeal to the Summary Appeal Court.

(b) **Prosecutions:** A joint Service Prosecuting Authority (SPA) has replaced the current single Service Prosecuting Authorities. The SPA will continue to remain independent of the chain of command and will be staffed by lawyers from the three services. The SPA will determine whether to prosecute an offender under service law and will be responsible for conducting the prosecution at trials by court-martial.

(c) **The Court-Martial:** The ad hoc system of court-martial has been replaced with a standing court-martial. It remains the means of dealing with serious offences. The court-martial comprises a civilian judge advocate and a panel of between three or five service members, depending on the seriousness of the offence charged.

(d) **Reviewing Authority:** The reviewing authority no longer have the power to review the finding or sentence of court martial. The convicted person has a right of appeal to the Court Martial Appeal Court (CMAC).

(e) **Redress of Complaint:** Service personnel retain the statutory right to complain on any matter relating to their service. The proposals on redress are aimed at more speedy resolution of complaints through pro-active case management and the delegation of powers from the Defence Council to an empowered panel independent of the chain of command.

Canada

The Canadian military justice system is based on the military justice system of the UK. Until the *National Defence Act* first came into effect in 1950, British statutes governed military discipline in the Canadian Army and in the Royal Canadian Air Force (RCAF). Canada's *Militia Act* (1927) and *Royal Canadian Air Force Act* (1940) provided that the *Army Act* of Great Britain and the *Air Force Act* of the United Kingdom applied to the Canadian Army and the Air Force, respectively. A Canadian statute, the *Naval Service Act* (1944), dealt with naval discipline.

During and immediately after the Second World War, military justice legislation applicable to the army and air force consisted of a mixture of British and Canadian norms. This state of affairs was widely criticized. As a result, the government took up a review of Canadian military legislation. This review culminated in the passing of the National Defence Act in 1950, to govern all three branches of the armed services under the Department of National Defence.

In 1968, the Army, Navy and Air Force were brought together to form the Canadian Armed Forces or Canadian Forces. This did not have a significant impact on the military justice system since the Code of Service Discipline already applied equally to the Army, Navy and Air Force.

The military justice system is regulated through the National Defence Act, the Queen's Regulations and Orders for the Canadian Forces and other supplementary regulations. The military justice statute, the Code of Service Discipline, forms part of the National Defence Act. The military justice system applies in peacetime as well as in times of war or armed conflict, and encompasses offences committed both within Canada and abroad. The system is based on two main pillars: the summary trial and the court-martial. The rules and procedures for courts-martial are similar to those applicable to ordinary criminal trials. The Court Martial Appeal Court constitutes the second tier of jurisdiction and hears appeals against sentences handed down by courts-martial. It comprises a panel of three civilian judges from the Federal Court of Canada. The Supreme Court of Canada provides the third tier of jurisdiction.

Australia

In Australia, before federation on 1 January 1901, there were separate

State naval and military forces. These were governed by State legislation that closely followed the English system. With the federation of the various States into the Commonwealth of Australia in 1901, a statute of the Parliament of Great Britain, namely the Commonwealth of Australia Constitution Act 1900 (UK), provided Australia with a written Constitution. The Constitution specified the powers of the Australian Parliament. The Constitution granted Federal Parliament exclusive powers to make laws for the Naval and military defence of the Commonwealth. Pursuant to this power, the Federal Parliament enacted the Defence Act 1903, the Naval Defence Act 1910, and the Air Force Act 1923. Since 3 July 1985, all the three arms of the Australian Defence Force have come under the provisions of a common act, the Defence Force Discipline Act 1982.

Like the USA, Canada and the UK, Australia has also seen numerous challenges to the legal validity of its military justice systems. In the last ten years, there have been several significant parliamentary and quasi-judicial inquiries into matters related to the military justice system in Australia. These inquiries have identified, to a greater or lesser degree, shortcomings in the military justice system and its processes. Most of these inquiries made substantial recommendations for change in the areas of legislation, policy and procedure. The Defence Legislation Amendment Act, 2006 has amended the Australian Defence Force Disciple Act, 1982 in accordance with these recommendations.

South Africa

During the years 1912 to 1957 British military law was applied in the Union of South Africa. The Defence Act of 1912 was in force up to 1957 when the existing, completely new Defence Act (Act 44), was passed by Parliament. South African military law, contained in the first schedule of the Act was called the Military Discipline Code (MDC). In the 1990s, South African laws were amended and a new constitution promulgated, affecting all spheres of society including the military. On 23 April 1999, the Military Discipline Supplementary Measure Act (MDSMA), or Act 16, was passed by the Republic of South Africa. The MDSMA, read with its Rules of Procedure and the Military Discipline Code (MDC), is aimed at maintaining discipline in the armed forces in peacetime as well as during war. The MDSMA has made certain important changes in the military justice system. It has established the Court of Military Appeals with full appeal and review competencies, the Court of Senior Military Judge, and the Court of Military Judge. In addition, the commanding officers have been authorized disciplinary power over minor offences. The system of *ad hoc* military tribunals (courts-martial) has been abolished.

The experiences of countries like the United States, the UK, Canada, South Africa and Australia suggests the desirability of making the rights and duties of the members of the armed forces ascertainable by reference to a single statute. These democracies have carried out large-scale revisions of their respective military codes to bring them in line with changes in international standards and the concept of the rule of law.

Fourth Military Code

Since the three service chiefs in India could not agree on a common code, there are reports that the armed forces are now planning a "Tri-Service Act" (TSA) only for the few military establishments which have a tri-service command set-up, i.e., personnel from all the three services. It will have the same provisions and processes as the other three mother legislations—the Army Act, 1950, the Air Force Act, 1950 and the Navy Act, 1957. The Parliamentary Standing Committee in its 2nd Report submitted to Parliament on 16 December 2009, has given tacit approval to the TSA, which would be applicable in a few establishments under joint command. If accepted, the armed forces will have four outdated legislations carried from the colonial era. The defects inherent in them will create more confusion than there is already.

A Common Code

Colonel Harry Summers, Jr., in his book, *On Strategy: A Critical Analysis of Vietnam War*, said that the people, the politicians and the army—the "trinity"—must all have the will to win if war is to be successfully conducted.

Modern military men and political leaders have to develop a mind-set to think strategically. Similarly national defence strategy must have the support of the people, the politicians, and the military in order to be successful. This idea applies equally to other issues like the development of weapons, the size of our military, the employment of women in combat roles and so on. We need to address these issues at the national level and answer the question, "What type of military justice system should we have to maintain morale and discipline within the armed forces?" We can no longer leave it to the military to decide this. It has to be viewed from the perspectives of politicians and the people as well. Once the people, the politicians and the military agree on the strategic aspects of military justice, the other related issues can be evolved.

For drafting a common code, it is imperative that the government constitute an 'expert committee' headed by a Member of Parliament. Each service should detail representatives who would be responsible for providing the day-to-day link to his own service on policy matters. In addition, incorporating a member from the Ministry of Law and Justice would ensure that time is not lost in future scrutiny. The drafting of a common code has to be a time-bound task andwhere minor differences within the services should be thrashed out on a day-to-day basis.

The expert committee would be required to gather information about the discipline systems in the armed forces of other countries. It would also have to get the view of a cross- section of personnel of all ranks in the military units (including field areas) and HQ staff, and training institutions like the Defence Services Staff College, College of Defence Management and the National College of Defence on the improvements considered necessary. Other relevant factors, including the most recent operational experiences and developments in civilian law would also have to be taken into account. This could be achieved in about six months, followed by the actual drafting of the Bill, which may take another twelve months. No doubt it will be a challenging task, but if pursued earnestly, the Bill could be submitted to the Parliament within a time-frame of about 18 months. A new orientation and a greater level of activity from the government, military academic institutions and the legal fraternity would be required to achieve this goal.

The government must stop processing a fourth military legislation meant for tri-service organizations. In order to bring jointness and operational efficiency in the three services, it is necessary that every uniformed military person is governed by the same law. While modernizing our system, the issues which need consideration are: (1) independence of the judge advocate general branch; (2) provisions relating to summary general and summary court-martial—whether these could be abolished; (3) uniformity in the power of minor punishment in the three services, its applicability to higher ranks with a provision for review by judicial authority; (4) ensuring procedural rights to a suspect/accused; (5) the right to bail and legal aid to the accused, at par with the civilian system; (6) reducing the role of convening authority in the disciplinary process; (7) provision for plea-bargaining; and (8) streamlining the process of redress of complaints.

Roadblocks

The biggest roadblock could be the attitude of the military hierarchy. The military has the reputation of being encumbered by its traditions and fixed ideas. The views of Sir Basil Liddell Hart, a military thinker and a soldier, would be relevant in this context: "There was only one thing more difficult than getting a new idea into the military mind and that was getting an old idea out."

The military carries the grave responsibility of protecting nations and ideals. It has to prove itself in the extreme confusion of war, when a single error may jeopardize the existence of a country. Perhaps this is the reason why the military mind relies so heavily on time-tested methods and practised routines, whether in dealing with the immediate problems of the battlefield, the details of logistics, or the manifold difficulties of long-term planning.

Usually, a debate is held before the enactment of an Act or an amendment to it. Political parties, academics and interested parties take part in such a debate. The background information and the proceedings of discussion are available for public scrutiny. In the US, the UK, Australia, Canada and South Africa, where changes in the military justice system have been made in the recent past, the civil society has made important contributions to the development of military law. Unfortunately, in the case of India, the information relating to military law remains 'secret' and not available for public scrutiny.

Since we do not have an enlightened civil society or a lawyers' forum that could be entrusted with the task of giving inputs for the modernization of military law, military-related research institutions would have to play a greater role in bringing changes in the system. Once agreed to by the service HQs, these research institutions could undertake certain tasks, like creating awareness on the advantages of a unified system of military justice, collecting the views of retired military officials, and gathering data related to the new system.

Since its inheritance in the 1950s, no serious attempt has been made towards the modernization of the military justice system in India. Some piecemeal amendments were made as and when the civil laws underwent change. However, the law still denies service personnel certain basic rights on the pretext that Article 33 of the Constitution abrogates their fundamental rights. Political and bureaucratic insensitivity to the service conditions of military personnel has stopped us from bringing in the changes made by other democracies. Even the decisions of the higher courts against our archaic system have not been taken too seriously. The Government took almost 25 years to introduce the Armed Forces Tribunal Bill, 2005, after the landmark decision of the Supreme Court in PPS Bedi's case.

Conclusion

A fair military justice system is vital for upholding the morale and discipline of the armed forces and for retaining public confidence in the armed forces. A system that fails to protect adequately the rights of those accused of misconduct will undermine discipline just as much as a system that fails to enforce the rules and protect the law abiding. In either case, the system's failure will eat away at morale, mutual trust and respect for authority. The existing system in the three services differs on various counts and gives too much power to commanders and too little assurance of due process and fairness to service personnel to be acceptable. There is a need for a new system, which will limit command authority, and balance it with procedure established by law and judicial authority.

The unification and modernization of the Army, Navy and the Air Force Act should be undertaken keeping in view our own experiences as well as developments in other democracies in this area. We cannot insulate ourselves from the changes in the systems followed in other countries, especially because our forces are internationally recognized and are part of peacekeeping missions the world over. Therefore, there is a need to create a common code of justice which will promote discipline in the armed forces.

CHAPTER 5

COMMAND RESPONSIBILITY IN ARMED CONFLICTS[1]

Introduction

International humanitarian law (IHL) has been defined as: "International rules, established by treaties and customs, which are specifically intended to solve humanitarian problems directly arising from international or non-international armed conflicts and which, for humanitarian reasons, limit the rights of the parties to a conflict to use the methods and means of warfare of their choice or protect persons and property that are, or may be, affected by conflict." The IHL has a twofold purpose. First, it is intended to protect non-combatants, or those who are not, or never were, taking part in the fighting, and second, it limits the methods and means by which fighting is carried out. The IHL is based on treaties as well as customs of war. The Geneva laws protect those not taking direct part in hostilities. The Hague laws establish the rights and duties of those actually engaged in fighting, and limit the methods that can be employed to harm the enemy. There is some overlap between the two, and the adoption of the 1977 Additional Protocols to the Geneva Conventions ended any distinction for all practical purposes. These rules apply to armed conflicts of all kinds—whether international or non-international armed conflicts.

The fundamental principles of laws of war can be summarized as follows: (i) Attacks must be confined to military objectives, and neither civilians nor civilian property may be attacked. If there is a doubt about whether a target is a civilian or military one, it must be assumed to be civilian. (ii) An enemy who has surrendered or who cannot take part in

1 The text of this Chapter is based on a talk delivered at the USI on 8 August 2007.

fighting any longer may not be killed or wounded. (iii) The wounded and sick must be cared for by whichever party to the conflict has taken them under its control. Medical personnel and equipment are exempt from attack. (iv) Prisoners of war and civilians who are in the power of an enemy must have their rights protected. (v) There are practical constraints on the methods and means of warfare that are allowed. In particular, those which cause unnecessary losses or sufferings are illegal. (vi) Reprisals are forbidden. (vii) Unavoidable civilian casualties are acceptable, but every effort should be made to keep them to a minimum, and they should be proportionate to the military advantage expected to be gained.

Role of the Armed Forces

The principle objective of the armed forces is to fight and win wars. The highly peculiar features of the armed forces are (1) centralized command, (2) hierarchy, (3) discipline, and (4) *esprit de corps* and self-sufficiency. The centralized command structure ensures that a continuous chain of command links the very lowest echelon with the supreme headquarter. The forces are arranged in a pyramid of authority, in which, each echelon owes explicit and peremptory obedience to the orders of its superior. The commanders at various hierarchical levels are responsible for ensuring that while participating in an armed conflict, the forces under their command follow the laws of war or the IHL. Command and leadership are not necessarily the same. The former is a legal status, an authoritative position recognized under the law. The latter comprises the skills and techniques necessary to influence soldiers to submit to the orders issued by those in authority or those holding the lawful status of command. The responsibility for the success or failure of a military mission falls squarely on the commander's shoulders. But, the commander's responsibility extends to more than just mission success. In the U.S. Army doctrine commanders are "responsible for everything their command does or fails to do".

In an armed conflict, each belligerent party bears the State responsibility for the conduct of the members of its armed forces. The modern doctrine of command responsibility can be defined as the responsibility of commanders for war crimes committed by subordinate members of their armed forces or other persons subject to their control. This responsibility includes the failure to prevent or punish subordinates for their unlawful actions. The concept of 'command responsibility' in armed conflicts embraces two issues. In the first place, it concerns the responsibility of a commander who has given an order to a subordinate to commit an act which is in breach of the law of armed conflict or whose conduct implies that he is not averse to such a breach being committed. It also covers the plea of the subordinate that he is not responsible for any breach because he was acting in accordance with the orders of or what he presumed to be the wishes of his commander, a plea that is more commonly described as that of 'compliance with superior orders'. The subordinate putting forward such a plea contends that the superior alone is responsible.

Historical

Around 500 BC, Sun Tzu wrote in *Ping Fa* (The Art of War) about the duty of commanders to ensure that subordinates conduct themselves with a certain level of civility in armed conflict. In 1439, Charles VII of France issued the Ordinance of Orleans, which imposed blanket responsibility on commanders for all unlawful acts of their subordinates, without requiring any standard of knowledge. About 200 years later, the Swedish King Adolphus ordered that: "No Colonell or Capitaine shall command his soldiers to doe any unlawful thing: which who so does, shall be punished according to the discretion of the Judges." The first modern attempt to codify what could be described as the laws of war was made in the 1907 Hague Convention. Article 3 of the Convention (IV) provided that if there was a violation of the articles or regulations, the belligerent State so violating them would be responsible for the acts committed by its military and would be liable to pay compensation for the same.

In 1919, subsequent to the termination of hostilities after WW I, the Commission on the Responsibility of the Authors of the War and on the Enforcement of Penalties was established. The Commission recommended action against some 895 alleged war criminals. However, for political reasons, only 12 German officers were brought to trial before the German Supreme Court and the longest sentence was four years of imprisonment.

The German Court accepted the defence of superior orders, which is the logical adjunct to the concept of command responsibility.

Until World War II, it had been common wisdom that criminal liability under international law could only be incurred where an individual had been personally involved in the commission of a crime. In the case of a military commander or civilian leader, this meant that to be liable he had to have taken a personal part in the commission of a crime as, for instance, by ordering that crime or by aiding and abetting it. One of the most significant advances of the post-war era was the development of a doctrine that attributes criminal responsibility to military and civilian leaders, not only where they have taken a personal or direct part in the commission of a crime, but also where they have failed to prevent or punish crimes of subordinates. The newly coined term 'command responsibility' provides for a penally enforceable minimum standard of responsibility for leaders and commanders with respect to the conduct of their subordinates. The recognition that military commanders and civilian leaders could be held accountable under international law for failing in their duties of supervision signified a qualitative leap in the way breaches of international criminal law are to be dealt with.

Trial of General Yamashita

The trial of General Yamashita is perhaps the most frequently cited WW II command responsibility case. It was the first international trial to find a military commander criminally liable for the crimes committed by his subordinates. Yamashita was the Commanding General of the 14th Army Group between 9 Oct 44 - 2 Sep 45 and the Military Governor of the Philippines. During this period, his troops committed widespread, brutal atrocities including acts of violence, cruelty and homicide on the civilian population resulting in the death of over 25,000 non-combatant men, women and children. Yamashita was charged with "unlawfully disregarding and failing to discharge his duty as a commander to control the acts of members of his command by permitting them to commit war crimes". Although it was not alleged that Yamashita had actually issued illegal orders, in finding him guilty, the US military commission found that the public notoriety of the crimes was such that the accused "must have known" of them and failed to take action to prevent them or punish those responsible.

The case against General Yamashita was that, between 9 October 1944 and 2 September 1945, in the Philippine Islands, "while commander of armed forces of Japan at war with the United States of America and its allies, he unlawfully disregarded and failed to discharge his duty as commander to control the operations of the members of his command, permitting them to commit brutal atrocities and other high crimes against people of the United States and of its allies and dependencies, particularly the Philippines; and he...... thereby violated the laws of war". The US Military Commission charged with trying him found that a military commander could in some cases be held criminally responsible when there is no effective attempt on his part to discover and control the criminal acts of his subordinates. The Commission did not lay down in any detail the conditions under which such consequences could ensue for a commander.

The Commission appears to have considered that a conviction under that legal theory did not require that the accused be shown to have known of the crimes committed by his troops, nor that he should have been able to control his troops at the time when the crimes were being committed. It was enough, the judgment suggests, that General Yamashita failed to maintain control over those troops. The law of 'command responsibility', as the Commission viewed it, was thus much removed from the fundamental requirements of personal fault and culpable mindset which criminal law generally requires for a criminal conviction. The standard of liability set out by the Military Commission amounted to a form of objective liability pursuant to which a commander could be held criminally responsible for crimes committed by his troops where he failed to discover and control the criminal acts of his subordinates and despite the absence of knowledge on his part that such crimes had been committed or, rather, regardless of any such awareness.

In appeal, the US Supreme Court ruled that: "T*he law of war presupposes that its violation is to be avoided through the control of the operations of war by commanders who are to some extent responsible for* *their subordinates.*" The Court held that there was an affirmative duty to take such measures as were within his power and appropriate to protect POWs and the civilian population. The standard applied by the court was that the atrocities were so widespread that *Yamashita* "must have known" of them despite no evidence of knowledge or direct connection to the accused. The Yamashita case came to be accepted as a precedent, not for the position that the Military Commission or the Supreme Court took in relation to the elements of the doctrine of superior responsibility, but for the statement of principle that a commander could be held criminally responsible under international law in relation to crimes committed by his men.

Geneva Conventions of 1949

The Geneva Convention of 1949 lays down that each belligerent Party bears responsibility under international law for the conduct of all members of its armed forces, and that the State is obliged to maintain discipline, law and order at all times. All members of armed forces are subject to the military and criminal code of the States they serve, and in case of infraction they are liable to be prosecuted before military or civil courts of that State. For example, the Third Geneva Convention (Article 129) states: "The High Contracting Parties undertake to enact any legislation necessary to provide effective penal sanctions for persons committing, or ordering to be committed, any of the 'grave breaches' of the present Convention." The 'grave breaches' to which Article 129 relates are further listed in Article 130 as (i) wilful killing, (ii) torture or inhuman treatment, including biological experiments, (iii) causing great suffering or serious injury to body or health, and (iv) compelling a POW to serve in the forces of the hostile Power, or depriving a POW of the rights of fair and regular trial.

Article 3 of the Geneva Conventions of 1949 (Common Article 3) states that in cases of armed conflict not of an international character occurring in the territory of one of the High Contracting Parties, each Party to the conflict shall be bound to apply as a minimum the provisions to protected persons: those not taking active part in hostilities; members of armed forces who have laid their arms; members of armed forces who are *horse de cambat* by sickness, wounds, detention etc. The acts prohibited against these persons are: (1) violence to life and person, in particular murder of all kinds, mutilation, cruel treatment and torture; (2) taking of hostages; (3) outrages upon personal dignity, in particular, humiliating and degrading treatment; and (4) the passing of sentences and the carrying out of executions without previous judgment pronounced by a regularly constituted court affording all the judicial guarantees which are recognized as indispensable by civilized peoples.

Additional Protocol I

The Additional Protocol I to the Geneva Conventions, adopted in 1977, was the first international treaty to codify the doctrine of command responsibility, creating an affirmative duty to repress grave breaches of international law. The provisions relating to command responsibility are contained in Articles 86 and 87 of the Protocol.

> **Article 86 - Failure to act**
>
> 1. The High Contracting Parties and the Parties to the conflict shall repress grave breaches, and take measures necessary to suppress all other breaches, of the Conventions or of this Protocol which result from a failure to act when under a duty to do so.
>
> **2.** The fact that a breach of the Conventions or of this Protocol was committed by a subordinate does not absolve his superiors from penal or disciplinary responsibility, as the case may be, if they knew, or had information which should have enabled them to conclude in the circumstances at the time, that he was committing or was going to commit such a breach and if they did not take all feasible measures within their power to prevent or repress the breach.
>
> **Article 87 - Duty of commanders**
>
> 1. The High Contracting Parties and the Parties to the conflict shall require military commanders, with respect to members of the armed forces under their command and other persons under their control, to prevent and, where necessary, to suppress and to report to

competent authorities breaches of the Conventions and of this Protocol.

2. In order to prevent and suppress breaches, High Contracting Parties and Parties to the conflict shall require that, commensurate with their level of responsibility, commanders ensure that members of the armed forces under their command are aware of their obligations under the Conventions and this Protocol.

3. The High Contracting Parties and Parties to the conflict shall require any commander who is aware that subordinates or other persons under his control are going to commit or have committed a breach of the Conventions or of this Protocol, to initiate such steps as are necessary to prevent such violations of the Conventions or this Protocol, and, where appropriate, to initiate disciplinary or penal action against violators thereof.

A commander is liable for grave breaches committed by a subordinate "if he knew, or had information which should have enabled him" to conclude in the circumstances at the time, that his subordinate was committing or was going to commit such a breach and did not take all feasible measures within his power to prevent or repress the breach. Apart from being liable to be considered a party to war crimes committed by his subordinates, a commander has a general duty to maintain discipline and this includes a duty to take action in respect of war crimes committed, or about to be committed by his subordinates or by other persons under his control. Protocol I places the responsibility on the high contracting parties to ensure that commanders prevent breaches, train their subordinates and take action against offenders.

The commanders are to prevent and, where necessary, suppress and report to the competent authorities about the breaches of the Geneva Conventions and Protocol I. This applies in relation to members of the armed forces under their command and also other persons under the control of commanders. The commanders are also responsible to make members of the armed forces under their command aware of their obligations under the Conventions and Protocol.

International Criminal Tribunal for former Yugoslavia and Rwanda

In the wake of the human rights violations committed in the former Yugoslavia, the United Nations Security Council, relying on Chapter VII of the United Nations Charter as authority, created the International Criminal Tribunal for the Former Yugoslavia (ICTY). The Security Council felt that there was a link between the maintenance of peace in the former Yugoslavia and the restoration of justice. A statute was drafted giving the court both substantive and personal jurisdiction over certain individuals and particular types of criminal activity. The intent of the United Nations Security Council was to create international criminal tribunals that would apply the customary international law standard of command responsibility. The *Yamashita* rules were applied in both tribunals, even though the Security Council apparently viewed the conflict in former Yugoslavia as being of an international character and the armed conflict in Rwanda as being purely internal in nature.

The ICTY has jurisdiction over four types of crime committed in the territory of former Yugoslavia since 1991: (i) grave breaches of the 1949 Geneva Conventions, (ii) violations of the laws or customs of war, (iii) genocide, and (iv) crime against humanity. It can try only individuals, not organizations or governments. It was the first international criminal court to enforce the existing body of international humanitarian law, and in particular, judicially determine aspects of its customary law.

The statute for the ICTY included a provision for holding commanders criminally responsible for the acts of their subordinates. Article 7(3) of the Statute reads:-

> 'The fact that any of the acts referred to in articles 2 to 5 of the present Statute was committed by a subordinate does not relieve his superior of criminal responsibility if he knew or had reason to know that the subordinate was about to commit such acts or had

> done so and the superior failed to take the necessary and reasonable measures to prevent such acts or to punish the perpetrators thereof.'

There are two standards of knowledge encompassed by Article 7(3): 'knew' and 'had reason to know'. 'Knew' refers to actual knowledge, which can be established either directly or through circumstantial evidence. The meaning of 'had reason to know' has been the most contentious aspect of command responsibility before the ICTY. The Appeal Chamber has held that the ordinary meaning of Article 86 of the additional Protocol indicated that the commander must have some information available to him, which puts him on notice of the commission of unlawful acts by his subordinates.

The ICTY has set a large number of legal and institutional precedents: (1) it identified and applied the modern doctrine of criminal responsibility of superiors, so-called *command responsibility*, clarifying that a formal superior-subordinate relationship is *not* necessarily required for criminal responsibility; (2) it removed uncertainty about the *level of knowledge* to be expected from a superior, whose subordinates were about to commit crimes he did not prevent, or about crimes actually committed by them; and (3) it expanded the legal elements of the crime of grave breaches of the Geneva Conventions of 1949 by further defining the test of overall control.

The strife in Rwanda was internal and the UN Security Council viewed the genocide and massive human rights violations as a threat to international peace and security. After receiving a request from the Rwandan government, the UN Security Council established an international criminal tribunal for the prosecution of persons responsible for "Genocide and Other Serious Violations of International Humanitarian Law Committed in the Territory of Rwanda and Rwandan citizens responsible (ICTR)." The Rwandan court was also authorized by the United Nations Security Council to hold individuals liable on a theory of command responsibility. The ICTR Statute reads:-

> 'The fact that any of the acts referred to in articles 2 to 4 of the present Statute was committed by a subordinate does not relieve

his or her superior of criminal responsibility if he or she knew or had reason to know that the subordinate was about to commit such acts or had done so and the superior failed to take the necessary and reasonable measures to prevent such acts or to punish the perpetrators thereof.'

The treatment of command responsibility was virtually identical in both the ICTY Statute and the ICTR Statute which suggests that the customary international law standard for holding commanders liable in internal armed conflicts is now the same as that for international armed conflicts. Both statutes were created by the United Nations Security Council and both tribunals, the only international tribunals since World War II and the only currently sitting international criminal tribunals, codify the *Yamashita* standard.

The Rome Statute of the International Criminal Court

The Rome Statute is unique in many ways. It has created a permanent tribunal, the ICC, to deal with all crimes of serious concern to the international community as a whole. Its jurisdiction and mandate are not limited to specific events in specific places, or to any specified time-frame. The Rome Statute provides that the ICC shall exercise jurisdiction over individuals, unlike the other permanent international tribunals, such as the International Court of Justice. The ICC's powers and functions include holding individuals accountable, and subjecting the accused to investigation, arrest, detention, prosecution and if found guilty, incarceration. The Rome Statute creates obligations on the part of state parties to provide the means to enforce these powers.

The doctrine of command responsibility has been codified in Article 28 of the Rome Statute of the International Criminal Court.

1. A military commander or person effectively acting as a military commander shall be criminally responsible for crimes within the jurisdiction of the Court committed by forces under his or her effective command and control, or effective authority and control as the case may be, as a result of his or her

failure to exercise control properly over such forces, where:-

(a) That military commander or person either knew or, owing to the circumstances at the time, should have known that the forces were committing or about to commit such crimes; and

(b) That military commander or person failed to take all necessary and reasonable measures within his or her power to prevent or repress their commission or to submit the matter to the competent authorities for investigation and prosecution.

2. With respect to superior and subordinate relationships not described in paragraph 1, a superior shall be criminally responsible for crimes within the jurisdiction of the Court committed by subordinates under his or her effective authority and control, as a result of his or her failure to exercise control properly over such subordinates, where:-

(a) The superior either knew, or consciously disregarded information which clearly indicated, that the subordinates were committing or about to commit such crimes;

(b) The crimes concerned activities that were within the effective responsibility and control of the superior; and

(c) The superior failed to take all necessary and reasonable measures within his or her power to prevent or repress their commission or to submit the matter to the competent authorities for investigation and prosecution.

Article 28 imposes individual responsibility on military commanders for crimes committed by forces under their effective command and control if they 'either knew or, owing to the circumstances at the time, should have known that the forces were committing or about to commit such crimes'. Interpreted literally, Article 28 adopts the stricter "should have known" standard. It is felt that this provision will serve as a deterrent, giving incentive to a commander to be aware of what his subordinates are doing. The offences dealt with under the Rome Statute are genocide, war crimes and crimes against humanity. The ICC is complementary to national jurisdictions and will intervene only where States are unable or unwilling to act.

The doctrine of command responsibility plays a fundamental role in 'regulating the behaviour of superiors and their subordinates in times of war'. In order to meet its international obligations, the UK has passed the Iinternational Criminal Court Act, 2001. The military manuals of the USA, Canada and Australia have also been amended to incorporate provisions relating to command responsibility.

The UN Convention for the Protection of All Persons from Enforced Disappearance, 2006

The principal of command responsibility is well established in the recently adopted UN Convention for the Protection of All Persons from Enforced Disappearance. Article 6 of this Convention provides:-

1. Each State Party shall take the necessary measures to hold criminally responsible at least:-

> (a) Any person who commits, orders, solicits or induces the commission of, attempts to commit, is an accomplice to or participates in an enforced disappearance;
>
> (b) A superior who:-
>
>> (i) Knew, or consciously disregarded information which clearly indicated, that subordinates under his or her effective authority and control were committing or about to commit a crime of enforced disappearance;
>>
>> (ii) Exercised effective responsibility for and control over activities which were concerned with the crime of enforced disappearance; and
>>
>> (iii) Failed to take all necessary and reasonable measures within his or her power to prevent or repress the commission of an

enforced disappearance or to submit the matter to the competent authorities for investigation and prosecution;

(c) Subparagraph (b) above is without prejudice to the higher standards of responsibility applicable under relevant international law to a military commander or to a person effectively acting as a military commander.

2. No order or instruction from any public authority, civilian, military or other, may be invoked to justify an offence of enforced disappearance.

India is a signatory to the UN Convention for the Protection of All Persons from Enforced Disappearance, 2006. However, the Convention has not yet come into the force. The UN Committee against Torture, in its general comment on the obligations of the Convention against Torture, has affirmed that "those exercising superior authority-including public officials cannot avoid accountability or escape criminal responsibility for torture or ill-treatment committed by subordinates where they knew or should have know that such impermissible conduct was occurring, or was likely to occur, and they failed to take reasonable and necessary preventive measures. The Committee considered it essential that the responsibility of any superior officials, whether for direct instigation or encouragement of torture or ill-treatment or for consent or acquiescence therein, be fully investigated through competent, independent and impartial prosecutorial authorities."

Command Responsibility in Peacekeeping Missions

The armed forces of a country may be deployed in UN multinational missions as part of the UN peacekeeping operations. The main purpose of deploying armed forces in peace missions is not to engage in military operations but to protect the lives of civilians from opposing militia groups and ensure the safe delivery of humanitarian assistance as a part of the agreement with the UN. There is no unified disciplinary system for all the military contingents in multi-force operations. The normal practice is to allow each visiting force to exercise its disciplinary process over its own personnel in the territory of the host State. There has been no instance where the UN has taken disciplinary action against its peacekeepers, though misconduct has been reported in many operations.

A common senior officer is placed in command of the multi-national force for passing orders to the national commanders, who in turn, command their own national contingents. The normal military structure operates within each national contingent in terms of superior-subordinate relationship. The national commanders have orders from their national superiors to obey the orders of the overall commander.

There may be a few differences among the different national contingents in matters of military equipment and other facilities. The main issues which matter in such settings are domestic military law and the international human rights treaties to which the country is a signatory. The rules of engagement issued to a national contingent may impose some limitations on the soldiers of visiting forces. The international laws applicable in such situations may include: (1) international humanitarian law set out in the UN Secretary-General Bulletin of 1999; (2) the Fourth Geneva convention of 1949, relating to protection of the civilians; (3) the Third Geneva Convention of 1949, relating to the protection of prisoners of war—if there is some degree of armed conflict between two or more states; and (4) Additional Protocol I to the Geneva Conventions of 1949, if the States to which the multinational forces belong are signatories to it.

A person who attacks a UN force or its property during an armed conflict will commit a war crime and can be tried by the ICC for violation of the Rome Statute. The liability of a state party to an international human rights instrument for a breach of human rights by members of its armed forces will not be extinguished merely because the armed forces are assigned to a multinational force. The extra-territorial reach of the criminal law of a State might encompass the activities of a soldier within the State, especially where this involves torture. The soldier may be at risk from the exercise of some form of criminal process if he later visits the State claiming such jurisdiction and he is arrested. Depending upon the extent of the extra-territorial effect of the jurisdiction, he might find himself being prosecuted in the State or be the subject of extradition proceedings to another State with such extensive jurisdiction.

Canadian Forces in Somalia

In December 1992, paratroopers from the Canadian Airborne Regiment arrived in Somalia to participate in humanitarian relief efforts. Their mission was to secure an area around the central Somali town of Belet Huen and distribute food to starving Somalis. In the beginning, the soldiers performed their mission with enthusiasm. Over time, however, many lost their motivation, and discipline started to slip. The paratroopers were harassed by the local citizens even while they tried to repair roads and hospitals. Somalis began to throw rocks at the food convoys. However, the greatest cause for the loss of morale was the "incessant stream of desperate Somalis sneaking into the Canadian compound at night to steal food and anything else they could scrounge".

The Canadians felt a deepening sense of frustration and despair. They were upset and felt that they were spending too much time routing out thieves rather than performing their mission. One officer gave an order that soldiers who caught Somalis in the compound were to "abuse" them. Another officer directed the men to shoot fleeing looters below the waist if they refused to stop after being ordered to do so.

A team of soldiers, including a sniper, wearing night vision goggles, began setting traps using food as bait. When Somalis grabbed the food, they were ordered to halt. If they ran, they were shot. There was some evidence that perhaps a few Somalis had been shot at point blank range and killed after being brought to the ground. The Canadian officers felt the rules of engagement were vague and believed the men were only doing their job. The most infamous incident was the torture and murder of a Somali man caught stealing in the compound. He was beaten, burned with cigarettes and tortured for three hours by two young enlisted soldiers before dying. Noncommissioned officers (NCO) in the area could hear the man's cries for help.

In disciplinary proceedings after the incident, the officer who gave the order to "abuse" Somalis contended that he merely meant for them to be "roughed up", not literally abused. One of the two soldiers charged attempted to hang himself after the incident and was determined to be mentally incompetent to stand trial. The other soldier involved was convicted and sentenced to five years' confinement. The NCO who instructed the two to not kill the Somali was convicted for failing to exercise proper control and received a nominal sentence. Although no commanders were prosecuted criminally for the acts of their subordinates, some received letters of reprimand. However, because of the abuses in Somalia, as well as other prior incidents of poor discipline, the Canadian government took the extreme measure of disbanding the Canadian Airborne Regiment.

Command Responsibility in Iraq War

In December 2003, an Iraqi auto repair shop owner in the Sunni Triangle made an obscene gesture as a platoon of US soldiers passed by his garage. The soldiers stopped and searched the shop. Although they found nothing, their platoon commander ordered them to take the shop owner to a bridge over the Tigris and throw him into the water. Apparently, the soldiers' tactic worked, because the next time the platoon passed by the auto repair shop, its owner greeted them with a polite wave. A few weeks later, the same squad decided to throw two more Iraqis off a bridge. This time, one of the Iraqis is believed to have drowned.

The commander of the battalion, Lt. Col. Nathan Sassaman, heard about the first incident and learned about the second incident only a few days after it occurred. He asked his deputy to investigate and, on the basis of what his deputy told him, Sassaman believed that no one had been harmed—that the stunt, though "dumb", was not criminal. He decided not to report the incident to his superior. When army investigators later started questioning Sassaman's men about the incident, Sassaman urged his subordinates to tell the investigators everything that they wanted to know—except "the part about the water". Sassaman's cover-up eventually came to light. Although the Uniform Code of Military Justice (UCMJ) provides for the court-martial of a commander who fails to investigate or punish an offence committed by his subordinates, Sassaman was awarded reprimand—a non-judicial punishment.

The US Army Field Manual 27-10 states that "commanding officers of US troops must ensure that war crimes committed by members of their forces against enemy personnel are promptly and adequately punished". However, most abuses in the war in Iraq were not reported and commanders were never punished.

Command Responsibility: Implications for India

The doctrine of command responsibility, developed primarily at the conclusion of WWII, holds that a commander may be criminally liable for the law of war violations committed by the forces under his command. Over the years, the doctrine has obtained the status of customary international law and has been codified in various formulations. Under this doctrine, if a commander fails to control his forces in such a way as to prevent, suppress, and punish law of war violations that he either knew about or was reckless about or negligent in failing to become aware of, he can be punished as if he committed the crimes engaged in by the forces under his command.

This doctrine is based on the unique position that the commander holds in a military organization. It is a recognition that the commander is the focal point for military discipline and order and it is the commander's responsibility to maintain command and control of his subordinate forces. The doctrine is also based on the traditional role of the military commander as the oracle for military justice. In essence, the doctrine is based on the recognition of the fact that there is often a very thin line separating a disciplined military force from a mob. It is the commander who stands on that line and by use of all the resources and authority available to him, ensures that his forces do not violate the laws of war. If they do, it is in large part attributable to the commander's failings.

The Indian armed forces have been involved in UN peacekeeping missions, as well as international and internal conflicts for the last 50 years. Though India is not a party to the Rome Statute, and has also not ratified the Additional Protocols, it is imperative that the concept of command responsibility be analysed, keeping in view the existing realities of armed conflict and developments in the international law.

In the last 20 years, the national legal system has made qualitative advances. This is due in large part to the impact of international human rights norms on national legislation. The international legal system now includes the concept of international criminal accountability for the commission of certain international crimes, and the emerging concept of the duty to protect the human rights of innocents. In March 2006, the UN General Assembly adopted the "Basic Principles and Guidelines on the Right to a Remedy and Reparation for Victims of Gross Violations of International Human Rights Law and Serious Violations of International Humanitarian Law". The UN document states that in cases of gross violations of international human rights law and serious violations of international humanitarian law constituting crimes under international law, States have the duty to investigate and to prosecute the person allegedly responsible for the violations. The Supreme Court of India has also tried to assimilate or incorporate the international standard into domestic law in a number of cases.

We ought to examine possible methods available to incorporate the superior responsibility standard into domestic military manuals. The international standard should be incorporated so that it does not appear that our commanders have a greater degree of immunity in military operations than those from the rest of the world. If we are to hold ourselves out as an armed force that supports the rule of law, the internationally accepted "knew or should have known" standard of command responsibility should be followed domestically. It is more likely to prevent war crimes because it places a greater burden on commanders to pay attention to the acts of subordinates and assign them an affirmative duty to stay informed. Moreover, adopting the superior responsibility standard will bring the Indian courts-martial practice in line with the customary international law of war. In Indian military law, a subordinate is bound to comply with superior orders, provided the command is lawful. For example, under Section 41 of the

Army Act, 1950, to be lawful, a command must satisfy the following conditions: (a) it must be a specific command given by a superior officer to an individual; (b) it must be capable of execution by the individual to whom it is addressed; (c) it must be justified by military law as well as civil law and by usages of service; and (d) it must relate to military duty; that is to say, disobedience to it must tend to impede, delay or prevent some military proceedings.

One of the unique aspects of military justice is that it serves as one of the primary tools that the commander has to maintain order and discipline within the force. If outside officials, government bureaucrats, courts, and international commissions step in and assume the disciplinary authority that was once reserved for commanders, it would raise a number of concerns. If Indian courts-martial practice is to conform to international law, the government would need to expand the culpability of commanders where their subordinates are committing violations of the law. Perhaps the best way to resolve the issue would be for Parliament to amend the Army Act, 1950 (and also the Air Force and the Navy Acts) to comport with the international standard. Among others, one significant advantage in following the amendment approach would be that the international standard for command responsibility would be clearly codified as domestic law. Such an amendment would allow the armed forces to continue their preference for and policy of trying service members alleged to have violated the law by a court-martial.

Conclusion

It is well established under international law that individual criminal responsibility is not limited to persons who have directly committed an international crime and personally perpetrated its material elements. The superiors of the direct perpetrators of international crimes can be held equally liable for these crimes, which that they have not personally committed but for which they are nevertheless responsible. While the theory of indirect command responsibility punishes a superior for an omission, direct command responsibility of superiors holds such persons responsible for the positive acts that have directly triggered or caused the commission of international crimes, such as ordering, soliciting, inducing, aiding and abetting the perpetration of a war crime or a crime against humanity. The theory of command responsibility whether direct or indirect, applies equally to military and civilian superiors. The 1977 Additional Protocol I to the Geneva Conventions and both the ICTY's and ICTR's Statutes refer to superiors and not to military commanders alone, while Article 28 of the Rome Statute clearly provides for civilian superiors' responsibility.

The most important factor in the reduction of war crimes is an assertive and proactive command structure that aggressively seeks to prevent its subordinates from committing atrocities. Recognizing this fact, the international community seeks to hold commanders personally liable for the crimes committed by subordinates if the commander "knows or should know" that the subordinates are involved in criminal conduct and the commander fails to take action to stop such acts. The doctrine of command responsibility serves as a deterrent to the commission of war crimes. It is perhaps beneficial from a policy standpoint for the armed forces to try those who violate the law of war as criminals under domestic law rather than as war criminals, which may trigger a host of international legal requirements based on the treaty obligations. Moreover, asserting that domestic jurisdiction exists to cover alleged violations of the law of war may prevent jurisdiction from being asserted by another country or an international tribunal.

CHAPTER 6

LAWS OF WEAPONRY[1]

Introduction

The basic tenet of international humanitarian law (IHL), also known as the law of armed conflict or the law of war, is that 'the right of combatants to choose their means and methods of warfare is not unlimited'. This principle is stipulated in Article 22 of the 1907 Hague Regulations Respecting the Laws and Customs of War on Land. Means of combat are the instruments used in the course of hostilities, specifically weapons. By contrast, methods of combat are the tactical or strategic procedures for conducting hostilities. The means are physical objects, while the methods are non-physical instruments. It is possible to employ a legitimate means of warfare through an illegitimate method or vice versa. The main reason for limiting the means and methods of warfare is to put some limitation on the barbarism of war and to assure a minimum of humanity.

Limitations on Weapons

The limitations or prohibitions on specific means and methods of warfare contained in IHL derive from three basic premises:-

1. The choice of the means and methods of warfare is not unlimited;
2. The use of means and methods that are of such a nature as to cause unnecessary suffering or superfluous injury is forbidden; and

---

1 The text of the chapter is based on a paper presented at the workshop on International Law on 8 January 2005, at the Army Institute of Law, Mohali.

3. The only legitimate object of war is to overpower or weaken the military forces of the enemy, not primarily to destroy and kill as much as possible.

From these general principles flow a series of detailed rules as to the prohibited means and methods of warfare. International humanitarian law starts from the assumption that the parties are allowed to use all methods not prohibited by the law. The fact that a means or method of warfare is not specifically prohibited by a concrete provision of IHL does not mean that this means or method is lawful. It must first be determined whether that means is compatible with the general principles of IHL, e.g., the principle of distinction (prohibition of indiscriminate attacks), and with the principle of humanity as enshrined in the rule on "unnecessary sufferings". Only if the weapons at stake do not violate these general principles can it be said that IHL does not prohibit them and that they are, therefore, lawful.

Indiscriminate Weapons

Weapons that cannot be specifically directed against military targets are forbidden because of their indiscriminate effect. Drifting contact mines and long-range unguided missiles fall into this category. A weapon is not indiscriminate simply because it may cause incidental or collateral damage. A precision-guided munition which can be directed at a military objective, but which may also miss its target because of a failure in its guidance system, is not an indiscriminate weapon because of this potential for failure. Conversely, uncontrolled balloon-borne bombs, like those released by the Japanese against the west coast of the United States during World War II, lack the capability of direction and are, therefore, unlawful.

Unnecessary Suffering

Anti-personnel weapons are designed to kill or disable enemy combatants and are lawful, notwithstanding the death, pain and suffering they inflict. Weapons that are designed to cause unnecessary suffering or superfluous injury are prohibited because their injurious effects are disproportionate to the military advantage that would be gained by their use. Laser weapons designed to cause permanent blindness, poisoned projectiles and soft-nosed lead (dum-dum) bullets fall into this category.

Laws of Weaponry

The international humanitarian laws applicable to weapons in warfare consist of the Laws of The Hague and the Geneva Laws. In addition, certain conventions have been held under the auspices of the United Nations that ban the use of specific weapons in warfare. Further, over the centuries, a body of rules and principles guiding the behaviour of belligerent states has developed as customary law. 'Custom' is understood as a widespread repetition, over a long period, of a specific type of conduct in the belief that such conduct is obligatory and should be respected by all.

The Geneva Conventions, adopted in their current form in 1949, govern the basic rules of IHL. The Conventions protect civilians, prisoners of war, and the sick and wounded. Two additional Protocols to the Geneva Conventions of 1949 were adopted in 1977. Additional Protocol I regulates international armed conflicts, and Protocol II regulates non-international armed conflicts. Under these provisions, parties in a conflict are required to observe these general rules: distinguish between non-combatants, including the civilian population, and combatants; attack only military objectives; and refrain from using weapons that cause unnecessary loss of life or excessive suffering. Several such rules are found in Protocol I, Part III, which governs the "Methods and Means of Warfare".

Article 51 of Protocol I forbids states from attacking civilians. Article 57 specifies, "Constant care shall be taken to spare the civilian population." Article 58 requires parties to "avoid locating objectives within or near densely populated areas." In addition, the Geneva Convention condemns the use of "human shields" by prohibiting the military from using the presence of non-combatants to protect themselves from the enemy. In cases not covered by IHL, the Martens clause applies. This mandates that civilians and combatants remain under the protection and authority of the principles of international law derived from established custom, from the principles of humanity and from the dictates of public conscience.

The laws relating to weapons made under the auspices of the United Nations are (1) Convention on the Prohibition of the Development, Production and Stockpiling of Bacteriological (biological) and Toxin Weapons and on their Destruction, 1971; (2) Convention on the Prohibition of the Development, Production, Stockpiling and Use of Chemical Weapons and on Their Destruction, 1993; (3) 1980 UN Convention on Prohibition or Restrictions on the Use of Certain Conventional Weapons which may be deemed to be Excessively Injurious or to have Indiscriminate Attack (CCW); and its five Protocols. These laws regulate or ban weapons like biological weapons, chemical weapons, blinding laser weapons and anti-personnel landmines.

Article 8 of the Rome Statute of the International Criminal Court (ICC) provides that serious violations of the laws and customs applicable in international armed conflict would amount to a "war crime". The following acts constitute serious violations:-

(1) Employing poison or poisoned weapons;

(2) Employing asphyxiating, poisonous or other gases, and all analogous liquids, materials or devices;

(3) Employing bullets which expand or flatten easily in the human body, such as bullets with a hard envelope which does not entirely cover the core or is pierced with incisions;

(4) Employing weapons, projectiles and material and methods of warfare which are of such a nature as to cause superfluous injury or unnecessary suffering, or which are inherently indiscriminate in violation of the international law of armed conflict, provided that such weapons, projectiles and material and methods of warfare are the subject of a comprehensive prohibition and are included in an annex to the Statute, by an amendment in accordance with the relevant provisions set forth in articles 121 and 123.

Prohibited Weapons in War: Conventional Weapons

Weapons which cause unnecessary suffering or superfluous injury are proscribed by the Regulations annexed to the Hague Convention of 1907 and by the Additional Protocol I of 1977. The 1907 Convention draws particular attention to the employment of poison and poisoned weapons. There are other conventions and laws in which attempts have been made by the international community to control the use of particular weapons. These are as follows:

1. **Poison or Poisonous Weapons.** Article 23 (a) of the Hague Regulations of 1899/1907 prohibits the employment of poison or poisonous weapons. The use of poison referred to in the document relates mainly to the poisoning of drinking water or foodstuff likely to be used by enemy forces, while poisoned weapons applies to poisoned arrows or spears. The repudiation of poison and poisonous weapons is an ancient one which draws upon the ethical beliefs of many cultures that the use of poison is cowardly and unworthy of a warrior. Article 8 (2) (b) (xvii) of the Rome Statute also calls "employing poison or poisoned weapons" a war crime.

2. **Incendiary and Explosive Bullets.** An incendiary bullet is intended to cause harm through a burn injury, while an exploding bullet is intended to cause harm through an explosive effect. The use of incendiary or exploding bullets weighing less than 400 grams against personnel is prohibited. The use of exploding rounds in an anti-aircraft or anti-vehicle role is not prohibited, although in combat such rounds may incidentally hit personnel as well as the intended target.

3. **Expanding Bullets.** An expanding bullet expands or flattens easily in the human body, e.g., a bullet which has a hard envelope that does not entirely cover the core, or is pierced with incisions. The use of expanding bullets (dum-dum) in international armed conflict is prohibited. The unlawfulness of expanding bullets is now one of the most well-known prohibitions in modern IHL. The prohibition

does not apply to domestic policing, in which soft-nosed bullets may be used because of their ability to remove a threat immediately and with the least risk of incidental injury to others.

4. **Poisonous Gases.** Following the extensive use of chemical weapons, such as chlorine and mustard gas, during the First World War, the international community agreed to strengthen the existing legislation on these weapons so as to prevent their future use. This led Member States of the League of Nations to sign the protocol for the prohibition of the use in war of asphyxiating, poisonous or other gases and of bacteriological methods of warfare on 17 June 1925, during the Conference for the Supervision of the International Trade in Arms and Ammunition and in Implements of War. This treaty, which is usually referred to as the Geneva Protocol of 1925, entered into force on 8 February 1928. The Protocol prohibits "the use in war of asphyxiating, poisonous, or other gases and of all analogous liquids, materials or devices" and also "extends this prohibition to the use of bacteriological methods of warfare".

5. **Landmines.** The 1997 Anti-Personnel Mine Ban Convention (AP MBC) prohibits the production, stockpiling, transfer and use of all anti-personnel mines. Although it has many of the characteristics of a disarmament treaty, its purpose is humanitarian. Countries like the USA, India and Pakistan have not signed the AP MBC. However, there is every reason to believe that the prohibition of anti-personnel mines will gradually be endorsed by customary international law.

   The 1980 Convention on Certain Conventional Weapons (CCW) has two protocols regulating all landmines, booby-traps and other devices. Protocol II of the CCW treats landmines at par with booby-traps, in so far as the prohibitions and restrictions are concerned. Article 5 places limitations on the employment of remotely delivered mines, especially by requiring the use of an effective self-neutralization mechanism to render such mines harmless once they stop serving military purposes.

In 1996, Protocol II was amended to prohibit the use of certain types of landmines equipped with (i) a mechanism designed to detonate the munition in response to the operation of commonly available mine detectors; or with (ii) an anti-handling device capable of functioning after the mine has been deactivated.1 The amended text forbids the use of non-detectable anti-personnel mines and stipulates that such mines must either be equipped with a self-deactivating device or be placed in an area marked, fenced and monitored by military personnel.

•**Booby-traps.** Article 6 of Protocol II of the 1980 Convention prohibits the use of booby-traps in all circumstances:

(i) In the form of "an apparently harmless portable object which is specifically designed and constructed to contain explosive material and to detonate when it is disturbed or approached";

(ii) In any way attached to or associated with internationally recognized protective emblems, sick, wounded or dead persons; burial or cremation sites; medical facilities, equipments, supplies or transportation; children's toys and other portable objects specifically designed for the feeding., health, hygiene, clothing or education of children; food or drinks; kitchen utensils or appliances, except in military locations; object of a religious nature; historic monuments, works of art or places of worship; animals and their carcasses;

(iii) Designed to cause superfluous injury or unnecessary suffering.

•**Anti-Vehicle Landmines.** An anti-vehicle mine is any munition placed under, on or near the ground and designed to be detonated or exploded by the presence of or proximity or contact with a vehicle.3 Anti-vehicle landmines are largely synonymous with "anti-armour mines" or "anti-tank mines", which are anti-vehicle mines of sufficient power to destroy armoured vehicles. Such weapons are also referred to as "Mines Other Than Anti-Personnel Mines" (MOTAPM). Anti-vehicle landmines may be deployed only against or to protect military objectives and feasible precautions must be taken to protect civilians from their effects.

•**Naval Mines.** Modern naval mines are technologically advanced and are controlled, meaning that they have no destructive capability until activated by some form of arming order. They can be supervised and hence, the principle of distinction has no bearing on them. Other sophisticated naval mines, designed to seek out and destroy submarines, obviously do not pose any risk to surface ships. Some naval mines are even fitted with sensors activated by particular types of surface warships. However, not every naval mine in use at present is so sophisticated. Naval mines not equipped with a high-tech target selection device or free-floating mines can indiscriminately endanger ships, including neutral vessels, merchant ships and passenger liners. These mines can also affect neutral territory if they get swept away by currents.

•**Torpedoes.** A torpedo, having run its course, may lie in water like a free-floating mine and cause danger to a neutral target. Article 1 (3) of the Hague Convention (VIII) prohibits the use of torpedoes which do not become harmless once they have missed their mark.

6. **Explosive Remnants of War (ERW).** The problem of explosive remnants of war has become more and more alarming in recent years. The rapidly expanding use of mass-produced cluster munitions, quality-control problems in the highly competitive international arms market and budgetary pressures in the defence industry have increased the likelihood of malfunctioning munitions posing a threat to the civilian population and military personnel long after a conflict has ended. In the 1991 Gulf War and the 2000 Kosovo conflict, ERW killed and injured more military personnel after the end of the conflict than during the conflict. ERW not only endanger the life of the civilian population, but also impede post-conflict reconstruction efforts, including the repatriation of displaced

civilians.

The CCW Protocol V was adopted in November 2003 to address the serious post-conflict humanitarian impact of ERW. The Protocol has been designed to eradicate the deadly threat that ERW pose to the civilian population and to humanitarian personnel working in post-conflict settings. It entered into force on 12 November 2006.

7. **Blinding Laser Weapons.** A "blinding laser weapon" is a weapon which is designed, as its sole combat function or as one of its combat functions, to cause permanent blindness to unenhanced vision. In 1996, a Protocol on Binding Laser Weapons (Protocol IV) was added to the 1980 Convention. Article 1 of the Protocol bans the use and transfer of laser weapons "specifically designed, as their sole combat function is to cause permanent blindness". The prohibition is inapplicable if the blinding effect is temporary or an incidental or collateral effect of the (military) employment of laser systems. Thus, lasers can be used for range-finding and target designation.

8. **Non-detectable Fragments.** Under Protocol I of the 1980 CCW, "it is prohibited to use any weapon, the primary effect of which is to injure by fragments which in the human body escape detection by X-rays". The rationale is that since such fragments cannot be detected by X-rays, they render medical treatment almost impossible and thereby, cause unnecessary suffering. Metal fragments produced by ordinary hand grenades are not affected by the protocol, which is applicable only to materials that cannot be detected by X-rays, such as plastic or glass.

9. **Environment Altering Weapons.** The Convention on the Prohibition of Military or Any Other Hostile Use of Environmental Modification Techniques (ENMOD), 1976 prohibits the military use of climate modification techniques that are intended or could be expected to cause "widespread, long-lasting, or severe" destruction or damage to the enemy environment.

10. **Incendiary Weapons.** The CCW, invokes certain rules which restrict the use of incendiary weapons. An incendiary weapon is any weapon or munition which is primarily designed to set fire to objects or to cause burn injuries to persons, through the action of heat and flame. Some examples are flame throwers, shells, rockets, bombs and other containers of incendiary substances. Weapons such as illuminants, tracers, smoke or signalling systems, and munitions designed to combine blast or fragmentation effects with incendiary effects are not regarded as incendiary weapons.

Under Article 2 (1) of Protocol III of the 1980 Convention, it is prohibited in all circumstances to make the civilian population/ objects the targets of attack by incendiary weapons. Article 2 (2) forbids belligerents States from making military objects/positions located within a concentration of civilians the target of attack by air-delivered incendiary weapons. Article 2 (3) proscribes such attack when the incendiary weapon is not air-delivered. Protocol III does not protect combatants from incendiary weapons (napalm) when they are away from the civilian population.

The specific rules regarding the use of incendiary weapons under the Conventional Weapons Convention are: (a) it is prohibited in all circumstances to attack the civilian population, individual citizens or civilian objects with air-delivered incendiary weapons; (b) it is prohibited in all circumstances to make any military objective located within a concentration of civilians the object of attack by air-delivered incendiary weapons; (c) it is prohibited to make any military objective located within a concentration of civilians the object of attack by other than air-delivered incendiary weapons, except where the military objective is clearly separated from the civilians and all feasible precautions are taken to minimize incidental loss of civilian life and damage to civilian objects; and (d) it is prohibited to make forests or other kinds of plant cover the object of attack by incendiary weapons except when such elements are used to cover, conceal or camouflage combatants or other military objectives, or they are themselves military objectives.

11. **Cluster Munitions.** A cluster bomb consists of two primary elements: a container or dispenser; and sub-munitions, called bomblets. They may be deployed from aircraft or ground-launchers, by rocket or artillery shell. There are four main categories of sub-munition: (i) anti-personnel; (ii) anti-tank; (iii) combined effects munition (an anti-tank bomblet with incendiary capacity); and (iv) landmines. A cluster bomb may contain as many as 250–300 sub-munitions. Cluster bombs are capable of turning huge areas of territory into killing fields to achieve primary military objectives. They may cause immediate fatalities or injuries and undermine the strategic objectives of enemy forces.

Because cluster bombs release many small munitions over a wide area, they pose risks to civilians both during attacks and afterwards. The failure rate of sub-munitions could be between 10 and 30 per cent. During attacks, the weapons are prone to indiscriminate effects, especially in populated areas.

On 30 May 2008, the new Convention on Cluster Munitions was opened for signature. The Convention prohibits all use, stockpiling, production and transfer of cluster munitions. The Convention concerns assistance to victims, clearance of contaminated areas and destruction of stockpiles. Article 5 of the Convention provides that the state parties, in accordance with applicable international humanitarian and human rights law, shall adequately provide age- and gender-sensitive assistance, including medical care, rehabilitation and psychological support, to the victims. Till now, the Convention on Cluster Munitions has been signed by 110 states, of which 21 have ratified it.

12. **Riot Control Agents.** Riot control agents are those liquids, gases and similar substances that are widely used by civil law enforcement agencies. Riot control agents, in all but the most unusual circumstances, cause transient effects that disappear within minutes of exposure. Tear gas is one example of a riot control agent. The use of such agents as a method of warfare is prohibited

by the 1992 Chemical Weapons Convention. Situations in which the use of riot control agents may be considered are:-

(a) To control rioting prisoners of war (POWs);

(b) In rescue missions involving downed aircrew or escaped POWs;

(c) To protect supply depots, military convoys and other rear echelon areas from civil disturbances and terrorist activities; and

(d) During civil disturbance where the military is providing aid to the civil power.

Weapons of Mass Destruction

1. **Biological Weapons.** Biological warfare is the intentional use of microorganisms and toxins, generally of microbial, plant or animal origin, to produce disease and death in humans, livestock and crops. The international community adopted the Convention on the Prohibition of the Development, Production and Stockpiling of Bacteriological (biological) and Toxin Weapons and on their Destruction on 10 April 1972 (BWC). The treaty entered into force on 26 March 1975. The BWC is designed to complement the prohibition of the use of biological weapons embodied in the 1925 Geneva Protocol.

   The BWC has been in force since 1975, but has no enforcement mechanism. In 1994, an ad hoc group was formed by the state parties to the BWC, which included the USA, to work towards the strengthening of the convention. For six years the parties worked on a draft protocol to the convention with a view to enhancing transparency and promoting compliance. On the last day of the conference (7 December 2001), however, the USA announced its opposition to the continuation of work by the ad hoc group.

2. **Chemical Weapons.** Chemical weapons are intended to kill, seriously injure or incapacitate living systems. Choking agents such as phosgene cause death; blood agents such as cyanide-based

compounds are more lethal than choking agents; and nerve agents such as *sarin* and *tabun* are still more lethal than blood agents. The use of chemicals (for example, poisoned arrows) as tools of war is almost as old as humanity. The Convention on the Prohibition of the Development, Production, Stockpiling and use of Chemical Weapons and on their Destruction was opened for signature on 13 January 1993, and entered into force on 29 April 1997 (CWC). The CWC prohibits the development, production, acquisition, stockpiling, retention, transfer and use of chemical weapons. It also forbids state parties to assist, encourage or induce anyone to be involved in such outlawed activities. Like the BWC, the CWC uses a general-purpose criterion to define its scope so that states parties have the right to conduct activities involving toxic chemicals for purposes not prohibited under the CWC. Similarly, the provisions of the CWC must also be implemented in such a way as to avoid hampering the economic and technological development of the states parties.

The CWC stipulates that the state parties must totally destroy their existing stockpiles of chemical weapons and the related production facilities located on their territory or under their jurisdiction, or control within 10 or, under certain conditions, 15 years after the CWC's entry into force. This destruction process must be completed in such a way as to ensure the safety of the population and the protection of the environment. Finally, the CWC establishes an international system for verifying compliance. This relies on several types of verification techniques and methods that allow for the protection of national security. This verification machinery, which includes declarations by the state parties, routine inspections as well as means (such as challenge inspections) to investigate allegations of violations of the treaty, is operated by the Organization for the Prohibition of Chemical Weapons (OPCW). The main element of the system is factual information obtained through verification procedures in accordance with the Convention that are independently conducted by the OPCW Technical

Secretariat, the sufficiency of such information being essential for successful operation.

3. **Nuclear Weapons.** A nuclear weapon is defined in Article 5 of the Treaty of Tlatelolco as "any device which is capable of releasing nuclear energy in an uncontrolled manner and which has a group of characteristics that are appropriate for use with warlike purposes". Nuclear weapons are characterized in particular by their destructive power, the suffering caused by their use, the difficulty in bringing aid to victims, the risk of escalation and proliferation, and the dangers which such weapons pose to the environment, future generations and the survival of humanity.

Nuclear weapons, unlike chemical or biological weapons, are not subject to any general treaty banning their use. However, they are within the ambit of the limitations on international armed conflicts. There are a number of treaties prohibiting the deployment of nuclear weapons in designated areas, such as Antarctica, outer space and the seabed, their testing, and even their possession by certain countries, establishing nuclear-free zones and creating non-proliferation obligations. The UN has, in various resolutions, encouraged the creation of nuclear-free zones, which have become a part and parcel of the nuclear non-proliferation regime. The proposal for the establishment of a nuclear-free zone in South Asia has been rejected by India because it feels that the matter requires a global rather than regional approach.

A number of authors argue that the existing conventions, such as the St Petersburg Declaration, 1968, The Hague Rules of 1907, the Geneva Gas Protocol, 1925, the Genocide Convention, 1948, the Geneva Conventions of 1949 and the Additional Protocols of 1977, make the use of nuclear weapons an infringement of international law. The position of the International Committee of the Red Cross (ICRC) on nuclear weapons (2002) is as follows:-

- The principles and rules of international humanitarian law, and in particular the principles of distinction and proportionality and the prohibition on causing superfluous injury or unnecessary suffering, apply to the use of nuclear weapons.

- In view of the unique characteristics of nuclear weapons, the States must ensure that these weapons are not used, irrespective of whether they consider them to be lawful or not.

- Nuclear weapons are characterized in particular by their destructive power, the unspeakable suffering caused by their use, the fact that it is extremely difficult to bring aid to victims, the fact that it is impossible to control their effects in space and time, the risk of escalation and proliferation which any use of nuclear weapons necessarily involves, and the dangers which such weapons entail for the environment, future generations and the survival of humanity.

- The States must take every appropriate measure to limit the risk of the proliferation of nuclear weapons and achieve a complete prohibition on nuclear weapons as well as the elimination of such weapons.

It can be argued that in a few situations, nuclear weapons can be used in conformity with the parameters of humanitarian law: (1) a strike upon troops and armour in an isolated desert region with a low-yield air-burst in conditions of no wind; and (2) detonation of ‘clean’ nuclear weapons against an enemy fleet in the middle of the ocean. In neither of these exceptional situations should the employment of nuclear weapons give rise to significant collateral damage to civilians. But these are hypothetical situations. Members of the nuclear club are aware of the colossal ramifications of a decision to unleash nuclear weapons in warfare.

Legal Review of New Weapons

For a state that is party to Additional Protocol I of 1977, determining the legality of new weapons is a treaty obligation pursuant to Article 36 of the Protocol. It states:-

> In the study, development, acquisition or adoption of a new weapon, means or method of warfare, a High Contracting Party is under an obligation to determine whether its employment would, in some or all circumstances, be prohibited by this Protocol or by any other rule of international law applicable to the High Contracting Party.

The aim of Article 36 is to prevent the use of weapons that would violate international law in all circumstances and to impose restrictions on the use of weapons that would violate international law in some circumstances, by determining their lawfulness before they are developed, acquired or otherwise incorporated into a state's arsenal. A state party to Additional Protocol I is required by Article 36 to carry out legal reviews of weapons it is developing or acquiring. Article 36 requires each state to determine whether the employment of "a weapon, means or method of warfare" that it studies, develops, acquires or adopts would, "in some or all circumstances", be prohibited by international law applicable to the state.

Scope of Article 36

Article 36 of Additional Protocol I refers to "weapons, means or methods of warfare". The material scope of the legal review under Article 36 is, therefore, very broad. It would cover:-

- Weapons of all types, be they anti-personnel or anti-material, "lethal", "non-lethal" or "less lethal", and weapons systems;
- The ways in which these weapons are to be used pursuant to military doctrine, tactics, rules of engagement, operating procedures and counter-measures;
- All weapons to be acquired, be they procured further to research and development on the basis of military

specifications, or purchased "off-the-shelf";

- A weapon which the state intends to acquire for the first time, without its necessarily being "new" in a technical sense;
- An existing weapon which is modified in a way that alters its function, or a weapon which has already passed a legal review but is subsequently modified; and
- An existing weapon where a state has joined a new international treaty which may affect the legality of the weapon.

When in doubt as to whether the device or system proposed for study, development or acquisition is a "weapon", legal advice should be sought from the weapons review authority. Article 36 is complemented by Article 82 of Additional Protocol I of 1977, which requires that legal advisers be available at all times to advise military commanders on IHL and "on the appropriate instruction to be given to the armed forces on this subject". Both provisions establish a framework for ensuring that armed forces will be capable of conducting hostilities in strict accordance with IHL, through legal reviews of planned means and methods of warfare.

In order to ensure that the new weapon adheres to international humanitarian law, a few states have constituted expert committee to determine: (i) the purpose of the new weapon; (ii) the factors which favour the introduction of the new weapons; (iii) the damage mechanism of the new weapon (blast, fragmentation, etc.); (iv) whether the new weapon is specifically designed to cause injury to personnel; (v) the human injuries that the new weapon is capable of inflicting; (vi) what other weapons, if any, would be capable of fulfilling the same purpose as the new weapon; (vii) whether the new weapon has been adopted by the armed forces of other states or by other agencies in the country or overseas and, if so, by which one; and (viii) whether evaluation data concerning the new weapons is available from the armed forces of other sates or from other agencies.

In assessing the legality of a particular weapon, the reviewing authority must examine not only the weapon's design and characteristics (the "means" of warfare), but also how it is to be used (the "method" of warfare), bearing in mind that the weapon's effects will result from a combination of its design and the manner in which it is to be used.4 However, other states, whether or not they are party to the Protocol I, must assess the lawfulness of their new weapons in order to ensure that they are able to comply with their international legal obligations during armed conflicts and other situations of violence. Having a "national mechanism" to review the legality of new weapons is especially relevant in view of emerging new weapons technologies, such as directed energy, incapacitants, behaviour change agents, acoustics and nanotechnology.

The International Committee of Red Cross (ICRC) has called on states to establish mechanisms and procedures to determine the conformity of weapons with international law.5 In particular, the 28th Conference declared: "In light of the rapid development of weapons technology and in order to protect civilians from the indiscriminate effects of weapons and combatants from unnecessary suffering and prohibited weapons, all new weapons, means and methods of warfare should be subject to rigorous and multidisciplinary review." However, very few states not party to Additional Protocol I have adopted formal weapons review procedures.

The obligation to review the legality of new weapons implies at least two things. First, a state should have in place some form of permanent procedure to that effect, in other words, a standing mechanism that can be automatically activated at any time that a state is developing or acquiring a new weapon. Second, such a procedure should be made mandatory, by law or by administrative directive, for the authority responsible for developing or acquiring new weapons.

Implications for India

The Government of India has signed and ratified the following treaties relating to IHL:-

1. Geneva Convention (I) for the Amelioration of the Condition of the Wounded and Sick in Armed Forces in the Field. Geneva, 12 August

1949.

2. Geneva Convention (II) for the Amelioration of the Condition of Wounded, Sick and Shipwrecked Members of Armed Forces at Sea. Geneva, 12 August 1949.

3. Geneva Convention (III) relative to the Treatment of Prisoners of War. Geneva, 12 August 1949.

4. Geneva Convention (IV) relative to the Protection of Civilian Persons in Time of War. Geneva, 12 August 1949.

5. Convention on the Rights of the Child. New York, 20 November 1989.

6. Optional Protocol to the Convention on the Rights of the Child on the involvement of children in armed conflict. New York, 25 May 2000.

7. Convention for the Protection of Cultural Property in the Event of Armed Conflict. The Hague, 14 May 1954.

8. First Protocol to the Hague Convention of 1954 for the Protection of Cultural Property in the Event of Armed Conflict. The Hague, 14 May 1954.

9. Convention on the prohibition of military or any other hostile use of environmental modification techniques. New York, 10 December 1976.

10. Protocol for the Prohibition of the Use of Asphyxiating, Poisonous or Other Gases, and Warfare. Geneva, 17 June 1925.

11. Convention on the Prohibition of the Development, Production and Stockpiling of Bacteriological (Biological) and Toxin Weapons and on their Destruction. Opened for signature at London, Moscow and Washington. 10 April 1972.

12. Convention on Prohibitions or Restrictions on the Use of Certain Conventional Weapons (CWC) which may be deemed to be Excessively Injurious or to have Indiscriminate Effects. Geneva, 10 October 1980.

13. CWC Protocol on non-detectable fragments (I), 1980.

14. CWC Protocol on prohibitions or restrictions on the use of mines, booby-traps and other devices (II), 1980.

15. CWC Protocol on prohibitions or restrictions on the use of incendiary weapons (III), 1980.

16. CWC Protocol on Blinding Laser Weapons (Protocol IV to the 1980 Convention), 13 October 1995.

17. CWC Protocol on Prohibitions or Restrictions on the Use of Mines, Booby-Traps and Other Devices as amended on 3 May 1996 (Protocol II to the 1980 Convention).

18. Amendment to the CWC which may be deemed to be Excessively Injurious or to have Indiscriminate Effects (with Protocols I, II and III). Geneva, 21 December 2001.

19. Convention on the Prohibition of the Development, Production, Stockpiling and Use of Chemical Weapons and on their Destruction. Paris 13 January 1993.

While the decision to sign or not sign a weapon-ban treaty could be based on a country's strategic perspectives and the arsenals of its possible adversaries, every country must establish a mechanism to review the legality of its weapon systems. Reviewing the legality of weapons is not a new concept. The first international instrument to refer to the legal assessment of emerging military technologies was the St Petersburg Declaration, adopted in 1868 by an international military commission. The Declaration addresses the development of future weapons in these terms: "The Contracting or Acceding Parties reserve to themselves to come hereafter to an understanding whenever a precise proposition shall be drawn up in view of future improvements which science may effect in the armament of troops, in order to maintain the principles which they have established, and to conciliate the necessities of war with the laws of humanity."

The only other reference in IHL to the need to carry out legal reviews of new weapons, means and methods of warfare is found in Article 36 of Additional Protocol I of 1977. Though the Government of India has not signed Additional Protocol I, the Protocol has received a customary status in IHL. The aim of Article 36 is to prevent the use of weapons that would violate IHL. The requirement that the legality of all new weapons be systematically assessed is one that applies to all States, regardless of whether or not they are party to Additional Protocol I. The necessity of legal reviews of new weapons is of particular importance today in the light of the rapid development of new weapons technologies.

In considering the compliance of the weapon, methods or means of warfare with a state's legal obligation under international law, five areas need to be considered:

- Treaty obligations of the state
- The principle that a combatant cannot use weapons of a nature that causes unnecessary suffering or superfluous injury
- Capability of distinction (accuracy) to avoid incidental loss of civilian life or damage to civilian objects
- Whether the weapon is likely to have a long-term, widespread or severe impact on the environment
- Final disposal of the weapon to ensure its compatibility with the future legal requirements under international humanitarian law.

The review procedure may include the operational analysis—the military utility of the weapon; the manner in which it is going to be used by a commander; its accuracy and legality; the medical aspect of injuries likely to be caused by the weapon; and its impact on the environment. The weapon review process provides an opportunity for states to anticipate legal challenges on the basis of the core principles of IHL and to take them into account in the development of the characteristics of new weapons and military equipment.

The UK's Legal Review Guidance, for example, suggests that required data should include: (i) a technical description of the equipment, including its range, speed, constituent material, reliability and accuracy; (ii) destructive radius of the weapon; (iii) nature of expected injury to persons; (iv) the design purpose and intended normal method of use of the weapon, including types of target; (v) test data as to accuracy, failure rate and sensitivity of unexploded munitions which fail live; and (vi) impact of unexploded munitions and debris on public health.

A weapon cannot be assessed in isolation from the method of warfare by which it is to be used. Thus, the legality of a weapon does not depend solely on its design or intended purpose, but also on the manner in which it is expected to be used on the battlefield. In addition, a weapon used in one manner may "pass" the Article 36 "test", but may fail it when used in another manner. This is why Article 36 requires a state "to determine whether its employment would, in some or all circumstances, be prohibited" by international law. In order to provide a tool to assist states in establishing weapons review mechanisms, in 2006 the ICRC drew up "A Guide to the Legal Review of New Weapons, Means and Methods of Warfare". It was prepared in consultation with close to 30 military and international law experts, including government experts from ten countries. As emphasized in the Guide, a new weapon—that is, a proposed means of warfare, cannot be examined in isolation from the way in which it is to be used—that is, without also taking into account the method of warfare associated with it. This Guide reflects the ICRC's interpretation of the subject based on the text of Article 36 of Additional Protocol I and the ICRC's Commentary on the Additional Protocols.

The Government of India must constitute an 'expert committee' to examine the legality of its new weapons or the new systems bought, manufactured or otherwise acquired, including the new weapon-related technology developed. Besides the technical description and performance, the committee must consider the weapon's mechanism of injury and environmental implications. This necessitates that the committee must have experts from various fields, including military engineering, logistics, legal, environment, administration and medical.

Conclusion

The St. Petersburg Declaration of 1868 declared that "the only legitimate object which States should endeavour to accomplish during war is to weaken the military forces of the enemy". It continued, "This object would be exceeded by the employment of arms which uselessly aggravate the sufferings of disabled men, or render their death inevitable." About 142 years after the St Petersburg Declaration, we are facing challenges to the application of IHL, which is being violated with impunity.

Protecting civilians and reducing unnecessary injuries to combatants is an imperative in IHL. It is forbidden to employ any weapon/method of warfare which causes "superfluous or unnecessary injuries"; or a weapon that cannot be directed against a specific military target. Though the term "superfluous or unnecessary suffering" has not been defined, the common interpretation of this phrase is the increase of sufferings without really increasing military advantages. Whether we are speaking of futuristic weapons, including microwave, infrasound and light-flash devices, environmental warfare, electronic warfare and cyber-weapons, or technological advances in conventional weapons, we must never forget the St Petersburg Declaration, which states that weapons which "uselessly aggravate the suffering of disabled men or render their death inevitable" are "contrary to the laws of humanity".

CHAPTER 7

INTERNATIONAL CRIMINAL COURT AND THE MILITARY LEGAL SYSTEM[1]

Introduction

The Rome Statute of the International Criminal Court (ICC) was adopted on 17 July 1998. The Court was given substantial powers, as it was intended to act as a true international court, self-reliant and independent of any particular state. The jurisdiction of the Court is based on the principle of complementarity: the court would not hear any case unless the State or States that would have municipal jurisdiction were "unwilling or unable genuinely" to prosecute the offender. From this concept of complementarity arises the possibility that the Indian military justice system may be exposed to significant international scrutiny.

India has not signed the Rome Statute. However, it has signed and ratified the following international instruments relating to the protection and preservation of human rights.

- The Geneva Convention (I) for the Amelioration of the Condition of the Wounded and Sick in Armed Forces in the Field of 12 August 1949
- The Geneva Convention (II) for the Amelioration of the Condition of Wounded, Sick and Shipwrecked Members of Armed Forces at Sea of 12 August 1949
- The Geneva Convention (III) Relative to the Treatment of Prisoners of War of 12 August 1949

---

1 The text of this chapter is based on a talk given at a seminar organized by the International Committee of the Red Cross in New Delhi on 13 January 2007.

- The Geneva Convention (IV) relative to the Protection of Civilian Persons in Time of War of 12 August 1949
- Convention on the Prevention and Punishment of the Crime of Genocide, 1948
- Convention on the Elimination of All Forms of Racial Discrimination, 1965
- International Covenant on Civil and Political Rights, 1966
- International Covenant on Economic, Social and Cultural Rights, 1966
- Convention on the Rights of the Child, 1989
- Convention on the Elimination of All Forms of Discrimination Against Women, 1979

There are no explicit provisions in the Indian Constitution regulating the incorporation and status of international law in the Indian legal system. However, Article 51 (c) of the Constitution stipulates, as one of the directive principles of state policy, that: "The State shall endeavour to foster respect for international law and treaty obligations..."

This Chapter will analyse the effectiveness of the Indian military justice system and the extent to which it can prosecute a military person for violations contained in the Rome Statute. It will also examine the provisions of the Geneva Convention in the Indian context, and the right to a fair trial available to a military accused in a trial by court-martial. In addition, it will explore the need for a systematic review of the Indian military justice system— not merely from the point of view of the offences it could try; but also the systems and procedures followed in a trial by court-martial and the appellate forums available to an accused—to make it compatible with the demands of international law.

Crimes under the Rome Statute

The object and purpose of the Rome Statute is to put in place effective arrangements for the trial of crimes over which the ICC has jurisdiction. Articles 6, 7 and 8 of the Rome Statute define the crimes over which the ICC has jurisdiction; that is genocide, crimes against humanity, and war crimes. These definitions also contain a list of acts that can amount to the said crimes when the threshold test for each crime is met.

A. Genocide

Article 6 of the Statute reproduces the definition of genocide provided in Article II of the UN Convention on the Prevention and Punishment of the Crime of Genocide, 1948. The Rome Statute and the Genocide Convention identify five specific acts committed with the intent to destroy, in whole or part, a national, ethnical, racial or religious group. The five acts are: killing members of the group, causing serious bodily or mental harm to members of the group, imposing conditions on the group calculated to destroy it, preventing births within the group and forcibly transferring children of the group to another.

B. Crimes against Humanity

The definition of crimes against humanity contained in Article 7 of the Rome Statute is broader than that contained in the statutes of the ICTY and ICTR. The list includes rape, sexual slavery, enforced prostitution, forced pregnancy, enforced sterilization, and any other form of sexual violence. It also includes the forced transfer of a population, enforced disappearance of persons and apartheid. Such acts, however, must be committed as part of a "widespread or systematic attack directed against any civilian population, with knowledge of the attack" and there must be "multiple commissions of [the specified act]... pursuant to or in furtherance of a State or organizational policy to commit such attack". These last requirements limit the scope of ICC jurisdiction over crimes against humanity, notwithstanding the comparatively broad list of offences. Since such crimes must be directed against a civilian group, and they must be committed in furtherance of a state policy, it would be comparatively difficult to prove such a charge. Hence, it is very unlikely that an Indian military person would be charged with crimes against humanity.

C. War Crimes

War crimes do not have the heavy evidentiary requirements of crimes against humanity. The Rome Statute divides war crimes into four categories: (a) grave breaches of the Geneva Conventions of 12 August 1949; (b) other serious violations of the laws and customs applicable in international armed conflict, within the established framework of international law; (c) in the case of an armed conflict not of an international character, serious violations of Article 3 common to the four Geneva Conventions; and (d) other serious violations of the laws and customs applicable to armed conflicts that are not of an international character, within the established framework of international law.

The definition of war crimes is of relevance to India, as its armed forces are deployed in humanitarian missions of the UN, and also internally, to aid civil power. The Indian armed forces have been involved in counter-insurgency operations in Jammu and Kashmir and the northeast since the 1950s. The excessive use of the armed forces in counter-insurgency operations has raised the question of violation of the common article 3 of the Geneva Conventions of 1949. Various human rights organizations in the country and abroad and foreign and local media have criticized the effectiveness of Indian laws in dealing with violations of human rights by armed forces personnel. They have also criticized the Armed Forces (Special Powers) Act, which gives enhanced power to the armed forces for dealing effectively with disruptive activities in specific areas.

Article 8, Paragraph 2 (b) of the Rome Statute is similar to Article 75 of the Additional Protocol I of 1977 to the Geneva Conventions of 1949, to which India is not a party. The provisions contained in the said paragraph severely restrict a state's discretion to choose the means and methods of warfare it considers appropriate to the military situation on the ground by enforcing a particularly high duty of care towards civilians. While many of the rules derived from the Additional Protocol I could be considered binding under customary international law, the Rome Statute still contains innovations — including a provision prohibiting attacks against buildings dedicated to religion, education, art, science or charitable purposes..." are outlawed. Article 8, para 2 (c) and (d) apply to non-international conflict situations under the Additional Protocol II of the Geneva Conventions of 1949.

The crimes listed under Article 8 (2) (a) of the Rome Statute correspond exactly to the relevant provisions of the Geneva Convention and are subject to the same limitations, i.e. they shall be qualified as crimes only when committed in an international armed conflict, and against persons protected under the relevant Geneva Conventions. Rape, sexual slavery, enforced prostitution, forced pregnancy and enforced sterilization occurring during international armed conflicts shall also be qualified as war crimes, provided they constitute a grave breach according to the Geneva Convention.

The Rome Statute states that "the Court shall have jurisdiction in respect of war crimes, in particular when committed as part of a plan or policy or as part of a large-scale commission of such crimes." While the ICC is guided to take cognizance of a suspected war crime only when it is a part of a large-scale policy, the words "in particular" make it clear that this is not a requirement. The language does not preclude jurisdiction over a *single* act defined in Article 8, para 2, and says nothing about the rank or status of the person committing that single act.

Complementarity

An important element of the principles guiding the ICC is that the national criminal justice processes should be used if they are adequate to ensure the investigation, prosecution and punishment related to a crime. This principle, called 'complementarity', is dealt with in the Preamble and in Articles 1 and 17 of the Rome Statute. For example, paragraph 4 of the Preamble states that the most serious crimes of concern to the international community must be punished by measures taken at the national level and by enhancing international cooperation. Paragraph 6 refers to the "duty of every State to exercise its criminal jurisdiction over those responsible for international crimes", while paragraph 11 plainly states that the ICC shall be complementary to national criminal jurisdictions. Article 17 spells out complementarity under the heading "Issues of Admissibility".

Article 17 — Issues of Admissibility

1. Having regard to paragraph 10 of the Preamble and Article 1, the Court shall determine that the case is inadmissible where:-

   (a) The case is being investigated or prosecuted by a State which has jurisdiction over it, unless the State is unwilling or unable genuinely to carry out the investigation or prosecution;

   (b) The case has been investigated by a State which has jurisdiction over it and the State has decided not to prosecute the person concerned, unless the decision resulted from the unwillingness or inability of the State genuinely to prosecute;

   (c) The person concerned has already been tried for conduct which is the subject of the complaint, and a trial by the Court is not permitted under Article 20, paragraph 3;

   (d) The case is not of sufficient gravity to justify further action by the Court.

The Statute is clear that national courts have the first right and duty to prosecute perpetrators of international crimes. However, the ICC is empowered to intervene not only where the existing national judicial machinery is insufficient to allow a successful prosecution, but also where national governments are unwilling to fulfil their responsibility to prosecute. Thus, though the principle of complementarity preserves national criminal jurisdiction as primary, it allows the ICC to step in when States fail to act and allow a person accused of genocide, war crimes or crimes against humanity from escaping justice altogether.

Command Responsibility

The modern doctrine of command responsibility can be defined as the responsibility of commanders for war crimes committed by subordinate members of their armed forces or other persons subject to their control. Command responsibility has two facets. The commander is held responsible when he has given an order to a subordinate to commit an act which is in breach of the law of armed conflict or when his conduct implies that he is not averse to such a breach being committed. The commander is also held responsible when a subordinate who has committed a breach of law pleads that he was acting in accordance with the orders of, or what he presumed to be the wishes of his commander, a plea that is commonly described as that of "compliance with superior orders". The subordinate putting forward such a plea contends that the superior alone is responsible.

The Rome Statute, consistent with well-developed customary international norms, gives the ICC jurisdiction over military commanders and certain civilians who are in a position of superiority. Such superiors can, in certain circumstances, be held individually liable for the crimes committed by their subordinates. For example, Article 28(a) of the Statute imposes individual responsibility on military commanders for crimes committed by forces under their effective command and control if they "either knew or, owing to the circumstances at the time, should have known that the forces were committing or about to commit such crimes". The doctrine of command responsibility serves as a deterrent to the commission of war crimes by forcing commanders to internalize some of the cost for directing or acquiescing to atrocities committed by their troops.

In Indian military law, a subordinate is bound to comply with superior orders, provided the command was lawful. For example, section 41 of the Army Act, 1950 provides that a command to be lawful must satisfy the following conditions: (a) It must be a specific command given by a superior officer to an individual; (b) It must be capable of execution by the individual to whom it is addressed; (c) It must be justified by military law as well as civil law and by usages of service; and (d) It must relate to military duty; that is to say disobedience to it must tend to impede, delay or prevent some military proceedings. A commander who has issued an illegal order is liable to explain his conduct.

To conform to the international standard, the Indian Army Act should be amended to create a basis of culpability for commanders equal to the international standard. It would perhaps be beneficial from a policy standpoint for the Indian armed forces to try those who violate the laws of war as criminals under domestic law rather than as war criminals, which may trigger a host of international legal requirements based on treaty obligations. Moreover, asserting that domestic jurisdiction exists to cover alleged violations of the laws of war may prevent jurisdiction from being asserted by another country or an international tribunal.

The Indian Military Justice System

The present Indian military justice system is contained in the Army Act, 1950, the Air Force Act, 1950 and the Navy Act, 1957. The provisions under these three Acts are generally identical; therefore, the term Army Act has been used henceforth.

Under the Indian military justice system, the court-martial is the single most important institution for disciplining military forces, preventing atrocities and punishing military offenders. Military tribunals (courts-martial) constituted under the Army Act are *ad hoc* with an aim to secure obedience to the commander. The rationale for dispensing justice through such *ad hoc* tribunals vested with varying powers is that military discipline requires the quick disposal of offences relating to armed forces personnel. Such tribunals (general court-martial, district court-martial, summary general court-martial and summary court-martial) are constituted under the provisions of the Army Act, depending upon the nature and gravity of the offence and the rank of the accused. The court-martial is a criminal court as per the definitions in the Indian Code of Criminal Procedure, 1973. It has no civil jurisdiction and it cannot enforce a contract or award damages in favour of an individual. By virtue of Section 152 of the Army Act, 1950, trial by the court-martial is a judicial proceeding and the court-martial is itself deemed to be a court within the meaning of the Code of Criminal Procedure, 1973.

The Army Act, Chapter VI, creates three categories of offences, which could be tried by the court-martial:-

(a) Offences which are specifically military in nature such as offences of misconduct in the face of the enemy, mutiny, desertion, absence without leave, disobedience of orders, sleeping on the post, violation of good order and discipline

(b) Civil offences committed at any place in or beyond India, but deemed to be offences committed under the Army Act (if charged under Section 69 of the Act)

(c) Offences of murder, culpable homicide not amounting to murder, or rape committed by a person subject to the Act against any person, if these offences are committed (i) while on active service, or (ii) at any place outside India, or (iii) at a frontier post specified by the central government

The Indian Army Act defines some war crimes as crimes under national law, and provides for universal jurisdiction over such crimes. Military personnel accused of breaches in the nature of torture, inhuman and degrading treatment, destruction of property etc. can be tried under different provisions of the Army Act. Some offences under the Army Act that can be equated with breaches of laws of war, are listed in the table given below.

Breach of IHL	Offence under the Army Act, 1950	Punishment under the Army Act, 1950
Appropriation of property	Section 36 (b): Breaking into house in search of plunder	14 years of rigorous imprisonment (RI)
Disobedience	Section 41: Disobedience of lawful command	14 years of RI
Making perfidious use of protective emblem	Section 45: Unbecoming conduct	Dishonourable dismissal (cashiering) for officers
Destruction of historic monuments, works of art, property	Section 64: Offences against property	7 years of RI
Inhuman treatment, wilfully causing great suffering	Section 46: Disgraceful conduct of a cruel kind	7 years of RI
Torture, inhuman treatment	Section 63: Act prejudicial to good order and discipline.	7 years of RI
Destruction of place of worship	Section 64 (b): Defiling of place of worship, wounding religious feelings	7 years of RI
Murder, rape on active service	Section 69, 70: Civil offences	Death

For serious offences, a military accused could be tried under the Indian Penal Code (IPC). For example, an officer of the rank of Captain of Indian Army was tried by a Summary General Court-Martial under Section 69 of the Army Act, 1950, for committing a civil offence, that is, robbery (under section 392 of the Indian Penal Code), at Hajiganj, Bangladesh on 11 December 1971. He was awarded the punishment of cashiering. The confirming authority considered that the punishment awarded by the court-martial was lenient and ordered for its revision by the court-martial. In revision, the same court sentenced him "to be cashiered and to suffer two years imprisonment". His writ petition under Article 32 of the Constitution was dismissed by the Supreme Court (For details see: *Capt Harish Uppal v. Union of India* AIR 1973 SC 258).

The IPC criminalizes certain acts that can amount to torture. The following criminal offences could be used to prosecute those responsible for torture:-

(a) Voluntarily causing hurt to extort confession is punishable by up to one year of imprisonment and a fine (Section 323 IPC). If the hurt caused is grievous, the maximum punishment is 10 years of imprisonment and a fine (Section 326 IPC).

(b) Wrongful confinement to extort confession or compel restoration of property, which carries a maximum punishment of three years of imprisonment and liability to pay a fine (Section 348 IPC).

(c) A public servant disobeying the law, with intent to cause injury to any person, is liable to a punishment of up to one year of imprisonment and/or a fine (Section 166 IPC).

(d) A public servant concealing the design to commit an offence that it is his/her duty to prevent is liable to punishment which depends on the imprisonment or fine provided for the concerned offence (Section 199 IPC).

In essence, the provisions contained in the Army Act do not cover 'superior responsibility' and 'war crimes' as defined under the Rome Statute. The Army Act, the Manual of Military Law (three volumes) and the Regulations for the Army (two volumes) do not deal with international humanitarian law provisions at all.

Another area that needs consideration is that the punishments authorized under the Indian military justice system are more severe than those under the prevailing civil-criminal justice system or the Rome Statute. The maximum punishment that could be awarded by the International Criminal Court under the Rome Statute is life imprisonment in addition to a fine. The table of punishments contained in the Army Act includes death; transportation for life; imprisonment, rigorous or simple, up to 14 years; cashiering (in case of officers); dismissal from service; reduction to the ranks; forfeiture of seniority or service; reprimand; and forfeiture or stoppage of pay and allowances.

A military commander plays an important role in the administration of military justice in India. He appoints investigating officers, decides the charges, selects the court members, controls their future service career, provides or may deny legal aid to the accused and reviews the findings of the court-martial. He can set aside the findings of the court-martial or send back the proceedings for review by the same court. There are of course problems with a system that gives the commander such absolute control over military justice matters. The rights of the individual soldier are rarely accorded much weight or consideration and commanders with such power can easily abuse the system to the point where the rule of law is replaced by a commander who operates as a law unto himself. Such absolute power in the hands of one person can also prevent any check on his authority. Besides, the rights available to an accused during a trial by a court-martial do not match the international standards.

Standards for Fair Trial During Court-Martial

Article 67 of the Rome Statute guarantees the highest standards of protection for the rights of the accused in all trials before the ICC. These rights need to be guaranteed by all States in every trial conducted at the national level, including trials of international crimes. The right to a fair trial and the other due process protections in the Rome Statute were derived principally from the International Covenant on Civil and Political Rights (ICCPR) and partly from the Universal Declaration of Human Rights, 1948.

The right to a fair trial is a norm of international human rights law designed to protect individuals from the unlawful and arbitrary curtailment or deprivation of their basic rights and freedoms, the most prominent of which are the right to life and liberty. It is guaranteed under Article 14 of the ICCPR, to which India is a signatory. Article 14 provides minimum procedural guarantees for an individual undergoing a trial for criminal charges. These rights are: (i) The right to a fair and public hearing, (ii) Equal access to, and equality before, the courts, (iii) The right to a competent, independent and impartial tribunal established by law, (iv) The right to a presumption of innocence until proved guilty according to law, (v) The right to prompt notice of the nature and cause of criminal charges, (vi) The right to adequate time and facilities for the preparation of a defence to the defendant and to his counsel, (vii) The right to a trial without undue delay, (viii) The right to defend oneself in person or through legal counsel of one's own choice and to free legal assistance, (ix) The right to an interpreter and the right to examine witnesses, (x) Prohibition of self-incrimination, (xi) Prohibition of double jeopardy, (xii) The right to appeal against conviction and sentence to a higher tribunal established according to law, and (xiii) The right to compensation for miscarriage of justice.

The Indian military justice system falls short of the international legal standards in that it is not free from command pressure, there are chances of its being applied with discretion and an accused may be denied legal representation on grounds of expediency. For example, Army Rules 96 provides that in every General Court-Martial and Discrict Court-Martial counsel shall be allowed to appear on behalf of the prosecution as well as accused. However, the convening officer may deny the same on the grounds of expediency. The military justice system has been criticized by the Indian Supreme Court on a number of occasions as being antiquated. Though the Armed Forces Tribunal has been established to entertain appeals from court-martial, this cannot remedy the fact that a trial before a court-martial itself denies the rights guaranteed under Article 14 of the ICCPR. There is thus, a need to amend the trial procedure contained in the Army Act and the Rules under it to meet the standards set in the Rome Statute.

The Geneva Conventions Act, 1960

India has passed the Geneva Conventions Act, 1960 to give effect to the Geneva Conventions of 1949. The punishment for grave breaches of the Conventions is contained in Section 3 of the Act. It provides that if any person within or without India commits or attempts to commit, or abets, or procures the commission by any other person of a grave breach of any of the Conventions, he shall be punished: (a) where the offence involves the wilful killing of a person protected by any of the Conventions, with death or with imprisonment for life; and (b) in any other case, with imprisonment for a term which may extend to 14 years. The Act further provides that a grave breach of the Geneva Conventions is a breach involving an act referred to in Article 50 of the First Geneva Convention, Article 51 of the Second Geneva Convention, Article 130 of the Third Geneva Convention and Article 147 of the Fourth Geneva Convention, committed against persons or property protected by that Convention.

Section 4 of the Geneva Act deals with the liability of a person who has committed offences outside India. It provides that when an offence is committed by any person outside India, he may be dealt with in respect of such offence as if it had been committed at any place within India at which he may be found. The competent court to try any offence under the Act shall be that of a chief presidency magistrate or a Court of Sessions. The Act further provides that **a person subject to the Army Act**, 1950, the Air Force Act, 1950, or the Navy Act, 1957, **who has committed a civil offence, shall be tried only by a military court** (court-martial). However, none of the grave breaches or violations of the Geneva Conventions have been incorporated into the Army Act, which has been amended on a few occasions after the Geneva Act came into force.

The competent courts shall not take cognizance of any offence under the Act, except on complaint by the government or of such officer of the government as the Central Government may specify by notification in the official gazette. Political officials can prevent the investigation of a case or the prosecution of an offender. The Act does not give a specific right to anyone to approach the court, nor does it give the victim the right to a remedy. Finally, if a complaint is made by the government or an authorized officer, questions relating to the application of the Convention to a conflict are to be determined by a government official, not the court.

In *Rev. Mons. Sebastiao Franciso Xavier dos Remedios Monteiro v. The State of Goa,* AIR 1970 SC 329, the Supreme Court gave the Geneva Act a restrictive interpretation. In this case, the appellant was a residence of Goa. After the annexation of Goa by India, he had a choice of becoming an Indian national or retaining Portuguese nationality. He chose the latter and was registered as a foreigner. He also obtained a temporary residential permit. His residential permit expired and he did not ask for renewal. He was ordered to leave India by the Lt Governor of Goa, who was empowered to discharge functions of the Central Government. He disobeyed the order and was prosecuted under the Foreigners Act and sentenced to 30 days of imprisonment. Since his appeal failed in the Sessions Court, and in the Court of the Judicial Commissioner, he approached the Supreme Court by a special leave. He claimed that his deportation was *ultra vires* the Geneva Act, 1960. The Sessions Court and the Court of the Judicial Commissioner had held that the Geneva Conventions Act, 1960 ceased to apply after Goa became part of the India.

In the Supreme Court, he challenged his deportation order as a violation of the Fourth Geneva Convention. The Court stated that the Act did not provide a cause of action for civil suits:-

> To begin with, the Geneva Conventions Act gives no specific right to anyone to approach the Court. The Act was passed under Article 253 of the Indian Constitution read with entries 13 and 14 of the Union List in the Seventh Schedule to implement the agreement signed and merely provides for certain matters based on the Geneva Conventions. What method an aggrieved party must adopt to move the municipal court is not very clear but we need not consider the point because of our conclusions on the other parts of the case.
>
> It will thus be seen that the Act by itself does not give any special remedy. It does give indirect protection by providing for breaches of

the Convention. The Conventions are not made enforceable by Government against itself nor does the Act give a cause of action to any party for the enforcement of the Conventions. Thus there is only an obligation undertaken by the Government of India to respect the Conventions regarding the treatment of civilian population but there is no right created in favour of protected persons, which the Court has been asked to enforce. If there is no provision of law which the courts can enforce, the court may be powerless and the court may have to leave the matter to what Westlake aptly described as "indignation of mankind".

Amendments to Military Manuals

In the last 20 years, the national legal system has made qualitative advances. This is due, in large part, to the impact of international human rights norms on national legislation. The international legal system now includes the concept of international criminal accountability for the commission of certain international crimes, and the emerging concept of the duty to protect the human rights of innocents. In March 2006, the UN General Assembly adopted the "Basic Principles and Guidelines on the Right to a Remedy and Reparation for Victims of Gross Violations of International Human Rights Law and Serious Violations of International Humanitarian Law". The UN document states that in cases of gross violations of international human rights law and serious violations of international humanitarian law constituting crimes under international law, States have the duty to investigate and prosecute the person allegedly responsible for the violations. The Supreme Court of India has, in a number of cases, tried to assimilate or incorporate the international standard into domestic law.

We ought to examine the possible methods available for incorporating the crimes spelt out in the Rome Statute and the standard of 'superior responsibility' into domestic military manuals. International standards should be incorporated so that it does not appear that our commanders have a greater degree of immunity in military operations than those from the rest of the world. If we are to claim that our armed forces support the rule of law, our military manuals should ensure a compatibility with the Rome Statute in relation to crimes, the rights of an accused during trial, and the internationally accepted “knew or should have known” standard of command responsibility. This would be more likely to prevent war crimes as it places a greater burden on commanders to be informed of the acts of their subordinates. Moreover, adopting the superior responsibility standard will bring the practice followed by Indian courts-martial in line with the customary international law of war.

Perhaps the best way to resolve the issue would be for Parliament to amend the Army Act (and also the Air Force and the Navy Act) to comport with the international standard. A significant advantage of such a course would be that the international standard would be clearly codified as domestic law and allow the armed forces to continue with their policy of trying service members alleged to have violated the law by a court-martial.

Conclusion

India is a parliamentary democracy with a free press, independent judiciary, active political parties and civic associations, and civilian-controlled armed forces. The Indian armed forces are known for their discipline, tradition and ethos in the entire world. They are known for their sense of propriety and just approach. It is for these basic humane qualities that the Indian armed forces are preferred over many other armies in the world in the formation of peace contingents representing the United Nations. Hence, the Indian military justice system should adopt a procedure that is not only open and objective, but also strives towards a liberal interpretation of the principles of natural justice. Shortcomings in the legal system should be removed by making suitable amendments to the military Acts to ensure their compliance with the Rome Statute.

CHAPTER 8

LEGAL ISSUES IN UNITED NATIONS PEACEKEEPING[1]

Introduction

Peacekeeping by the United Nations (UN) is a relatively recent development. It began with a primarily military model of observing ceasefires and separating combatants after inter-State wars. UN observers were first deployed in Palestine in 1948 and military forces were first used by the Security Council in 1956 during the Suez crisis. The 1988 award of the Nobel Peace Prize to the 50,000 soldiers who served the UN in the preceding four decades was an important sign of the renewed public interest in peacekeeping. Blue berets and blue helmets have recently gained much favour and public recognition.

Peacekeeping has witnessed significant growth since the 1990s and has become a cornerstone of the international community's response to international crises. Today nearly 100,000 UN peacekeepers—soldiers and military officers, police and civilian personnel—from as many as 115 countries monitor and observe peace processes that emerge in post-conflict situations and assist conflicting parties in implementing the peace agreement they have signed. Such assistance comes in many forms, including promoting human security, confidence-building measures, power-sharing arrangements, electoral support, strengthening the rule of law, and economic and social development.

---

1 The text of this chapter is based on a talk delivered at the USI on 22 May 2009.

United Nations and Peacekeeping Missions

The UN was established to "save succeeding generations from the scourge of war" and one of its main purposes is to maintain international peace and security. Peacekeeping, although not explicitly provided for in the UN Charter, has evolved into one of the main tools used by the UN to achieve this purpose. The Charter gives the UN Security Council primary responsibility for the maintenance of international peace and security. In fulfilling this responsibility, the Security Council may adopt a range of measures, including the establishment of a UN peacekeeping operation. The legal basis for such action is found in Chapters VI, VII and VIII of the Charter. While Chapter VI deals with the "Pacific Settlement of Disputes", Chapter VII contains provisions related to "Action with Respect to the Peace, Breaches of the Peace and Acts of Aggression". Chapter VIII of the Charter also provides for the involvement of regional arrangements and agencies in the maintenance of international peace and security, provided such activities are consistent with the purposes and principles outlined in Chapter I of the Charter.

UN peacekeeping operations have traditionally been associated with Chapter VI of the Charter. However, the Security Council need not refer to a specific Chapter of the Charter when passing a resolution authorizing the deployment of a United Nations peacekeeping operation and has never invoked Chapter VI. In recent years, the Security Council has adopted the practice of invoking Chapter VII of the Charter when authorizing the deployment of UN peacekeeping operations into volatile post-conflict settings where the State is unable to maintain security and public order. The Security Council's invocation of Chapter VII in these situations, in addition to denoting the legal basis for its action, can also be seen as a statement of firm political resolve and a means of reminding the parties to a conflict and the wider United Nations membership of their obligation to give effect to Security Council decisions.

Mandate and Authority of Peacekeeping Missions

The guidelines for peacekeeping operations provide that peacekeeping is a UN presence in the field (normally involving military and civilian personnel), with the consent of the conflicting parties to implement or monitor the implementation of arrangements relating to the control of conflicts (ceasefires, separation of forces, etc.) and their resolution, or to ensure the safe delivery of humanitarian relief. Peace enforcement may be needed when all other efforts fail. The authority for enforcement is dealt with in Chapter VII of the Charter, and includes the use of armed forces to maintain or restore international peace and security in situations in which the Security Council has determined the existence of a threat to peace, breach of peace or act of aggression.

Under the Charter of the UN, it is the Security Council that normally creates and defines peacekeeping missions. It does this by providing the mission with a mandate—a description of the mission's tasks. To establish a new peacekeeping mission, or change the mandate or strength of an existing mission, nine of the Security Council's 15 Member States must vote in favour. However, if any one of the five permanent members—China, France, the Russian Federation, the United Kingdom or the United States—votes against the proposal, it fails.

Most peacekeeping operations are established and implemented by the UN itself, with the troops supplied by member states serving under UN operational command. In other cases, where direct UN involvement is not considered appropriate or feasible, the Security Council authorizes regional and other international organizations, such as the European Union (EU), African Union (AU), North Atlantic Treaty Organization (NATO), Economic Community of West African States (ECOWAS) or "coalitions of willing countries", to implement certain peacekeeping or peace enforcement functions.

Force Structure, Privileges and Immunities

The UN does not have its own military force; it depends on contributions from Member States. As of 31 January 2010, 115 countries have contributed 99,943 military, police and civilian personnel to UN peacekeeping. Most troops are provided by developing countries, like Pakistan, Bangladesh,

India and Nigeria. In contrast, developed countries provide most of the funding (the USA tops the chart with 26% of the total funding, followed by Japan, Germany, the UK and several others).

Each UN peacekeeping mission is a separate entity and operates under different circumstances. Troops from different countries have different national military rules. The task of the missions is always different and, therefore, the Status of Forces Agreement (SOFA) may differ from mission to mission. The peacekeeping forces have status, privileges and immunities which are granted to UN personnel while carrying out peacekeeping operations under the (i) UN Convention on Privileges and Immunities of 13 February, 1946; (ii) UN Convention on Safety of UN and its Personnel, adopted by the General Assembly on 9 December, 1994; and (iii) Secretary General's 2003 bulletin, Special Measure for Protection from Sexual Exploitation and Sexual Abuse.

Advantages of UN Peacekeeping

UN peacekeeping is both effective and cost-effective when compared to the costs of conflict and the loss of life and economic devastation. UN peacekeeping operations are cheaper as they have the distinct advantage of having a built-in mechanism for globally sharing the financial, material and personnel costs. Peacekeeping missions play a vital role in providing a bridge to stability and eventual long-term peace and development. Another distinct advantage of UN peacekeeping is its multinational nature, which provides impartiality and legitimacy. The staff members are experienced in post-conflict peace-building operations, and the structure for coordinating international assistance is well oiled.

Human Rights in Peacekeeping Missions

International human rights law is an integral part of the normative framework for UN peacekeeping operations. The Universal Declaration of Human Rights, which is the cornerstone of international human rights standards, emphasizes that human rights and fundamental freedoms are universal and guaranteed to everybody. UN peacekeeping operations should be conducted with full and due regard for human rights, and should seek to advance human rights.

UN peacekeeping personnel—whether military, police or civilian—must understand how the implementation of their tasks intersects with human rights. Peacekeeping personnel must ensure that they do not become perpetrators of human rights abuse. They must be able to recognize violations or abuse of human rights, and be prepared to respond appropriately within the limits of their mandate and their competence. UN peacekeeping personnel should respect human rights in their dealings with colleagues and the local people, both in their public and private lives.

International Humanitarian Law

International humanitarian law (IHL), also known as "the law of war" or "the law of armed conflict," restricts the means and methods of armed conflict. IHL is contained in the four Geneva Conventions of 1949 and their two Additional Protocols of 1977, as well as in rules regulating the means and methods of combat. IHL also includes conventions and treaties on the protection of cultural property and the environment during armed conflict, as well as the protection of victims of conflict.

IHL is designed to protect persons who do not participate, or are no longer participating, in hostilities; and it maintains the fundamental rights of civilians, victims and non-combatants in an armed conflict. It is relevant to UN peacekeeping operations because these missions are often deployed in post-conflict environments where violence may be ongoing or conflict could reignite. Additionally, in post-conflict environments there are often large civilian populations that have been targeted by the warring parties, prisoners of war and other vulnerable groups to whom the Geneva Conventions or other humanitarian law would apply in the event of further hostilities. UN peacekeepers need to have a clear understanding of the principles and rules of IHL and observe them in situations where they apply.

The UN and International Responsibility

The UN has, in general, assumed responsibility for the activities of UN peacekeeping forces. The UN perceives its international responsibility to be an aspect of its international legal personality and its capacity to bear international rights and obligations. The UN Secretariat has stated, "As a subsidiary organ of the United Nations, an act of a peacekeeping force is, in principle, imputable to the Organization, and if committed in violation of an international obligation entails the international responsibility of the Organization and its liability in compensation." On the basis of this premise, the UN has acknowledged its responsibility for the conduct of peacekeepers participating in the UN Operation in the Congo ('ONUC') and the UN peacekeeping force in Cyprus. The Secretariat did clarify that the international responsibility of the UN is conditional upon the assumption that the operation in question is executed under its 'exclusive command and control' and hence, considered a subsidiary organ of the UN. That is, only peacekeeping operations conducted under UN command and control have the legal status of a UN subsidiary organ. In other operations, such as joint operations, responsibility lies where 'effective command and control' or 'operational command and control' is vested.

Command and Control in the Current Peacekeeping Missions

In a UN peacekeeping operation, all components of the mission—military, police and civilian—come under the 'operational authority' of the Head of Mission, typically a Special Representative of the Secretary-General, but in some cases a Force Commander or a Chief Military Observer. More pertinently, peacekeepers contributed by the Member States come under the 'operational control' of the Force Commander, the head of the military component of a peacekeeping operation. As for military personnel provided by Member States, they are placed under the operational control of the UN Force Commander or head of military component, but not under UN command. The UN Secretariat is careful not to assert that it has command over peacekeepers, as the laws and national policies of many Member States forbid command of their armed forces to be handed over to a foreign commander. For example, Canadian law does not permit national command of Canadian forces to be exercised by a foreign commander at any time, but permits 'operational control' to be vested in a foreign commander.

The national contingent commander is normally the most senior officer from the Member State on the ground. In some cases, he serves as the Commanding Officer of the contingent and in other cases, he serves on the Force Commander's staff or in other staff capacities within the peacekeeping operations. He has the authority to represent his contingent on all matters pertaining to his contingent. The force commander in peacekeeping operations is authorized to direct the forces so that the national contingent commander may accomplish specific missions or tasks which are usually limited by function, time, or location or a combination.

UN Peacekeeping Tasks

The range of tasks assigned to UN peacekeeping operations has expanded significantly in response to shifting patterns of conflict and to best address emerging threats to international peace and security. Although each UN peacekeeping operation is different, there is a considerable degree of consistency in the types of mandated tasks assigned by the Security Council. These could be as follows:

1. **Conflict Prevention** involves the application of structural or diplomatic measures to keep intra-state or inter-state tensions and disputes from escalating into violent conflict. Ideally, it should build on structured early warning, information-gathering and a careful analysis of the factors driving the conflict. Conflict prevention activities may include the use of the Secretary-General's 'good offices', preventive deployment or confidence-building measures.

2. **Peacemaking** generally includes measures to address conflicts in progress and usually involves diplomatic action to bring hostile parties to a negotiated agreement. The UN Secretary-General, upon the request of the Security Council or the General Assembly or at his own initiative, may exercise his or her 'good offices' to facilitate the resolution of the conflict. Peacemakers may also be envoys, governments, groups of states, regional organizations or the UN.

In addition, peacemaking efforts may be undertaken by unofficial and non-governmental groups, or by a prominent personality working independently.

3. **Peacekeeping** is a technique designed to preserve the peace, however fragile, in an area where fighting has been halted, and to assist in implementing agreements achieved by the peacemakers. Over the years, peacekeeping has evolved from a primarily military model of observing ceasefires and the separation of forces after inter-state wars to incorporate a complex model of many elements—military, police and civilian—working together to help lay the foundations for sustainable peace.

4. **Peace Enforcement** involves the application, with the authorization of the Security Council, of a range of coercive measures, including the use of military force. Such actions are authorized to restore international peace and security in situations where the Security Council has determined the existence of a threat to the peace, breach of the peace or act of aggression. The Security Council may utilize, where appropriate, regional organizations and agencies for enforcement action under its authority.

5. **Peace-building** involves a range of measures targeted to reduce the risk of parties lapsing or relapsing into conflict by strengthening national capacities for conflict management at all levels. It is a complex, long-term process of creating the necessary conditions and laying the foundation for sustainable peace and development. Peace-building works by addressing the deep-rooted, structural causes of violent conflict in a comprehensive manner. Peace-building measures address core issues that affect the functioning of society and the State, and seek to enhance the capacity of the State to effectively and legitimately carry out its core functions.

However, in today's scenario, the boundaries between conflict prevention, peace-making, peacekeeping, peace-building and peace enforcement have become increasingly blurred. Peace operations are rarely limited to one type of activity. While UN peacekeeping operations are, in principle, deployed to support the implementation of a ceasefire or peace agreement, they are often required to play an active role in peace-making efforts and may also be involved in early peace-building activities. UN peacekeeping operations may also use force at the tactical level, with the authorization of the Security Council, to defend themselves and their mandate, particularly in situations where the State is unable to provide security and maintain public order.

Peacekeeping operations commonly support local authorities in the following: (i) the implementation of a peace agreement; (ii) the maintenance of stability through military and police interventions; (iii) disarmament, demobilization and reintegration of former combatants; (iv) the supervision of ceasefires and troop withdrawal and manning of buffer zones; (v) the return of refugees and internally displaced persons to their homes; (vi) the delivery of humanitarian services to those in need; (vii) restructuring and reform of local armed forces and police; (viii) the maintenance of law and order; (ix) strengthening of court and judicial systems and prison facilities; (x) the promotion and protection of human rights; (xi) the conduct and monitoring of elections (for example, UN peace missions have supported elections in seven post-conflict countries—Afghanistan, Burundi, Haiti, Iraq, Liberia, the DRC and Timor); and (xii) the promotion of development and economic reconstruction.

Use of Force

Peacekeeping is a non-coercive instrument, based on the consent and cooperation of the parties. Force is not the means which it utilizes to achieve its mandate. However, peacekeepers at all times retain the right to self-defence, in which case force may be used as a last resort. The right to self-defence ends with the threat that gave rise to it; retaliation is not self-defence.

The peacekeeper's right to self-defence does not end with the defence of his/her own life. It includes defending one's comrades and any persons entrusted to one's care, as well as defending one's post, convoy, vehicle, or armed and ammunition. Each peacekeeping operation is expected to function as a single, integrated unit and an attack on any one of its members or sub-units engages the right to self-defence of the operation as a whole.

The environments in which UN peacekeeping operations are deployed are often characterized by the presence of militias, criminal gangs and other spoilers who may actively seek to undermine the peace process or pose a threat to the civilian population. In such situations, the Security Council has given UN peacekeeping operations "robust" mandates authorizing them to "use all necessary means" to deter forceful attempts to disrupt the political process, protect civilians under imminent threat of physical attack, and/or assist the national authorities in maintaining law and order. By proactively using force in defence of their mandates, these UN peacekeeping operations have succeeded in improving the security situation and creating an environment conducive to reconstruction.

Human Rights Violations

There is an obvious link between human rights and conflict. Where rights are violated, conflict is more likely to arise, and conflict inevitably brings with it human rights violations. Post-Cold War conflicts have mainly been of an internal nature and have often been rooted in gross violations of human rights, ethnic tensions and discrimination, fights for the control of natural resources, and people's struggle to achieve freedom from oppression, social justice and democratic government. These conflicts have involved deliberate targeting of civilians, mass population displacement, the use of child soldiers, violence against ethnic and religious groups, gender-based and sexual violence, deliberate destruction of property and crops, mutilation and other violations.

Accordingly, human rights violations are part of the operational reality that peace operations and peacekeepers have to confront. Addressing human rights problems is an essential aspect of finding solutions to conflicts. Thus, it is important for peacekeepers to be aware of and understand human rights norms, their relevance to their mandate and tasks, and how they can contribute to the promotion and protection of human rights through their action.

Accountability of Peacekeepers

The maintenance of the best possible relations with the civilian population in an area of operations is essential and the importance of the enforcement of acceptable behaviour, on leave as well as duty, can hardly be overemphasized. The peacekeepers are to adhere to the 'Ten Rules: For the code of personal conduct for blue-helmet'. The 'Ten Rules' are as follows:-

1. Dress, think, talk, act and behave in a manner befitting the dignity of a disciplined, caring, considerate, mature, respected and trusted soldier, displaying the highest integrity and impartiality. Have pride in your position as a peacekeeper and do not abuse or misuse your authority.

2. Respect the law of the land of the host country, their local culture, traditions, customs and practices.

3. Treat the inhabitants of the host country with respect, courtesy and consideration. You are there as a guest to help them and in so doing, will be welcomed with admiration. Neither solicit nor accept any material reward, honour or gift.

4. Do not indulge in immoral acts of sexual, physical or psychological abuse or exploitation of the local population or United Nations staff, especially women and children.

5. Respect and regard the human rights of all. Support and aid the infirm, sick and weak. Do not act in revenge or with malice, in particular when dealing with prisoners, detainees or people in your custody.

6. Properly care for and account for all United Nations money, vehicles, equipment and property assigned to you and do not trade or barter with them to seek personal benefits.

7. Show military courtesy and pay appropriate compliments to all members of the mission, including other United Nations

contingents, regardless of their creed, gender, rank or origin.

8. Show respect for and promote the environment, including the flora and fauna, of the host country.

9. Do not engage in excessive consumption of alcohol or traffic in drugs.

10. Exercise the utmost discretion in handling confidential information and matters of official business which can put lives into danger or soil the image of the United Nations.

The nearly 100,000 personnel serving in 20 UN missions come from a variety of military cultures and have received diverse types of training. Problems arise when individual members of the armed forces commit serious crimes or are even generally suspected to have done so. This can create general resentment and can reflect upon the population's perception of an entire force. Imposing a common code of conduct and discipline on such a heterogeneous force poses a huge challenge. The problem has been highlighted by several cases of sexual abuse and misbehaviour by UN personnel in recent years. Some instances in which peacekeepers have been involved in cases of indiscipline are given below.

Indiscipline: Somalia

In March 1993, the UN mission UNOSOM II was launched to deliver humanitarian aid and restore order in Somalia, which was suffering from a severe famine, general anarchy, and domination by warlords following the collapse of the government. The Canadian government selected the Canadian Airborne Regiment (CAR) as Canada's contribution to this operation for the restoration of peace. The forces were deployed in Somalia in January 1993. There were reports that the aid material was being stolen by the warlords as well as the locals, and was being bartered for weapons. The Canadian forces found that there was also a constant stream of locals pilfering from the Canadian camp itself. These thefts from the camp were a major irritant, and also a risk to the safety of the soldiers. A Canadian commanding officer had tacitly encouraged abuse of any thieves who were caught.

On 16 March 1993, the CAR captured a Somali teenager, Shidane Arone, who had sneaked into the camp. Arone was locked in an empty bunker that had often been used as a cell, and was placed under the guard of Master Corporal Clayton Matchee and Trooper (Private) Kyle Brown, both members of 2 Commando. Matchee, who had been drinking heavily, almost immediately began to severely beat Arone, punching him in the ribs, hitting him in the head with his baton, and putting out cigarettes on his foot. Brown participated somewhat in this abuse, but was mostly an observer. He took 16 photographs of the beating. During the several hours that the beating went on, several other soldiers visited the bunker and observed the events; many others were within earshot of the bunker and could hear what was going on.

Matchee and Brown left the unconscious Arone after several hours of this torture. When an officer returning from patrol checked on Arone, he found that he had no pulse and the base medics confirmed that the boy was dead. A death in custody automatically triggers an investigation, and two days later, Matchee and Brown were arrested and charged with the murder. Matchee later attempted suicide; the attempt failed but caused massive brain damage, making him unfit to stand trial. Brown was found guilty of manslaughter.

Brown claimed in his defence that he had informed every officer he could find of the happenings in the bunker and had requested them to intervene. He stated that when the officers declined to put an end to the torture, he began documenting the event with photographs.

It was found that 16 people had passed through the area where Arone was tortured and that during the night, his screams could be heard throughout the surrounding area. The Commanding Officer of the Airborne, Lieutenant Colonel Mathieu, was tried twice by courts-martial and acquitted of wrong-doing both times. The Officer Commanding of 2 Commando, Major Anthony Seward, was also court-martialed under Article 124 of the National Defence Act for negligent in performance of duties. He was convicted and sentenced to 3 months' imprisonment and dismissal with disgrace from the Canadian Forces. A number of his subordinate supervisors were also court-martialed and found guilty under Article 124.

Soon after the death of Arone came to public attention, other actions by the Airborne also began to be scrutinized. Days earlier, a patrol from the Reconnaissance Platoon had shot and killed a young Somali night-time infiltrator and seriously injured another. There were a few other reports of racial abuse and torture of the locals.

At first, Canadian military officials told the media, and also minister Campbell, that Arone had likely died from natural causes. The issue created a public outcry in Canada. The high regard the Canadian people had for their armed forces, especially the peacekeepers, was damaged. Highly placed members of the military leadership were accused of fraudulently altering documents prior to handing them over to journalists. The existence of other documents was denied, and some others were destroyed.

Canada was not the only country to face problems in Somalia. There were severe casualties on all sides in the warlord-dominated chaos. The Battle of Mogadishu resulted in 500–1000 Somali militia and civilian deaths, as well as 18 American and two Pakistani deaths, following which the US decided to leave the country. Soldiers of other countries also faced charges of misconduct: Italian troops were photographed appearing to rape a Somali woman and Belgian soldiers took photographs of themselves urinating on and burning Somalis.

In 2008, a Warrant Officer of the Uganda Army, while on the UN peacekeeping mission in Somalia, allegedly fathered a son with a Somali woman. His acts were detrimental to the rules, standing orders, operations and proceedings of the peacekeeping force.

Indiscipline: Other Countries

- **2008:** Indian peacekeepers (three soldiers, including a Lt Col) in Congo faced allegations of sexual exploitation and child abuse. The troops were withdrawn and sent back to India. The Defence

Minister ordered a thorough investigation into the charges.

•2008: Three Indian peacekeepers, including a Lt Col, were accused of assaulting and "sexually propositioning" a local resident in Congo to recover $480 which they paid to buy gold from him that proved to be fake. They were found guilty of illegally detaining and assaulting a gold trader, but were let off with a "warning". The United Nations banned them from taking part in any future peacekeeping missions.

•2007: Sri Lankan soldiers (110) in the UN peacekeeping mission in Haiti were repatriated after a preliminary investigation found that they had paid for prostitutes, including a few who were under-aged.

•2007: Pakistani troops facilitated the illegal transfer of gold from Congolese miners to buyers based in Kenya.

•2006: Thirteen military personnel were repatriated from Congo to their home countries on disciplinary grounds. The action taken by the Member States included three demotions in rank, four custodial sentences and five dismissals from the armed services.

•2005: Pakistani troops in the eastern town of Mongbwalu were accused of giving guns to local rebel in return for gold.

•2004–06: the UN Department of Peacekeeping investigated 319 peacekeeping personnel over allegations of sexual exploitation and abuse across its 16 missions. A total of 179 personnel were dismissed or repatriated following the inquiries. Because prostitution is legal in many countries which contribute troops, some peacekeepers who raped girls tried to disguise it as prostitution by giving them money or food. Not one person, however, has been prosecuted for these serious crimes.

•2003: Nepalese troops were accused of sexual abuse while serving in Congo. Disciplinary action was taken against them under the Nepal Army Act.

- **2001:** Seven Danish peacekeepers were accused of sexually abusing a 13-year-old girl in Eritrea while on leave from the UN Mission in Ethiopia and Eritrea.

Action against Peacekeepers

The allegations of war crimes and violations of human rights by the peacekeepers were shocking for civil society. They necessitated a change in the legal parameters of multinational peacekeeping operations. These abuses have undermined the UN administration and the credibility of every peacekeeping mission. Such conduct achieves the opposite of these missions' ideal of bringing 'peace and security'.

The UN force commander cannot exercise any authority over the accused peacekeeper. The UN force commander has general responsibility for good order and discipline of the operation. He may make investigations, conduct inquires and require information, reports and consultations for the purpose of discharging this responsibility. Generally, the responsibility for disciplinary action in national contingencies, however, rests with the commander of the national contingents. The most the UN could do in the examples cited above was to return the peacekeeper to his country.

If it is alleged that a member of the UN peacekeeping force has committed a serious breach of discipline or is guilty of an act amounting to a 'war crime', the question arises as to how and where the person is to be tried. The actual issue that emerges is who has the criminal jurisdiction over these crimes. For the victims of crimes committed by members of a UN peacekeeping force, the legal position is very complicated: who is the admissible defendant on their claim for compensation? Is it the host State or the sending State that is responsible for reparations? Is it the UN that exercises control, the overall force commander or the commander of the violator, or the violator in person? The UN has no power to try the offending soldiers, who are subject to the disciplinary authority of their own military. There are several possibilities of trials of UN forces personnel. The accused members of the UN peacekeeping force can be tried by the national court of the receiving State where the crime was committed, or by the sending

State, or by the international criminal court.

1. Trial in Receiving State

The trial of a peacekeeper by the receiving State would be most ideal as the witnesses could easily testify and the related evidence could also be placed before the court. It would be necessary for the courts to follow the rules of 'fair trial' as contained in Article 14 of the International Covenant on the Civil and Political Rights. The state machinery, however, would have to be capable of conducting such a trial. For example, the situation in Somalia, Rwanda and Haiti was such that total governance had collapsed, making the trial of a UN member virtually impossible.

When UN peacekeepers are stationed in the territory of a foreign State with that State's agreement, there arise certain issues of concurrent jurisdiction over alleged crimes perpetrated by them as between the courts of the sending and receiving States. These matters are usually dealt with by the provisions of the Status of Forces Agreement (SOFA). States are generally unwilling to submit their military personnel to local national jurisdiction for any violations during the course of duty.

2. Trial in the Sending State

There is a possibility of trial of UN peacekeepers by the military court or civil courts of the sending state. In the USA, it was argued in the case of *Jennings v. Markley* (1961) that the alleged US soldier would not fall under US jurisdiction, since he was a member of the UN force in Korea. The court rejected the argument and stated that US military personnel remain subject to US court-martial jurisdiction, irrespective of UN military jurisdiction. The Canadian court gave a similar ruling in the *Re Brown and Fisher* (1994) case and affirmed the primacy of national court-martial jurisdiction in cases involving charges of unlawful conduct by members of national contingents serving in UN forces. Another problem is that in a trial in the sending State, there would be difficulty relating to the victim's testimony, with the victim unlikely to testify in a foreign court. Also, the military courts of sending States may be tempted to shield their personnel.

Trial in the sending State also gives rise to the question of uniformity of practice and its implications for the UN forces, especially where personnel from two different countries are involved in a crime. Within any multinational force, uniformity of military practice is a question of considerable significance in terms of morale and fairness. Where the same offence carries grossly disproportionate punishment in different national contingents, the morale of the whole force may be seriously undermined. For instance, the punishment of death penalty has been abolished in Nepal, while it exists in Bangladesh, India, Pakistan and Sri Lanka. There are different procedures being followed in a trial by the military court, and also in matters of legal aid, review, appellate processes and the jurisdiction of the civil courts over the court-martial. In India, the Armed Forces Tribunal will have jurisdiction over the orders, findings and sentence awarded by a court-martial, whereas no such forum exists in Bangladesh, Nepal, Pakistan and Sri Lanka.

3. Trial in the International Criminal Court

The Rome Statute of the International Criminal Court (ICC) was adopted on 17 July 1998. The Rome Statute is unique in many ways. First, it has created a permanent tribunal, the ICC, to deal with all crimes of serious concern to the international community as a whole. Second, it provides that the ICC shall exercise jurisdiction over individuals, unlike the other permanent international tribunals, such as the International Court of Justice. The ICC's powers and functions include holding individuals accountable, and subjecting the accused to investigation, arrest, detention, prosecution and if found guilty, incarceration.

The ICC can exercise jurisdiction over a military accused if his state is a signatory to the Rome Statute of ICC. It has jurisdiction over war crimes, which have been divided into four categories: (a) grave breaches of the four Geneva Conventions of 12 August 1949; (b) other serious violations of the laws and customs applicable in international armed conflict, within the established framework of international law; (c) in the case of an armed conflict not of an international character, serious violations of Article 3 common to the four Geneva Conventions; and (d) other serious violations of the laws and customs applicable to armed conflicts that are not of an international character, within the established framework of international law. Most of the crimes committed in the past by the UN peacekeeper would come under one of these categories.

A person who attacks a UN force or its property during an armed conflict will commit a war crime and can be tried by the ICC for violation of the Rome Statute. However, the liability of a commander or members of a multinational force for a breach of international humanitarian law or human rights is not well defined. Every UN peacekeeping operation consists of military personnel provided by different states. In theory, the UN force commander has general responsibility for good order and discipline of the operation. He may make investigations and conduct inquiries; however, the responsibility for disciplinary action in national contingents rests with the commander of the national contingent. In the case of an alleged crime, the most the UN administration can do is to send the peacekeeper back to his home country. Once there, the peacekeeper is subject to the military laws of his country; it is at that country's discretion whether to prosecute the peacekeeper.

After the establishment of the ICC, there was a fear in the USA that American soldiers in UN peacekeeping operations might be held accused before that court. The issue of immunity of peacekeepers, therefore, arose in 2002, when the USA threatened the Security Council that it would make use of its veto right even in the area of peacekeeping operations unless UN personnel were granted blanket immunity from prosecution by the ICC. The Security Council passed a resolution prohibiting the ICC from prosecuting current or former UN peacekeeping personnel from countries not a party to the Rome Statute. Subsequently, the USA has signed bilateral agreements with different states that their soldiers will not fall within the jurisdiction of the ICC.

Immunity of UN Peacekeepers

Senior UN officials enjoy the benefit of full diplomatic immunity and military personnel are regularly granted immunity under SOFA. However, UN personnel are not absolutely immune from legal liability. They are usually granted a functional immunity, which seeks to protect the interests of the UN rather than benefiting the agent personally. The protection granted by the UN Charter is intended to safeguard the efficient functioning of the organization. In the context of UN peacekeeping operations, the SOFA plays an important role. Military personnel are usually granted immunity under a SOFA. As a result, criminal prosecution of an accused peacekeeper in the host State is usually excluded.

Insufficiency of the Existing System and Possible Remedies

The UN ignored, denied and actively suppressed crimes by peacekeepers till as recently as 2004. Since many of the allegations were difficult to prove in a court of law, the countries concerned tried to defend their accused peacekeepers either by taking no action or awarding minor punishments. However, in the wake of the most recent peacekeeper abuse scandal, there has been progress towards accountability for sexual exploitation and abuse committed in UN peacekeeping operations. In his package of reform, the former UN Secretary-General, Kofi Annan, admitted to being "especially troubled by instances in which United Nations peacekeepers are alleged to have sexually exploited minors and other vulnerable people." He repeated his policy of zero tolerance of such offences, and reaffirmed the United Nations' commitment to respect, adhere to and implement international law, fundamental human rights and the basic standards of due process. Annan appointed Prince Zeid al-Hussein, Jordan's ambassador to the UN with personal civilian peacekeeping experience in Bosnia, to study the abuses and make recommendations on improving the accountability of UN peacekeeping missions.

Prince Zeid's report, submitted in March 2005, concluded that sexual exploitation of women and girls by UN security and civilian personnel in Congo was significant, widespread and ongoing. The report made recommendations in four general areas: (i) creation of a common set of rules; (ii) formation of a professional investigation capability; (iii) introduction of measures to insure organizational, managerial and command responsibility; and (iv) establishment of procedures to ensure individual disciplinary, financial and criminal responsibility. His recommendations included withholding the salary of guilty peacekeepers and putting the money in a fund to care for the victims, requiring troop-contributing countries to prosecute perpetrators identified by the UN investigative teams, and making soldiers financially liable for "peacekeeper babies" they have fathered as determined by DNA testing.

In April 2005, the Special Committee on Peacekeeping Operations held a review session to discuss the report and recommended that the General Assembly adopt the detailed rules in the Secretary-General's 2003 bulletin, Special Measures for Protection from Sexual Exploitation and Sexual Abuse, as the uniform standard on sexual exploitation and abuse for every category of UN peacekeeping personnel.

Today, there is clear support at the political level to remove from service any UN employee who engages in sexual exploitation and abuse. The most severe administrative penalty that the UN is empowered to inflict is the termination of a civilian appointment and the immediate repatriation of a military member of a contingent who is found to have committed sexual exploitation and abuse by a UN investigation. This could be followed by sanctions for contingent commanders who do not enforce the standards. What is needed is a commitment from the troop-contributing countries to prosecute their nationals who commit crimes within peacekeeping operations.

The Department of Peacekeeping Operations: Conduct and Discipline Units

The Department of Peacekeeping Operations (DPKO) and Member States have put in place a comprehensive package of reforms to prevent misconduct by civilian and uniformed peacekeeping personnel and take swift action where breaches of UN standards have occurred. The conduct and discipline units in the DPKO were established in November 2005 as part of a package of reforms in UN peacekeeping to strengthen accountability and uphold standards of conduct in the UN.

The headquarters of the 'conduct and discipline' team maintains global oversight on the state of discipline in all peacekeeping operations and provides overall direction in the areas of conduct and discipline in field missions. The units in peacekeeping operations act as principal advisers to heads of mission on all conduct and discipline issues involving all categories of peacekeeping personnel in the missions. The conduct and discipline units address all forms of misconduct, including acts of sexual exploitation and abuse, by UN peacekeeping personnel.

In order to strengthen the rule of law in a failed state, the DPKO has identified four basic areas: police, prisons, courts and human rights. The DPKO thus recommends the creation of units dedicated to each of these areas in new peacekeeping operations. The civilian police component undertakes a range of transitional policing responsibilities and plays a major role in support of efforts to restructure and retrain national police forces. The corrections component supports the reconstruction of prisons and the training and resourcing of national corrections officers. The legal and judicial system support component supports the rebuilding, reopening and effective functioning of the national court system. The human rights and protection component promotes the protection of human rights and the creation and functioning of mechanisms that seek to provide transitional justice.

Reparations for Victims

In 2005, the UN General Assembly has adopted basic principles and guidelines on the right to a remedy and reparation for victims of gross violations of international human rights and serious violations of international humanitarian law. The states are obliged to provide effective remedy to victims, including equal and effective access to justice; assistance; and adequate, effective and prompt reparation for harm suffered. It provides:-

1. *Restitution* should, whenever possible, restore the victim to the original situation before the gross violations of international human rights law or serious violations of international humanitarian law occurred. Restitution includes, as appropriate: restoration of liberty, enjoyment of human rights, identity, family life and citizenship, return

to one's place of residence, restoration of employment and return of property.

2. *Compensation* should be provided for any economically assessable damage, as appropriate and proportional to the gravity of the violation and the circumstances of each case, resulting from gross violations of international human rights law and serious violations of international humanitarian law. This includes compensation for: (a) physical or mental harm; (b) lost opportunities, including employment, education and social benefits; (c) material and moral damages and loss of earnings, including loss of earning potential; and (d) costs required for legal or expert assistance, medicine and medical services, and psychological and social services.

3. *Rehabilitation* should include medical and psychological care, as well as legal and social services.

Memorandum of Understanding

The next step towards peacekeeper accountability depends on the development of the new model memorandum of understanding (MOU) for troop-contributing countries that is being considered by the Special Committee on Peacekeeping Operations. The model MOU, which is being drafted with the goal of eliminating sexual exploitation and abuse, can go far in addressing the tangle of administrative and legal issues involved. It would also give the UN the reliable leverage it now lacks vis-à-vis recalcitrant troop-contributing countries regarding their responsibilities.

This also requires the cooperation of the troop-contributing countries in areas such as pre-deployment training in human rights, participation in investigations, post-repatriation disciplinary action (including prosecution) and follow-up to the UN. Troop-contributing countries' responsibilities in these areas should be addressed in the model MOU, and the agreement between the UN and countries participating in peacekeeping operations.

The model MOU should be specific about responsibilities and requirements within a strategy of eliminating sexual exploitation and abuse.

It must highlight the following:-

- Basic pre-deployment training in international human rights and humanitarian laws. The substantive human rights issues that need to be addressed in training to enable military peacekeepers to effectively and competently perform their functions include the overall human rights and international humanitarian law framework, human rights of women (including issues of sexual exploitation, trafficking and other forms of violence against women), refugees, rights of children, internally displaced persons, minorities, use of force, arrest and detention, international tribunals and conduct of peacekeepers.
- The responsibilities of commanders to ensure their contingent's participation in preliminary investigations.
- The provision of a military prosecutor by the troop-contributing countries to participate in investigations.
- Disciplinary action by the troop-contributing countries against contingent commanders who have been repatriated for failure to cooperate with an investigation.
- Recovery of payments by the UN from troop-contributing countries for contingent commanders who are repatriated for failure to cooperate with an investigation.
- Deduction from future payments to troop-contributing countries funds paid to any member of their contingent who is found guilty of sexual exploitation and abuse.
- Establishment of processes by the UN and troop-contributing countries for paternity claims, and the referral of cases by troop-contributing countries to the national civil courts (where it is concluded that the allegations are well founded) for domestic prosecution.
- Creation by the UN of a "trust fund for victims". The fund should

be utilized for awarding compensation to the victims.

Recommendations

The incidents of sexual abuse, prostitution and other incidents of serious misconduct have tarnished the reputation and effectiveness of the UN peacekeeping operations. There is a need to adopt a zero-tolerance policy towards crimes committed by the peacekeepers. The troop-contributing countries need to enforce the highest possible standard of conduct among military officials selected for peacekeeping missions. The troop-contributing countries, along with the UN, need to strengthen their efforts to detect and prevent abuse. In case of serious violations of human rights and international humanitarian law, the immunity granted to UN peacekeepers and other personnel needs to be waived. The UN should publicly name and shame those countries whose peacekeepers are found to have committed abuses during the peacekeeping missions.

The UN and troop-contributing states need to create an independent and impartial forum in which erring peacekeepers can be tried for alleged violations. A UN-administered judicial tribunal could be formed to try serious violations. It may consist of international judges and must adhere to the fair-trial guarantees contained in Article 14 of the ICCPR. There is also a need to establish an independent mission-based ombudsman, who is completely independent of the UN Secretariat and backed by a Security Council mandate. He should have the power to investigate alleged criminal acts of the members of the UN peacekeeping forces.

The long-term solution would be that the UN should create its own UN military police force to meet the peacekeeping demands. Besides necessary weapon training, the force personnel could be imparted training in the human rights and international humanitarian law. They should be subject to a common code of discipline. In reality, what the military personnel are expected to do in the peacekeeping missions is not what they are trained in. The former UN Secretary-General, Dag Hammarskjold, had said, "Peacekeeping is not a job for soldiers, but only soldiers can do it." A military police force trained in peacekeeping and enforcement missions by experts would be a better option than the existing one.

Conclusion

United Nations peacekeeping operations have evolved during the past five decades to assume a central role in maintaining peace in the international community. This trend has been reinforced since the end of the Cold War, after which the Security Council, in the absence of the East-West conflict, has assumed greater responsibility in matters related to international security. Standards of conduct in peacekeeping missions must be based on three key principles: (i) competence, efficiency and integrity; (ii) zero-tolerance of sexual abuse and exploitation; and (iii) accountability of commanders who fail to enforce the standards of conduct. The peacekeeping operations should be conducted with full respect for human rights and should seek to advance human rights through the implementation of their mandates. The peacekeepers must have a clear understanding of the principles and rules of international humanitarian law and observe them in situations where they apply.

Peacekeeping is a difficult task. It is performed in a hostile environment in the midst of a different culture, language and customs. United Nations peacekeeping operations are highly visible and generate high expectations. Accordingly, UN peacekeeping personnel should be careful to mitigate the possible negative consequences of the mission's presence. They must adhere to national laws, refrain from violating fundamental human rights standards, respect the local culture, and maintain the highest standards of personal and professional conduct.

CHAPTER 9

PROTECTION OF ENVIRONMENT DURING ARMED CONFLICT[1]

Introduction

Throughout human history, the environment has been one of war's many victims. Thucydides records the Greek tactic of scorching the earth during the Peloponnesian Wars. The Romans salted the soils of Carthage after winning the Punic Wars. The Dutch breached their dykes in 1792 to prevent a French invasion. In World War I, the British set afire Romanian oilfields to prevent the Central Powers from capturing them; in World War II, Germany and the Soviet Union engaged in "scorched earth" tactics; and in the Korean War, the United States bombed North Korean dams.

During the Vietnam War, the United States destroyed nearly 20% of Vietnam's forests, including 54% of its mangrove forests, through chemical defoliants, bulldozers and bombings. To counter the use of forest as cover by the North Vietnamese and Viet Cong, the United States cleared nearly three-quarters of a million acres of land using the Rome Plow, a heavy tractor with large blades. It also dropped herbicides over huge expanses of South Vietnam. Similarly, in a futile attempt to arrest the flow of supplies southward along the Ho Chi Minh trail, the US military seeded clouds, hoping that the ensuing rain would render the track impassable.

Towards the end of the First Gulf War, Iraq burned hundreds of oil wells and dumped massive amounts of oil into the Persian Gulf. The United States and its allies dropped more than 47,500 cluster bombs, containing 13,167,500 bomblets. NATO forces destroyed major oil refineries, and

---

1 The text of this chapter is based on a talk delivered at USI on 20 January 2010.

pharmaceutical and petrochemical plants in Kosovo, causing significant damage to the environment. The civil war in the Congo has decimated the country's wildlife, killing thousands of elephants, gorillas and okapis.

During the most recent fighting – between 27 December 2008 and 18 January 2009 – Israeli Defence Forces (IDF) conducted a major combined military operation in the Gaza Strip. The operation comprised bombardment by land, sea and air, and incursions into the Gaza Strip by Israeli troops, causing serious environmental damage. The ongoing conflicts in Afghanistan and Iraq have had serious repercussions on the environment. More than two decades of war have played havoc with the physical environment and caused tremendous loss of natural resources of these countries. In particular, landmines have had a devastating effect on the environment, compounding the already existing problems, such as deforestation and overuse of marginal wildlife species.

What is Environment?

Many international treaties and conventions have attempted to define environment in the context of war, most with only limited success. One of the most descriptive definitions of the environment is found in the 1977 United Nations Convention on the Prohibition of Military or Any Other Hostile Use of Environmental Modification Techniques (ENMOD). The ENMOD Convention defines environment as "the Earth, including its biota, lithosphere, hydrosphere and atmosphere, or ... outer space." However, this definition provides little clarity. Based on this definition, it is difficult to imagine any form of warfare that would not have serious environmental effects.

Other definitions of the environment can be found at national level. For example, the United States' Toxic Substance Control Act (TSCA) provides that the environment "includes water, air, and land and the interrelationship which exists among and between water, air, and land and all living things." Under the Environment Protection Act (1986) of India, the environment includes water, air, and land and the inter-relationship which exists among and between water, air, and land, and human beings, other living creatures, plants, micro-organisms and property.

Despite the inability of the international legal community to agree on a useful definition of the environment, it is clear that the trend in the international community is to view the environment as a very broad and inclusive entity. In fact, the lack of precision seems to be the result of not wanting to narrow the scope of legal coverage for the environment. Therefore, although a specific definition may be useful in a general sense, the lack of clarity and the consequent broader coverage of environmental protection may prove more valuable over time.

Classification of Environmental Damage

Arne Willy Dahl (1997), Judge Advocate for the Norwegian Armed Forces, has classified war-related environmental damage into six groups: (1) destruction of the human environment; (2) destruction of the cultivated environment; (3) destruction of the natural environment of economic importance; (4) destruction of the natural environment of non-economic value; (5) general environmental degradation; and (6) environmental manipulation as a tool in warfare.

A simple alternative, non-scientific, non-legal classification is provided by Lanier-Graham (1993), namely (1) intentional direct destruction of the environment during war; (2) incidental direct destruction; and (3) indirect or induced destruction as a medium- or long-term consequence of war but still attributable to war. Graham's 'intentional direct destruction', refers to the deliberate attack on cultivated and uncultivated lands and resources where the objective is indeed environmental destruction for its own sake, as for example with the setting of oil-fires during the Gulf War. An example of 'incidental direct destruction' would be soil disturbance by battle tanks moving from one location to another, where environmental damage is collateral but not the primary objective of the action undertaken. Finally, 'indirect or induced destruction' may occur as a result of the migration of human population on account of war that, in turn, may exert undue environmental stresses.

Military Activities and the Environment

Military activities have a significant impact on the environment. Nuclear as well as conventional weapons pose a serious threat to the environment. The preparation, including the testing, development, production and maintenance, of conventional and nuclear weapons has generated large quantities of hazardous, toxic and radioactive substances. The use and disposal of such weapons also generate toxic or hazardous substances that lead to a large scale depletion of natural resources and degradation of the environment.

Today, the world's eight nuclear-weapon states (China, France, Russia, the United Kingdom and the United States) have 36,000 nuclear bombs, containing 5,000 megatons of destructive energy—more than sufficient to destroy the world. A single large nuclear weapon could release explosive power comparable to all the energy released from the conventional weapons used in all past wars. Nuclear weapons have the potential to destroy the entire ecosystem of the planet. Those already in the world's arsenals have the potential of destroying life on the planet several times over.

During the Gulf War, American and British forces introduced armour-piercing ammunition made of depleted uranium (DU), a radioactive waste. By war's end, more than 290,000 kg of depleted uranium contaminated equipment and the soil on the battlefields of Saudi Arabia, Kuwait, and southern Iraq. DU is not only chemically toxic like other heavy metals such as lead, but it is also an alpha particle emitter with a radioactive half-life of 4.5 billion years. DU weapons contaminate impact areas with extremely fine radioactive and toxic dust. In addition to the fine uranium dust created by impacts, depleted uranium fragments and intact DU penetrators also pose a hazard. DU is acknowledged to cause kidney damage, cancers of the lung and bone, non-malignant respiratory disease, skin disorders, neuro-cognitive disorders, chromosomal damage, and birth defects.

Depleted uranium contamination is unlikely to be cleaned up by the victor or the vanquished because of the great cost and the possibility of further environmental damage. The cleaning up of DU involves removing the top layer of soil, which could be potentially devastating to an environment, especially if depleted uranium contaminates arable land or wetlands. Further, the cost involved in removing the topsoil from contaminated areas could be astronomical. For example, the cost of cleaning up 290,000 kg of depleted uranium on thousands of hectares in Saudi Arabia, Kuwait, and Iraq would be tens of billions of US dollars.

Landmines and unexploded military ordnance (UXO) also pose a serious threat to the environment, livelihood and process of sustainable development, affecting not only the present but also future generations. They prejudice economic development by disrupting the biosphere's life support systems and diminishing the capacity of the environment to supply natural resources. Mines deny access to natural resources, promote the rapid and unsustainable exploitation of marginal and ecologically fragile environments, deplete biological diversity by destroying flora and fauna, contaminate the surrounding soil and water with highly toxic substances, and destroy the ecosystem itself by disrupting soil and water processes.

Landmines kill livestock as well as wildlife. In Libya, between 1940 and 1980, mines and other UXO have killed more than 125,000 camels, sheep, goats, and cattle. There were about 264,000 goats and sheep killed in Afghanistan, at a value of about $31.6 million dollars. The same holds for cows, horses and camels. In Libya, gazelles have disappeared from sites that were mined during World War II. In Croatia, brown bears are regular victims. In India, landmines have killed barking deer, clouded leopards, snow leopards, and tigers.

The intensity of environmental damage from wars has been remarkably proportionate to the technological advancement in warfare. The more advanced the arms and ammunition, the greater is the damage to the environment. There are currently some 40 armed conflicts going on in the world involving tens of millions of people. Many of these are taking place in locations that are critical to the maintenance of biodiversity, such as, Africa, South Asia and Latin America.

It is estimated that, on an average, a US soldier in Iraq or Afghanistan uses 60 litres of oil each day, through vehicles such as tanks, trucks, helicopters, or by calling air strikes. This means approximately 13.25 million litres of oil is used every day by US forces in those two conflicts. This is more than the amount of oil used each day in the whole of Bangladesh.

Active and Passive Environmental Warfare

Virtually all wartime acts will have some effect on the environment. However, we can classify environmental damage as either passive or active. This classification would allow for differentiating the severity of international law violations based on the target of the attack rather than on the effects of the attack and, therefore, provide the international community the opportunity to determine the intent of the actor and seek more appropriate remedies for such violations.

Active environmental warfare requires the "intentional use" of the environment as a weapon of waging armed conflict. Employing the environment as an "instrument of warfare" has been defined as "the use of the environment that might cause damage to the enemy or interference with an enemy military or combat activity". This can occur through the operation of any conceivable instrument, such as conventional or unconventional weapons, natural forces, or resources. Active environmental warfare includes inducing earthquakes or other natural disasters, weather manipulation, and climate modification, where these activities are intentionally conducted to disrupt enemy movements or to destroy enemy forces. Other examples include redirecting waterways or releasing stored water to flood trafficable areas, seeding clouds to produce rain, setting forest fires to direct military forces, and fouling internal waters to prevent the movement of forces. Active environmental warfare involves the deliberate harnessing of the environment as an instrument for conducting hostilities. In this sense the environment is not just the field upon which war takes place, but an actively used tool of war.

In contrast to active environmental warfare, passive environmental warfare includes acts not specifically designed to use the environment for a particular military purpose but rather that have a degrading effect on the environment. These wartime acts may be completely unrelated to the environment in terms of the intent of the parties, yet they still have consequences that directly affect the surrounding environment. An example of passive environmental warfare is the use of artillery. While artillery bombardment is not a use of the environment, it has secondary environmental effects such as the destruction of plant life and the disruption of natural habitats. The disruption of the natural environment could also be caused by the mass movement of large armoured vehicles. In this case, it may not be the intent of the belligerents to cause environmental damage, but it occurs as a secondary effect of waging war.

Therefore, in active environmental warfare the environment is the weapon, whereas, in passive environmental warfare, the environment is the victim of wartime acts.

Protection of Environment: The International Humanitarian Law (IHL)

The existing rules of the IHL for the protection of the environment aim not to prevent damage altogether, but rather, to limit it to a level deemed tolerable. Unfortunately, there is reason to fear that the use of particularly devastating means of warfare (whose effects are often still unknown) could wreak such large-scale destruction as to render illusory the protection afforded to civilians under the IHL. Indeed, severe environmental damage could seriously hamper or even prevent the implementation of the provisions to protect the victims of armed conflict. Two treaties under IHL have provisions relating to the protection of the environment.

1. **The Convention on the Prohibition of Military or Any Other Hostile Use of Environmental Modification Techniques (ENMOD), 1976.** The ENMOD was convened in response to the severe damage suffered by Vietnam's environment as a result of the United States' use of chemicals and defoliants. Article I of the Convention states: "Each State Party to this Convention undertakes not to engage in military or any other hostile use of environmental modification techniques having widespread, long-lasting or severe effects as the means of destruction, damage or injury to any other

State Party."

The ENMOD Convention was intended to prohibit the military use of climate modification techniques that are intended or could be expected to cause "widespread, long-lasting, or severe" destruction or damage to the enemy environment. These three terms are defined as follows: *Widespread*: encompassing an area on the scale of several hundred square kilometres; *Long-lasting*: lasting for a period of months, or approximately a season; and *Severe*: involving serious or significant disruption or harm to human life, natural and economic resources, or other assets.

The key phrase in ENMOD is "environmental modification techniques", and Article II of the Convention defines these as: "Any technique for changing – through the deliberate manipulation of natural processes – the dynamics, composition or structure of the Earth, including its biota, lithosphere, hydrosphere and atmosphere, or of outer space." Therefore, the idea behind the ENMOD is the prohibition of tactics, which utilise the environment itself to cause destruction or injury to the enemy. While the ENMOD does not pre-empt the customary principle of military necessity, it does refine the balancing of environmental damage with military necessity by providing an upper limit on the acceptable level of environmental damage.

2. **Protocol I of 1977 Additional to the Geneva Conventions of 1949.** Articles 35 and 55 of Protocol I specifically address the protection of the environment during periods of armed conflict. Article 35 begins by restating two principles developed in St Petersburg and The Hague: the right to choose means of warfare "is not unlimited" and it is prohibited to employ "methods of warfare of a nature to cause superfluous injury or unnecessary suffering". Article 35(3) further strengthens the protection of the environment by stating that "it is prohibited to employ methods of warfare which are intended, or may be expected, to cause widespread, long-term, and severe damage to the natural environment".

While Article 35(1) mentions the protection of the environment as a basic rule, Article 55 is entirely devoted to the environment and thus represents the only truly "environmental" provision in Protocol I. Article 55 states:-

> *Care shall be taken in warfare to protect the natural environment against widespread, long-term, and severe damage. This protection includes a prohibition of the use of methods or means of warfare, which are intended or may be expected to cause such damage to the natural environment and thereby prejudice the health or survival of the population.*

Article 55 appears to present the highest threshold of environmental damage within Protocol I. This threshold derives from the second sentence of Article 55, prohibiting the causation of environmental damage where that damage has the potential for consequent human injury. The prohibition appears only to apply where environmental damage would have the potential to cause consequent harm to humans.

The purpose of Protocol I and the ENMOD was to reaffirm the earlier 1949 Geneva Conventions, and to address the widespread awareness of the environmental destructiveness of war that grew out of the Vietnam era. Previously, the international community had paid little attention to the consequences of war on the environment, as illustrated by the failure to mention the environment in the four Geneva Conventions following the Second World War. Media coverage during the Vietnam War, coupled with an increasing worldwide awareness of the environment, led to the adoption of Protocol I and the ENMOD.

These two treaties prohibit different types of environmental damage. While Protocol I prohibits recourse to environmental warfare, i.e., the use of methods of warfare likely to upset the vital balance of nature, the ENMOD prohibits what is known as geophysical warfare, which implies the deliberate manipulation of natural processes and may trigger "hurricanes, tidal waves, earthquakes, and rain or snow". Despite growing international concern about the effect of war on the environment, neither of these agreements has been universally adopted. There is also a danger that discrepancies in these laws might hamper their effective implementation in the future.

As opposed to the cumulative threshold of harm contained in Protocol I (*widespread*, *long-term*, and *severe damage*), the three criteria in ENMOD are disjunctive: only one of which need to be fulfilled to constitute a breach of the Convention. The aim of ENMOD Convention is to prohibit all military manipulations of the natural environment, which is reflected in the relatively low requirements for breach.

3. **Rome Statute of the International Criminal Court (ICC).** The most recent work in the field has been adoption of the Rome Statue of the International Criminal Court, granting the Court jurisdiction over certain acts causing environmental damage. By Article 8.2(b)(iv), the following acts committed during international armed conflict constitute war crimes:-

> *Intentionally launching an attack in the knowledge that such an attack will cause incidental loss of life or injury to civilians or damage to civilian objects or widespread, long-term and severe damage to the natural environment which would be clearly excessive in relation to the concrete and direct military advantage anticipated.*

This provision is interesting for a number of reasons. There are two significant modifications as regard the protection of environment. First, the Rome Statute requires both intention and knowledge of the outcome rather than either intention or expectation as set forth in the Protocol. Second, for the act to qualify as a war crime, the damage to the natural environment must be clearly excessive in relation to the military advantage anticipated.

Criminal responsibility will therefore extend to those who order operations with the knowledge that widespread, long term, and severe damage will occur. Pursuant to Article 28 of the Rome Statute, a commander or superior who "knew, or owing to the circumstances, should have known" that those under his or her command and/or control were committing environmental crimes and "failed to take all necessary and reasonable measures within his or her power to prevent or repress their commission" is subject to prosecution. Indeed, commanders or superiors will be criminally responsible even if they merely fail to "submit the matter to the competent authorities for investigation and prosecution."

Indirect Environmental Protection

The law of armed conflict places limits on the conduct of combatants engaged in armed conflicts. The law functions by balancing the various values and needs at stake, such as the need of the military in fighting a war weighed against the protection of civilians. The four Geneva Conventions of 1949 and two Additional Protocols of 1949, which are concerned with the protection of victims of war and civilians, limit the use of particular weapons. In the course of providing protection for people, a number of provisions do expressly address the protection of the environment. The rules of the IHL treaty that can be considered to indirectly protect the environment during armed conflict can be clustered into five categories: (i) rules limiting or prohibiting certain weapons and methods of warfare like the Chemical Weapons Convention, 1993 (CWC), the Hague Convention IV of 1907 regulating the means and methods of warfare; (ii) clauses protecting civilian objects and properties; (iii) clauses protecting cultural heritage sites; (iv) rules concerning installations containing dangerous forces; and (v) limitations on certain specifically defined areas. The CWC specifically prohibits destroying chemical weapons by "dumping in any body of water, land burial and open pit burning", thereby ensuring that the human and environmental costs of disposal are minimal.

The 1981 Convention on Prohibitions or Restrictions on the Use of Certain Conventional Weapons which may be Deemed to be Excessively Injurious or to have Indiscriminate Effects (CCW) also provides protection to the environment. The CCW and its additional Protocols restrict the use of inhumane weapons. Protocol III of this convention, which concerns prohibitions and restrictions on the use of incendiary weapons, is a case in point. Article 1 contains definitions, and Article 2 contains a specifically applicable provision: "It is prohibited to make forests or other kinds of plant cover the object of attack by incendiary weapons except when such natural elements are used to cover, conceal or camouflage combatants or other military objectives or are themselves military objectives."

Protection of Environment: International Environmental Law

One of the basic principles relating to the protection of the environment is reflected in the Trail Smelter arbitration. In this decision, the United States was awarded damages from Canada because of air pollution that had drifted across the border. The decision stated what has become a foundation for much of current international environmental law: "No State has the right to use or permit the use of its territory in such a manner as to cause injury by fumes in or to the territory of another...." This principle was confirmed and extended to a wartime environment in the Corfu Channel case in which the International Court of Justice held Albania responsible for not warning British warships that mines had been placed in its territorial waters. The Court held that it was "every State's obligation not to allow knowingly its territory to be used for acts contrary to the rights of other States."

This principle was expanded in the Lac Lanoux arbitration and the Nuclear Tests case. The environment was directly affected in these cases, which not only confirmed the application of the "no harm" principle to the environment, but also the basic principle that nations must cooperate in avoiding adverse effects on their neighbours through a system of impact assessment, notification, consultation, and negotiation. These decisions are significant because they represent a clear indication that international law does not allow unilateral degradation of the environment at the expense of another nation, and that the "no harm" principle is a firm principle of international environmental law.

The "no harm" principle is found in the 1972 Stockholm Declaration of the United Nations Conference on the Human Environment. At the conclusion of the UN-sponsored conference, representatives of 103 nations adopted a declaration expressing their combined understanding of States' roles in this area. Principle 21 of the Stockholm Declaration states:-

> *States have, in accordance with the Charter of the United Nations and the principles of international law, the sovereign right to exploit their own resources pursuant to their own environmental policies,*

and the responsibility to ensure that activities within their jurisdiction or control do not cause damage to the environment of other States or of areas beyond the limits of national jurisdiction.

Principle 26 of the 1972 Stockholm Declaration focuses exclusively on nuclear weapons. It provides: "Man and his environment must be spared the effects of nuclear weapons and all other means of mass destruction. States must strive to reach prompt agreement, in the relevant international organs, on the elimination and complete destruction of such weapons."

The 1982 World Charter for Nature adopts a more general approach, stating the "general principle" that "nature shall be secured against degradation caused by warfare or other hostile activities", and declaring that "military activities damaging to nature shall be avoided". The phrasing of the 1992 Rio declaration gets closer to the point, but is still ambiguous. Although not legally binding, the text of Principle 24 could be interpreted either as requiring States to respect those rules of international law which provide protection for the environment in times of armed conflict, or as requiring States to respect international law by protecting the environment in times of armed conflict. Despite the absence of a provision expressly protecting the marine environment against the consequences of an armed conflict, it can be assumed that under the Convention on the Law of the Sea, 1982, such protection exists with regard to pollution of the sea.

Most environmental treaties, including those on civil liability for damage, are silent on the issue of their applicability following the outbreak of military conflicts. In fact, most of them have provisions that exclude their applicability in the case damage resulting from armed conflict.

Protection of Environment: Human Rights Law

Human rights law may provide additional guidance on State conduct affecting the environment and natural resources during the armed conflict. Both treaty law and customary international law contain rules that ensure that the basic social and political rights of individuals are respected, including those linked to environmental protection. At the national level, the right to a healthy environment has been officially recognized in most national constitutions adopted after 1992 (the Rio Conference). The 2009 United Nations Fact finding Mission on the Gaza Conflict, appointed by the President of the Human Rights Council, has demonstrated that the human rights approach and investigations related to it can offer an avenue for mediation in the case of environmental damage during armed conflict.

Protection of Environment: Customary International Law

The fundamental principles of customary international law applicable to the protection of the environment are those of humanity, discrimination, proportionality, and military necessity. The principle of humanity, also known as the "principle of unnecessary suffering and destruction", proscribes the use of means of warfare which cause unnecessary suffering not justified by legitimate military objectives. The principle of discrimination provides that the means and methods of warfare must distinguish between military and civilian targets. The principle of proportionality is a fact-specific concept requiring that the force employed by the attacker not be disproportionate to the military advantage sought. The principle of military necessity (or military advantage) states that a combatant may use only the level of force "required for the partial or complete submission of the enemy" that incurs the least "loss of time, life, and physical resources" in the attainment of a legitimate military objective. While at first glance, it might appear that the military necessity exception trumps all restrictions on the conduct of war, it is still subject to the limits of humanity, discrimination and proportionality.

These rules of customary law were developed to protect humans and their property, and may only be indirectly protective of an environment, which is not intended to be the direct beneficiary of these principles.

The UN Security Council

The acts of the United Nations Security Council during the 1991 Gulf War has created a legal precedent for future armed conflicts. In April 1991, the Security Council passed Resolution 687, holding Iraq liable under international law for "any direct loss, or damage, including environmental damage and the depletion of natural resources." It has set an important pattern for future responses to similar environmental degradation.

The ICRC Guidelines

In 2004, the International Committee of the Red Cross drew up guidelines concerning the protection of the environment against the effects of armed conflict. It provides that the general principles of international law such as the principle of distinction and the principle of proportionality provide protection to the environment. The guidelines state that care should be taken in warfare to protect and preserve the natural environment. The military or any other hostile use of environmental modification techniques having widespread, long-lasting or severe effects as the means of destruction, damage or injury to any other State party is prohibited. Attacks against the natural environment by way of reprisals are prohibited. Under the guidelines, the States are urged to enter into further agreements providing additional protection to the natural environment in times of armed conflict. The guidelines provide that the states must take all measures required by international law to avoid:

(a) making forests or other kinds of plant cover the object of attack by incendiary weapons except when such natural elements are used to cover, conceal or camouflage combatants or other military objectives, or are themselves military objectives;

(b) attacks on objects indispensable to the survival of the civilian population, such as foodstuffs, agricultural areas or drinking water installations, if carried out for the purpose of denying such objects to the civilian population;

(c) attacks on works or installations containing dangerous forces, namely dams, dykes and nuclear electrical generating stations, even where they are military objectives, if such attacks may cause the release of dangerous forces and consequent severe losses among the civilian population and as long as such works or installations are entitled to special protection under Protocol I additional to the Geneva Conventions;

(d) attacks on historic monuments, works of art or places of worship which constitute the cultural or spiritual heritage of peoples.

Implementation

The existing international legal framework contains many provisions that either directly or indirectly protect the environment or govern the use of natural resources during armed conflict. In practice, however, these provisions have not always been effectively implemented or enforced. Except in the case of Iraq, which was held accountable for damages caused during the 1990-1991 Gulf War, no other State or individual has been held responsible for environmental harm caused during armed conflict and the environment continues to be the silent victim of armed conflicts worldwide.

It is now widely recognized that the planet faces a diverse and growing range of environmental challenges which can only be addressed through international cooperation. To protect the natural environment as one of our fundamental security needs, we have to recognize that all species have a right to exist, that humans should only take what the natural environment can sustainably contribute to our life support system, and that nations should not assume that warfare and preparation for warfare justify environmental destruction. War is indiscriminate and can bring harm or destruction to life anywhere and the preservation of the global ecosystem is essential for the sustenance of the global population.

Recommendations

In order to ensure that environmental violations committed during war are punished, the provisions of international law that protect the environment in times of conflict should be fully reflected at the national level. States should adopt and reflect the ICRC Guidelines on the Protection of the Environment during Armed Conflict (1994) in national legislation and military manuals. The armed forces should develop the expertise to:

1. Understand, monitor and report damage to natural ecosystems.
2. Repair, restore and regenerate land and aquatic ecosystems.
3. Clean up contaminated sites within military bases and training areas.
4. Carry out waste and energy audits and develop programmes to achieve savings.
5. Manage the repair, re-use and recycling of materials including office paper, oil, sewage and metals.
6. Reduce the greenhouse effect through improved fuel and engine use.
7. Use military satellite and information-gathering systems to monitor and share local and global environmental data.
8. Cooperate with all other environment protection agencies to achieve and maintain the highest standard of air, land and water quality and biodiversity protection.

All military personnel should be educated in international and national 'best environmental practice' and environmental law requirements. Military manuals should contain clear instructions in this regard. Offences should be punishable by both military and civilian courts.

The International Law Commission (ILC), should examine the effectiveness of the legal framework to identify the gaps and barriers to enforcement, and to explore the possibilities for clarifying and codifying this body of law. A new legal instrument should be developed for place-based protection of critical natural resources and areas of ecological importance during international and non-international armed conflicts. This could include the protection for watersheds, groundwater aquifers, agricultural and grazing lands, parks, national forests, and the habitat of endangered species. At the outset of any conflict, critical natural resources and areas of ecological importance should be delineated and designated as 'demilitarized zones', and parties to the conflict should be prohibited from conducting military operations within their boundaries.

Conclusion

The issue of the destruction of the environment is one of the most disturbing aspects of armed conflicts. Destruction of the environment through the excessive human demands placed on it and due to the harmful effects of the production, testing, stockpiling and use of military weapons is the major concern of the international community. Following the 1991 Gulf War, concern was reawakened about the environmental effects of war. As for the ENMOD and Protocol I, several major belligerent countries are not parties to it. Besides, the specific environmental provisions of these agreements, which only prohibit destruction that is widespread, long-lasting, and/or severe, raise difficult questions of legal interpretation and scientific evaluation.

In its 1996 Advisory Opinion on the Legality of the Threat or Use of Nuclear Weapons, the International Court of Justice stressed that "the obligations of States to respect and protect the natural environment," applied equally "to the actual use of nuclear weapons in armed conflict". We have to decide whether the human need for aggression to settle local, national or international disputes should be allowed to outweigh environmental integrity. This would involve a reinterpretation of the interaction between international environmental law and international humanitarian law. Certain practices, such as slavery, genocide and torture, have been deemed illegal by the international community to the extent that they can never be undertaken, even if essential to defend national sovereignty. Why should international environmental desecration not be similarly proscribed?

CHAPTER 10

ARMED FORCES AND HUMAN RIGHTS[1]

Introduction

The armed forces of a nation are created to safeguard its boundaries against external aggression and maintain its integrity and sovereignty. Their primary purpose is to fight wars, if the need arises. The fighting of war involves loss of life, injury and destruction of property. Some might argue that during a war there is little room to consider the human rights of those who are fighting it. However, human rights are applicable at all times even in armed conflicts, by virtue of the fact that people are human and they always possess these rights. Though human rights treaties allow parties to derogate them in times of war, the 'hard-core' rights remain non-derogable. These are the right to life, the right against torture and other inhuman treatment, the right against slavery and retroactive criminal legislation or punishment.

Recent human rights jurisprudence has stressed the importance of this, and the continued applicability of certain judicial guarantees that are essential in order to give effective protection to the 'hard-core' rights. Like human rights law, humanitarian law is based on the premise that the protection accorded to victims of war must be without any discrimination. This is also a fundamental rule of human rights and is specified in the UN Charter as well as in all human rights treaties. To quote one example, Article 27 of the Fourth Geneva Convention of 1949 states: "*....all protected persons shall be treated with the same consideration by the Party to the conflict in whose power they are, without any adverse distinction based, in particular, on race, religion or political opinion.*"

---

1 The text of this chapter is based on a talk delivered at the USI on 14 March 2007.

Humanitarian law is devoted to the protection of human life. Victims of conflict are not to be murdered as this amounts to an unnecessary act of cruelty. Such persons are protected by the 1949 Geneva Convention; which was extended by the 1977 Protocol I. The protection of the life of combatants during hostilities is not guaranteed whilst they are fighting. However, humanitarian law is not absolutely silent even on this point. The rule prohibits the use of weapons of a nature that causes superfluous injury or unnecessary suffering. It accepts the incidental loss of civilian life subject to the principle of proportionality. The Additional Protocol I (AP I) on international armed conflict overlaps with human rights law.[3] Article 75 of the AP I, relating to Fundamental Guarantees, is directly derived from the ICCPR. Article 72 (Field of Application) of AP I says:-

> The provisions of Section III are additional to the rules concerning humanitarian protection of civilians and civilian objects in the power of a Party to the conflict contained in the Fourth Convention, as well as to other applicable rules of international law relating to the protection of fundamental human rights during international armed conflict.

The term human rights has been defined in the Protection of Human Rights Act, 1993. It means the rights relating to life, liberty, equality and dignity of the individual guaranteed by the Constitution or embodied in the International Covenants and enforceable by courts in India.

Role of the Armed Forces

In the Indian context, the operational roles of the armed forces can be summed up as follows.

I. Combat Activities: Attacks, raids and direct action.

II. Non-Combat activities:-

   a. Domestic assistance to civil authorities.

      i. Aid to civil authority—assistance during natural calamities.

ii. Security assistance—riot control, maintenance of law & order.

b. National assistance:-

i. Humanitarian assistance.

- Disaster relief
- Military civil assistance
- Refugee management
- Martial law
- Unconventional warfare
- Evacuation operations

ii. Security assistance.

- Combating terrorism
- Counter-insurgency
- Special reconnaissance
- Psychological operations
- Training to paramilitary forces

iii. Peace operations—international assistance; peacekeeping operations

As the fundamental purpose of the armed forces is to fight during an armed conflict, the needs of the individual were (earlier) treated as subservient to this purpose. The armed forces also had a hierarchical structure based on rank, with an obligation to obey the orders of superiors. The officers had formal education, while the soldiers were generally uneducated. Military organizations usually considered it inappropriate to treat all ranks equally in relation to certain aspects of military life. However, all this has changed in the last 50 years, due largely to the international human rights laws. The impact of international human rights laws will be examined in the context of the changing role of the armed forces and awareness of human rights.

The armed forces are an integral part of a democratic state and society. Their role is not merely to defend the state and its citizens against internal and external threats but also to protect and uphold the human rights and fundamental freedoms on which democratic societies are based. As representatives of the State, armed forces personnel are bound to respect human rights and international humanitarian law in the exercise of their duties. It follows that they must be entitled to the same rights and protections as all other persons, subject to certain limitations imposed by military life. When the human rights and fundamental freedoms of members of the armed forces are protected within their institution, they will be more likely to uphold these while carrying out their duties.

International Human Rights Laws

The concept of human rights developed after WW II. It was rarely used in relation to the armed forces because a soldier remained at the mercy of his military superiors, whose task was to enforce military discipline. Soldiers were given certain rights to complain about unfair treatment to their superiors. This right to make a complaint, however, cannot be compared to challenging a breach of human rights. There was no one standard of fair treatment for a military soldier, as they functioned under systems that operated differently in different parts of the world. Military punishments varied and generally exceeded the degree of severity of criminal sanctions available in the civil courts. Corporal punishments or the death penalty were not uncommon.

Today, there are a large number of international human rights instruments which have a bearing on the human rights of soldiers. These are:-

a. The Universal Declaration of Human Rights (UDHR), adopted by the UNGA in 1948.

b. The International Covenant on Civil and Political Rights (ICPPR), 1966.

c. The International Covenant on Economic, Social and Cultural Rights (ICESCR), 1966.

d. The UN Convention on the Elimination of All Forms of Discrimination against Women (CEDAW), 1981.

e. The Convention against Torture and Other Cruel, Inhuman or Degrading Punishment, 1984.

f. The Four Geneva Conventions of 12 August 1949 and Protocols I and II, Additional to the Conventions.

g. United Nations: Basic Principles on the Independence of Judiciary, adopted by the UNGA in 1985.

h. United Nations: Standard Minimum Rules for the Treatment of Prisoners, adopted by the UNGA in 1955 and amended in 1977.

i. The Rome Statute of the International Criminal Court, 1998.

j. The UN Basic Principles and guidelines on the right to a remedy and reparation for victims of gross violations of international human rights laws and serious violations of international humanitarian law, 2005.

k. The UN Convention for the Protection of All Persons from Enforced Disappearance, 2006.

While some human rights instruments are intended to have a global application (in the sense that they are open for adoption by all States), others are geographically limited in their application. A very broad spectrum of human rights is protected by the combined text of the ICCPR and ICESCR. A very obvious feature of human rights instruments is that they recognize, at least implicitly, that some human rights are deserving of a higher degree of protection than others and that they may not be abrogated under any circumstances.

There is a need to consider the human rights of military personnel. A soldier's life is expected to be tough. He is trained to live in difficult situations, be able to face the enemy anytime and bring victory in war. If the need arises, he is expected to sacrifice his life for the nation. An army which ignores the human rights of its soldiers may find it difficult to recruit and retain soldiers. The 'civilianization' of the military justice system has taken place in a number of democratic countries. In some countries, military discipline procedure is used to deal with only relatively minor military offences, while more serious offences are dealt with by civilian courts. In Germany, military offences are also tried by the civil courts. In some States, where the European Convention on Human Rights has been in force from early 1950, soldiers have themselves initiated the drive to make the disciplinary procedure compliant with human rights standards. They have appealed in the European Court of Human Rights for alleged breaches of human rights. This has resulted in a change in the military disciplinary procedures to ensure compliance with the Convention.

The Impact of Human Rights Laws

1. **Informal Discipline System.** Military commanders the world over have been given statutory powers to dispose of minor offences committed by members. This is an informal way of dealing with disciplinary matters which can be termed non-judicial summary trial. It has many advantages. Summary trials can be held quickly, and avoid the formality of a court-martial. The punishment awarded is not expected to have any adverse effect on the career of the accused. The human rights issues that might arise in such cases are whether (a) the punishment awarded could amount to torture, degrading or inhuman treatment, and (b) if the cumulative effect of the punishment is serious, whether the accused had the right to refuse summary trial and face a court-martial, where detailed procedural rights are available.

The observance of human rights may not be necessary in summary trials. However, the impact of a minor punishment on the future career of a soldier demands the observance of the rules of 'natural justice'. For instance, a single punishment entry in the conduct sheet may make a soldier ineligible for UN missions. In cases where the punishment available to a commanding officer (CO) is such as to amount to deprivation of the soldier's liberty, the observance of rules of fair trial becomes mandatory.

There is nothing wrong with empowering a CO to impose the punishment of deprivation of liberty. In fact, it may be necessary for the operational effectiveness of a unit. However, what is necessary is to afford the accused the right to opt for trial by a military court-martial, instead of being dealt with summarily by the CO. An affected person must be given the right to appeal from the decision of his CO to the judicial tribunal or court. The establishment of a Summary Appeals Court in the UK, in 2000, has had a beneficial effect on the summary process by laying down principles with which COs would be unlikely to disagree. Incidentally, when this Summary Court was established, there were apprehensions in the minds of critics that it would open a floodgate of complaints from affected persons.

The punishment awarded in a summary trial should also not be degrading and humiliating. It must not be such as to arouse in its victim feelings of fear, anguish and inferiority. In 1992, the Army Act, 1950 was amended to abolish the award of 'field punishment' which was considered degrading and inhuman. In the Indian context, an affected person must have the right to represent against minor punishments and also the right to appeal in the proposed Armed Forces Tribunal.

2. **Formal Disciplinary System.** The right to a fair trial is a norm of international human rights law designed to protect individuals from the unlawful and arbitrary curtailment or deprivation of their basic rights and freedoms. It is guaranteed under Article 14 of the ICCPR, which provides that "everyone shall be entitled to a fair and public hearing by a competent, independent and impartial tribunal established by law." Article 14 contains a catalogue of 'minimum guarantees' for an individual undergoing a trial

for criminal charges. These rights are:-

1. The right to a fair and public hearing.
2. Equal access to, and equality before, the courts.
3. The right to a competent, independent and impartial tribunal established by law.
4. The right to a presumption of innocence until proved guilty according to law.
5. The right to prompt notice of the nature and cause of criminal charges.
6. The right to adequate time and facilities for the preparation of a defence to the defendant and to his counsel.
7. The right to a trial without undue delay.
8. The right to defend through legal counsel of one's own choice and to free legal assistance.
9. The right to an interpreter and the right to examine witnesses.
10. Prohibition of self-incrimination.
11. Prohibition of double jeopardy.
12. The right to appeal against conviction and sentence to a higher tribunal established according to law.
13. The right to compensation for miscarriage of justice.

The Indian military justice system falls short of these standards in that it is does not provide free legal aid, it is not free from command influence and there are chances of its being applied with discretion. In the eyes of an outsider or an observer, courts-martial can easily be subject to manipulation by military commanders who convenes them and select the panel from among the officers under their command. While these problems affect all military trials, they are invariably exacerbated when the victim is a civilian. Ironically, the military justice system, with its inherent defects, is seen as being unjust by both the accused who feel that they are being treated unfairly, and the victims of abuse who feel that justice has not been done.

3. **Freedom of Association.** In India, the right to the freedom of association is severely restricted for members of the armed forces. It is felt that this right could give rise to two distinct problems with regard to armed forces personnel. The first is the question of military discipline and possible interference with the *esprit de corps*. The second relates to issues of allegiance and outside influence. It is feared that such influence may induce soldiers (or sailors or airmen) to act together in defiance of the orders of superiors in the military chain of command. The weight of numbers could then lead to senior officers losing control of an army unit. In most of the armed forces following the British military legal system, mutiny is considered to be a serious military offence.

However, in some countries representative bodies are permitted and certain constraints have been placed to limit their membership to members of the armed forces or restrict their powers, for instance forbidding strikes or other forms of industrial action. The right of armed forces personnel to the freedom of association is granted in 22 out of 39 countries of the Council of Europe. Of these, only seven allow the right to collective bargaining and none afford the right to collective action. Democracies like Hungary, Sweden and Germany allow trade unions in the armed forces.

Sweden's first association for military personnel was established almost a hundred years ago. The Swedish Association of Military Officers (SAMO) has a membership of 9,500 officers of all ranks. The association promotes the interests of military officers allowing them to take part in the process of decision-making, which influences their working conditions. Strikes or other offensive actions are allowed only during the negotiation period and not while an agreement is still valid. SAMO also cooperates at the governmental level on general defence issues (however, not on political matters such as foreign policy or the national budget). The advantage of the Swedish model is that officers feel more satisfied with their work because of the knowledge that their concerns are being addressed.

German soldiers have had the right to be members of trade unions and professional associations since the re-establishment of the armed forces in 1955. With 210,000 members representing all ranks and status groups, the Soldier's Association represents the general, ideological, social and career interests of its members, as well as their families. The union is represented at the level of barracks, battalions, regional executive boards and at the federal level. It is politically and financially independent of any authority and of any political party and is financed solely by members' fees. Being the authoritative organization for service personnel, it is consulted by parliament and elected governments when preparing any legislation affecting the interests of servicemen, their families and their surviving dependents. The Association also maintains close contact with the political parties, parliament, parliamentary groups and committees as well as the Minister of Defence. Its main focus is to take care of the interests of armed forces personnel sent on international missions.

In Russia, the All-Russian Professional Union of Servicemen was set up in 1992, a period during which the army was facing many challenges brought about by the disintegration of the Soviet Union. The organization concentrated its initial efforts on the establishment of regional bodies and is now represented in 70 out of 80 national regions. At the national level it promotes the social, legal, economic and professional interests of armed forces personnel. Many of its members are active at various levels of parliament, government and public administration. One of the Union's major achievements has been the provision of protection and assistance to families of military personnel who died during missions.

In France, the law prohibits armed forces personnel from membership of political parties and professional associations. The French system of professional participation takes place through institutions at three levels: at the department of defence, the level of the armed forces, and at the unit level. At the department of defence level, participation is allowed though a High Council, composed of members selected at random by the members of the seven armed forces councils. The High Council's core competence is to advise on conditions of service and on statutes or regulations pertaining to conditions of service. The councils at the level of the armed forces are responsible for studying questions relating to working conditions and to represent personnel of the forces on the topics submitted to the High Council. The representative bodies at the unit level deal with the day-to-day work of the unit, in particular work organizations; the conduct of exercises; and individual questions.

In the Indian context, the very nature of the requirement of obeying the orders of a superior makes compromise or negotiation difficult. The restriction on the right of assembly can be used to conceal poor physical treatment of soldiers, unpopular activities required of a soldier, poor leadership, discriminatory treatment of soldiers, irrational orders and poor management. While officers and soldiers are permitted by military law to make individual complaints about their treatment at the hands of superiors, the processing of their complaints remains outdated. In some cases, relatives of armed forces members have taken the lead and attracted considerable publicity. Thus, there is a need for an independent body to consider the requirements of various segments within the armed forces. It could avoid a 'near-mutiny' situation which was faced by the Indian Air Force after the Fifth Pay Commission. Today more attention is needed to improve the working conditions of the military who should enjoy their human rights to fullest possible extent. Recognition of the rights of armed forces personnel is a reflection of the maturity of a democracy.

4. **Gender Discrimination and the Right to Equality.** The issue of gender discrimination in the armed forces has been raised on a number of occasions. Though women have been working in the armed forces as medical and nursing officers since independence, the armed forces have been sceptical of their ability to perform the role of a soldier. In November 1991, the Ministry of Defence approved the induction of women officers into non-combatant branches of the Army, non-flying branches of the IAF and the Navy. Subsequently, approval was also accorded for the induction of women into the technical and flying branches of the IAF. The first batch of women officers was commissioned in June 1993, the same year that

India ratified the UN Convention on the Elimination of Discrimination Against Women (CEDAW). Today, we have over 2000 women officers working in various services/branches of the armed forces, against a total strength of 53000 officers, not including those in the medical services. The percentage of women in our armed forces works out to (Table 1) far below those of other countries.

Table 1: Percentage of women in the armed forces

COUNTRY	**PERCENTAGE OF FEMALE SOLDIERS**
USA	17
CANADA	16.9
HUNGARY	16
SPAIN	15.4
SOUTH AFRICA	13
FRANCE	12.8
UK	9.0
POLAND	8.4
GERMANY	6.0
INDIA	3.7 (of officers' strength)

In India, women officers are not given permanent commission and also not assigned any combat-related task. The Chiefs of Staff Committee (COSC) has recently advised the government against allowing women in roles that may require "close combat". However, in 2009, the government has approved permanent commission in the legal and education branches of the three services.

There have been cases where women officers have alleged sexual harassment and the organization has taken prompt measures against the wrongdoer. However, in a few cases the organization has adopted a policy of "not reported hence not known". In a case where a commanding officer was involved in the sexual harassment of a lady officer, the organization chose to be silent because there was no written complaint from the victim. Such cases of sexual harassment can be significantly reduced by: (a) developing a definitive policy that is clearly and regularly communicated to all the ranks; (b) providing a grievance procedure for reporting sexual harassment to one other than the alleged harasser; (c) prompt, thorough and documented investigations of all complaints; (d) swift remedial action to protect the victim from further harassment; and (e) enforcing sexual harassment policies quickly, consistently and aggressively. The present procedure of addressing all grievance applications to the commanding officer needs change.

The greatest challenge (in this context) before the country is to create an enabling environment and make institutional arrangements that would ensure the equal participation of women in every sphere. In pursuance of this goal, efforts must be made to ensure that all members of the armed forces receive the same benefits and are treated equally, as mandated by the Constitution. Hopefully in the years to come the defence system will be more technologically advanced and battles will increasingly depend on technology than on muscle power. Also, in the future, perhaps the physical and psychological differences between men and women will be taken into consideration while designing training programmes and creating functional environments to enable women to perform combat roles.

5. **Redress of Grievance.** The instances of suicide and fratricidal killing in the armed forces are on the rise. There are more than 100,000 grievance cases pending in the courts and services headquarters. Delay in the finalization of such cases causes undue stress, hardship and misery to the aggrieved soldier. It is this which has resulted in cases where armed forces personnel have taken the extreme step of committing suicide or killing their superiors. In a civilized democratic society, the State guarantees that every citizen can approach prescribed grievance redress forums against an individual or the State. In relation to the armed forces, this right has been expressly provided in the Army Act, the Navy Act and the Air Force Act, whereby an individual may complain up to the Chief of the Staff (Central Government in the case of officers) for the redress of grievances.

The system of processing grievance petitions is faulty. The Armed Forces Tribunal also does not have any jurisdiction in grievances relating to leave, postings, transfers, summary disposals and trials. The government has apprehensions that the review of these matters by an independent judicial forum would affect operational effectiveness and discipline in the forces. Viewed from a different perspective, the exclusion of these matters from the purview of the Tribunal may prompt aggrieved personnel to approach the higher civil courts.

In the past, servicemen rarely questioned the decisions of their superiors and approaching superior civil courts for the redress of grievances was unheard of. Officers and men were motivated by the famous quotation of Chetwode embodying the lofty ideals of service before self, prominently displayed as a guiding motto in military training establishments. With the democratic breeze sweeping the country, the ethos of the armed forces has undergone considerable change. Officers and men no longer think it objectionable to fight for their rights. There is a need for a grievance redress system, administered fairly, effectively and promptly and to improve transparency.

6. **Allegations of Human Rights Violations.** In the last five decades India has witnessed an increase in instances of violent conflict which have been termed variously as terrorism, insurgency, militancy, proxy war and

armed rebellion. The existing police forces have often proved inadequate in dealing with the perpetrators of large-scale violence and the armed forces have been called upon to aid the civil power. The Indian armed forces have been involved in counter-insurgency operations in Jammu and Kashmir and the north-east since the 1950s.However, the involvement of the armed forces in countering insurgency has become a controversial issue. There have been allegations that members of the armed forces have taken advantage of the Armed Forces (Special Powers) Act (AFSPA) to unleash their own brand of terror. It has also been claimed that the provisions of the AFSPA are against the international norms of human rights.

Indian law permits members of the Indian armed forces who are accused of crimes to be prosecuted by either the military or civilian justice system. However, the AFSPA requires prior approval of the central government for civilian prosecutions of military personnel. The armed forces may take over a case from the civil authorities for the trial of soldiers by a court-martial under the Army Act.

Though the armed forces are effectively prosecuting soldiers and officers for abuses committed under special powers, the civil liberties organizations doubt the effectiveness of the military judicial system. In May 2004, the Chief of the Army Staff informed the National Human Rights Commission that 131 army personnel, including officers, had been punished for human rights violations in J&K since 1990 (fewer than ten per year). The sentences included two life imprisonments, 59 rigorous imprisonments, and 11 instances of one year's imprisonment and dismissal. However, to date, the armed forces have not publicly released details of any of the cases: no incidents described, no names of those sentenced, and no information on the crimes committed. The human rights activists, and national and international NGOs have urged the Government of India to hold the trial of human rights abuses in civilian courts.

7. **Human Rights in Multinational Operations.** The armed forces of a country may be deployed in UN multinational missions as part of UN peacekeeping operations. The main purpose of deploying armed forces in peace missions is not to engage in military operations but to protect the

lives of civilians from opposing militia groups and to ensure the safe delivery of humanitarian assistance as a part of the agreement with the UN. There is no unified disciplinary system for all the military contingents in multi-force operations. The normal practice is to allow each visiting force to exercise its disciplinary process over its own personnel in the territory of the host State. Any possibility of the UN taking disciplinary action against its peacekeepers is not visible in example, though misconduct has been reported in many operations.

A common senior officer is placed in command of the multi-national force for passing orders to the national commanders, who in turn, command their own national contingents. The normal military structure operates within each national contingent in terms of superior/subordinate relationship. The national commanders have orders from their national superiors to obey the orders of the overall commander. The main issues which matter in such settings is domestic military law and the international human rights treaties to which the country is a signatory. The rules of engagement issued to national contingents may impose some limitations on the soldiers of visiting forces. The international laws applicable in such situations may include:-

1. International humanitarian law set out in the UN Secretary General Bulletin of 1999

2. The Fourth Geneva Convention of 1949, relating to protection of civilians

3. The Third Geneva Convention of 1949, relating to protection of POWs—if there is some degree of armed conflict between two or more states

4. Additional Protocol I to the Geneva Conventions of 1949, if the States to which the multinational forces belong are signatories to it. The forces may accord POW status to members of rebel groups. However, the multinational forces in Iraq (after 30 June 2004) had the power to intern insurgents, where necessary, for imperative

reasons of security. The action of the US to intern civilians and rebels in various prisons came under attack from human rights organizations.

A person who attacks a UN force or its property during an armed conflict will commit a war crime and can be tried by the International Criminal Court for violation of the Rome Statute. The liability of a State party to an international human rights instrument for a breach of human rights by members of its armed forces will not extinguish merely because the armed forces are assigned to a multinational force. The extra-territorial reach of the criminal law of a State might encompass the activities of a soldier within the State, especially where this involves torture. The soldier may be at risk from the exercise of some form of criminal process if he later visits the State claiming such jurisdiction and is arrested. Depending upon the extent of the extra-territorial effect of the jurisdiction, he might find himself being prosecuted in the State or be the subject of extradition proceedings to another State with such extensive jurisdiction.

8. **Conscientious Objection to Military Service.** The Universal Declaration of Human Rights and the International Covenant for Civil and Political Rights (ICCPR) do not explicitly mention the right to conscientious objection to military service. However, in 1993, the UN Human Rights Committee, the body of experts monitoring the implementation of the ICCPR, adopted General Comment No. 22 on the right to freedom of thought, conscience and religion, and affirmed that the right to conscientious objection to military service can be derived from Article 18 of the ICCPR. The Committee was of the view that the ICCPR does not explicitly refer to a right to conscientious objection, but such right can be derived from it, inasmuch as the obligation to use lethal force may seriously conflict with the freedom of conscience and the right to manifest one's religion or belief.

A large number of military personnel in the US, the UK and Israel have claimed the right to refuse to perform military service (conscientious objection) on the basis that such rights derived from their freedoms under Article 18. In response to such claims, a growing number of States have, in their laws, exempted from compulsory military service citizens who genuinely hold religious or other beliefs that forbid the performance of military service and provided them the choice of alternate national service. The Australian Defence Act 1903 grants a total exemption from military service on the grounds of conscientious belief for those who can prove that the doctrine of their religion forbids them to bear arms or perform military service. Conscientious objection and selective conscientious objection are available to persons conscripted to serve in the Australian Defence Forces. In the US, under the Military Selective Act, section 456 (j), no person is required to be subjected to combatant training and service in the armed forces, 'who by reason of religious training and belief, is conscientiously opposed to participate in war in any form'. A member of the armed forces may seek either separation or assignment to non-combatant duties for reasons of conscientious objection. This is achieved by administrative discharge and is discretionary within the military service concerned. In the US, during the Vietnam War, over 170,000 officers and men were classified as 'conscientious objectors' between 1965 and 1970.

The Israeli military justice system has tackled conscientious objection to military compulsory service, as well as to the use of force in a particular operation. Military service and conscientious objection are regulated by the Defence Service law of 1986. It requires all Israeli citizens and residents to perform military service—three years for men and two years for women. Section 36 (1) of the Defence Service Law gives the Minister of Defence a general discretion to exempt anyone from military service. The law also provides for various types of exemption from military service, discriminating between men and women. Women are exempted on reasons of conscience. A woman requesting such exemption has to present her case to a Committee composed of civilians. In December 2002, the Israeli Supreme Court reaffirmed the possibility of granting exemption from military service for reasons of conscientious objection.

Other armed forces may have to face similar situations in the near future as the ICCPR and national constitutions give the right to freedom of expression; which has been influenced by "new developments in political and ethical thoughts".

Human Rights and Combat Effectiveness

Contrary to the traditional view respect for human rights actually serves to increase combat effectiveness. There are three ways of creating a military culture based on respect for human rights. First, the attitude of officers should be moulded to secure the welfare of the individuals under their command and to lead them by example. A sense of justice and self-discipline must also be inculcated in them. Second, obedience should be ensured not by big penalties but by small sanctions. Third, an atmosphere of mutual trust and interdependence should be fostered by delegating authority and encouraging personal initiative. The creation of such a culture would automatically do away with abuse, without the need for a comprehensive system of rules.

Conclusion

The armed forces act as mirrors and standard-bearers for the values democratic societies are built on and the members of the armed forces cannot be expected to respect human rights in their operations without their own rights being protected: these are two sides of the same coin. Any limitations on human rights must be provided for by law and should be consistent with international treaty obligations. they should be applied only when necessary and strictly in proportion to the intended aim.

Being the largest democracy in the world, India is rightly expected to live up to the basic principles of human rights and humanitarian law. The Indian legal and constitutional framework, based on respect for human rights, is extremely conducive, sensitive and responsive to the implementation of international norms. The Indian armed forces have by now established a proud and enviable record of compliance with the dictates of international standards, to which their military manual by and large conforms. Various engagements across India's borders, as well as those under the aegis of the United Nations have largely demonstrated this compliance.

The existence of proper mechanisms to protect the rights of armed forces personnel should ultimately result in decreasing the number of human rights violations in the armed forces. The Parliament should not ignore human rights within the armed forces as an internal problem of the military leadership. On the contrary, parliamentarians should build cross-party consensus for dealing with human rights violations, incorporating human rights (of armed forces personnel) into the mandate of the Parliamentary Standing Committee on Defence, and conducting regular reviews of policy and legislation.

CHAPTER 11

THE ARMED FORCES (SPECIAL POWERS) ACT[1]

Introduction

In the last five decades, India has witnessed an increase in instances of violent conflict which have been variously dubbed as terrorism, insurgency, militancy, proxy war and armed rebellion. The existing police forces have often proved inadequate to deal with the perpetrators of large-scale violence and the armed forces have been called upon to aid the civil power. The involvement of the armed forces in countering insurgency has become a controversial issue. There have been allegations that the members of the armed forces have taken advantage of the Armed Forces (Special Powers) Act (henceforth referred to as the AFSPA) to unleash their own brand of terror. It has also been claimed that the provisions of the Act are against the international norms of human rights.

Civil liberties organizations have dubbed the AFSPA a colonial instrument, modelled on the Armed Forces Special Power Ordinance, 1942, which was enacted to neutralize the Quit India Movement. They have accused the Indian government of violating the international standards of human rights as defined by the Constitution and the International Bill of Human Rights. The Armed Forces have often been accused of extra-judicial execution of innocent civilians, illegal imposition of curfew, rape, molestation and sexual harassment of women, torture, forced labour and large-scale looting of homes and granaries under the powers vested in them by the AFSPA.

---

1 The text of this chapter is based on a talk delivered at North-East India Studies Programme, Jawaharlal Nehru University, New Delhi, on 14 October 2009.

This chapter examines the role of the armed forces operating under the AFSPA in the light of these allegations

The Indian Armed Forces

The Indian armed forces are quite unique. They are the only apolitical forces of the third world and are looked upon as a nationalist institution. Yet no one, including the greatest political leaders, is quite clear about their role or significance in modern Indian society. Nehru wanted the armed forces to work for peace. Gandhi demanded that the army "plough land, dig wells, clean latrines and do other constructive work to turn the people's hatred of them into the love". Civilian control over the military is one of the basic tenets of a democratic system. But politicians and bureaucrats do not understand the principle of civilian control and its implication. It should be interpreted to mean ultimate political control by Parliament and the cabinet. In practice, it should mean the control exercised by the Defence Minister under the guidance of the Prime Minister.

In reality, the India Armed Forces are controlled by civilian officials in the Ministry of Defence. The bureaucracy has become the front-end of the defence establishment, exercising control and supervisory functions, and acting as gatekeepers. The service chiefs are supervised by the defence secretary on policy matters and officials lower down the bureaucratic chain on routine affairs. Nothing changes the precedence given to the bureaucracy over the armed forces. Not even wars, in which the forces are called upon to make supreme sacrifice in the service of the nation.

The Indian soldier has a hard life. He has to struggle with an inadequate salary, poor accommodation, restrictions on leave, a paltry pension and an ineffective system of grievance redress. A retired officer writes, "The loneliness of being away for long periods of duty in counter-insurgency areas, coupled with a growing sense of dismay at the callousness of the civilian administration and political authority, produce a frustration that is virtually complete. While trying to clean up the mess created by bureaucratic and political ineptitude, the soldier is also putting his own neck on the line. The sense of honour that has been instilled in soldiering prevents him from walking away and leaving the mess as it was."

Aid to Civil Power: Counter-Insurgency Operations

When conflicts in the civil society are left to foster unchecked for a long time, they escalate into destructive threats to the nation. This is when the armed forces are usually called in to rein in the chaos created by political failure to fulfil promises to the people, excessive use of force, political killings, extra-judicial executions of suspected militants and failure of the civil administration and judicial machinery. Analysis shows that the armed forces are not called in at the 'preventive' stage. They are called in at the 'active' stage and are given hardly any intelligence or operational support by the civil administration. Without this support, it becomes difficult for the armed forces to isolate terrorists/ insurgents from the sympathetic local population. Added factors are the natural hostility of the people towards the security forces and the occasional complicity of the local police with the insurgents.

The Indian armed forces have been involved in counter-insurgency operations in Jammu and Kashmir and the North-East since the 1950s. The excessive use of the armed forces to aid civil authority has raised the question of violation of human rights. Various human rights organizations in the country and abroad and the foreign and local media have criticized the effectiveness of Indian laws dealing with the violation of human rights by armed forces personnel. They have also criticized the special laws giving enhanced power to the armed forces for dealing effectively with disruptive activities in specific areas. The special law in question is the AFSPA.

Under normal circumstances, law and order is a state subject in India. However, when a state becomes helpless in dealing with the law and order situation and discharging its primary duty of affording protection to citizens, the Union (Central Government) may declare the whole state or a part of it a disturbed area under the AFSPA and send armed forces in aid of civil powers.

AFSPA: Analysis

The AFSPA is a small legislation with six sections. Section 1 contains the title of the Act and the territorial limits to which the provisions of the Act are applicable. Section 2 sets out the definition of terms like "armed forces". However, the term "disturbed area" has not been defined. It has been described as "an area which is for the time being declared by notification under Section 3 to be a disturbed area". In the 1972 version of the AFSPA, the armed forces were defined as "the military and Air Force of the Union so operating". In the 1958 version of the Act, the definition was the "military forces and the air forces operating as land forces". Section 2(c) states that all other words not defined in the AFSPA have the meanings assigned to them in the Army Act of 1950.

Section 3 of the Act states how an area can be declared disturbed. It grants the power to declare an area disturbed to the Central Government and the Governor of the state, but does not describe the circumstances under which the authority would be justified in making such a declaration. It only requires that such authority be "of the opinion that the whole or parts of the area are in a dangerous or disturbed condition such that the use of the Armed Forces in aid of civil powers is necessary". This definition was challenged in the case of *Indrajit Barua v. State of Assam* AIR 1983 Del 513. The court decided that the lack of precision in the definition of a disturbed area was not an issue since the government and the people of India understand its meaning. The Delhi High Court held that the term "disturbed area" defies any definition. It held, "A disturbed area has to be adjudged according to the location, situation and circumstances of a particular case. Section 3 of the AFSPA lays down that a notification in respect of disturbed area may be issued in regard to an area which "is in such a disturbed or dangerous condition that the use of armed forces in aid of civil power is necessary."

However, there are acts which define the term more concretely. The Disturbed Areas (Special Courts) Act, 1976 states that when "a state government is satisfied that (i) there was, or (ii) there is, in any area within a state extensive disturbance of public peace and tranquility, by reason of differences or disputes between members of different religions, racial, language, or regional groups or castes or communities, it may ... declare such area to be a disturbed area".

The 1972 amendments to the AFSPA extended the power to declare an area disturbed to the Central Government. In the 1958 version of the AFSPA, only the state governments had this power. The Central Government has the power to overrule the opinion of the Governor of a state and declare an area disturbed.

Section 4 sets out the powers granted to the military stationed in a disturbed area. These powers are granted to commissioned officers, warrant officers or non-commissioned officers (NCOs). This section allows armed forces personnel to use force for a variety of reasons. The designated members of the armed forces can shoot to kill, under the powers of Section 4(a), for the commission or suspicion of the commission of the following offences: acting in contravention of any law or order for the time being in force in the disturbed area prohibiting the assembly of five or more persons, carrying weapons, or carrying anything which is capable of being used as a firearm or ammunition. To justify the invocation of this provision, the officer needs to be "of the opinion that it is necessary to do so for the maintenance of public order" and give "such due warning as he may consider necessary".

The armed forces officer/warrant officer or NCO can destroy property under Section 4(b) if it is an arms dump, a fortified position or shelter from where armed attacks are made or are suspected of being made, if the structure is used as a training camp, or as a hide-out by armed gangs or absconders. They can arrest anyone without a warrant under Section 4(c) who has committed or is suspected of having committed a cognizable offence and use any amount of force "necessary to effect the arrest". Under Section 4(d), they can enter and search without a warrant to make an arrest or to recover any property, arms, ammunition or explosives which are believed to be unlawfully kept on the premises. This section also allows the use of force necessary for the search. There is a contention that drastic powers have been conferred on low-ranking officials like non-commissioned officers.

Section 5 states that after the military has arrested someone under the AFSPA, it must hand that person over to the nearest police station with the "least possible delay". There is no definition in the Act of what constitutes the least possible delay. This provision has been interpreted as depending on the specific circumstances of each case; there is no precise amount of time after which the section is violated. In *Bacha Bora v. State of Assam* (1991) 2 GLR: 119, the divisional bench of the Guwahati high court held that the "least possible delay" means "within the shortest possible time", though no arbitrary time limit can be set down as it may not be possible in many cases to precisely quantify the period of time by reference to hours, dates or months.

A few human rights activists have claimed that the AFSPA is draconian, arbitrary and gives the right to kill. In reality, the imposition of the AFSPA and subsequent safeguards avoid any possibility of arbitrariness in the exercise of power under the Act. The provisions of the AFSPA can be applied in only the following special cases.

1. The Central Government must be satisfied that the normal law and order situation has deteriorated up to the extent that it has created a disturbed or dangerous situation.

2. The state police force is not in a position to stop infiltration or undesirable forces.

3. The powers conferred by the statute can be exercised only in the specified area and in no other state.

4. The powers can be exercised only in respect of those who are violating law and order.

5. Before exercising the powers, a warning is required to be given to those who are violating the law in force.

6. The military person exercising the powers is answerable to the organization for any breach in the policy directives issued by the organization.

Section 6 of the AFSPA stipulates that no legal proceeding can be brought against any member of the armed forces acting under the AFSPA without the permission of the Central Government. Section 6 gives the Central Government the discretion to grant or refuse sanction for instituting prosecution against any person in respect of anything done in the exercise of the powers conferred by the Act. It does not suffer from arbitrariness as the order of the Central Government refusing or granting sanction under Section 6 is subject to judicial review. Section 6 of the AFSPA was reviewed in the case of *Indrajit Barua v. Union of India* (1983). The high court justified this provision on the grounds that it prevents the filing of "frivolous claims".

The armed forces need special legal protection and powers in the areas where they operate. It is imperative to use special legislation "from the point of view of morale as well as operational efficiency to protect the rights of soldiers". The Supreme Court of India, in the case of *Naga People's Movement of Human Rights* AIR 1998 SC 431, upheld the AFSPA. A five-judge bench upheld the instructions issued by the Central Government that gave a list of do's and don'ts to be observed while acting under the AFSPA as these provide effective checks against any misuse or abuse of the powers conferred. The Supreme Court opined that these instructions (see Appendix A) should be treated as binding by members of the armed forces. It further observed that a complaint regarding the misuse or abuse of the powers conferred by the Act should be thoroughly enquired into and if it is found that there is substance in the allegation, the victim should be suitably compensated by the state and the requisite sanction under Section 6 of the Act should be granted for the institution of prosecution against the person responsible for such violation.

AFSPA and Human Rights

The Universal Declaration of Human Rights, adopted by the General Assembly in 1948, provided the basis for the formulation of covenants and conventions. Three documents—The Universal Declaration of Human Rights (UDHR), the International Covenant on Civil and Political Rights (ICCPR), 1966 and the International Covenant on Economic, Social and Cultural Rights (ICESCR),1966, along with two protocols—the Optional

Protocol to the ICCPR and the Second Optional Protocol to the ICCPR, constitute the International Bill of Human Rights. The Convention against Torture and other Cruel and Inhuman or Degrading Treatment or Punishment was adopted by the General Assembly on 10 December 1984 and came into force on 26 June 1987. The Convention on the Elimination of All Forms of Discrimination against Women was adopted by the General Assembly on 18 December 1979 and came into force on 3 September 1981. In addition, the Convention on the Rights of the Child was adopted by the UN General Assembly on 20 November 1989 and came into force on 2 September 1990. A World Conference on Human Rights was held in Vienna in 1993 and was attended by about 7000 participants representing 171 countries, including India.

It has been claimed by certain bodies that the AFSPA, by its form and application, violates the UDHR, the ICCPR, the Convention Against Torture, the UN Code of Conduct for Law Enforcement Officials, the UN Body of Principles for Protection of All Persons Under any form of Detention, and the UN Principles on Effective Prevention and Investigation of Extra-Legal and Summary Executions. Specifically, the AFSPA violates the articles of the UDHR that relate to the following: (a) free and equal dignity and rights; (b) non-discrimination; (c) life, liberty, security of person; (d) provisions against torture; (e) equality before the law; (f) effective remedy; (g) provisions against arbitrary arrest; and (h) right to property.

The Second Periodic Report under the ICPPR was submitted by India to the UN Human Rights Committee in March 1991. The Committee found Section 4 of the AFSPA to be incompatible with Articles 6, 9 and 14 of the ICCPR, which was ratified by India on 10 April 1979. In response to the UN Human Rights Committee, the Attorney General of India justified the AFSPA under Article 355 of the Indian Constitution, which makes it the duty of the Union to protect each state from external aggression. He said that the AFSPA was necessary given the context of the North-East, where there is "infiltration of aliens into the territories mingling with the local public, and encouraging them towards this [secession]", and that "the ICCPR does not encourage secession and governments are not encouraged to promote it".

International Humanitarian Law (IHL)

The four Geneva Conventions of 1949 along with the two Additional Protocols constitute the body of international humanitarian law. The significant provisions of the four Geneva conventions can be summarized as (i) outlawing violation of right to life; (ii) prohibiting cruel treatment and torture; (iii) protecting personal dignity; (iv) providing for treatment of the wounded and sick during hostilities; and (v) prohibiting discrimination on the basis of race, colour, religion, nationality, etc. Article 3, common to all the four Geneva Conventions, also extends basic protection to all personnel not taking part in hostilities. Protocol II of June 1977 introduces more detailed rules in the case of armed conflicts of a non-international nature. The issues addressed are (i) fundamental guarantee of humane treatment and non-discrimination to all persons not directly involved in hostilities; (ii) special provisions in respect of persons where liberty is restricted; (iii) general protection for civilian population; (iv) prohibition of forced movement and starvation as a method of combat; (v) protection of objects indispensable to the survival of the civilian population, cultural objects and places of worship; (vi) prohibition of taking of hostages and outraging of personal dignity; and (vii) prohibition of violence to life and persons, in particular murder, mutilation, cruel treatment and torture.

The Government of India has signed and ratified the four Geneva Conventions. The principles of IHL also find fair mention in the different provisions of the Constitution of India. Part III (Fundamental Rights), Part IV (Directive Principles) and Part IVA (Fundamental Duties) of the Constitution together ensure the basic rights embodied in IHL. The rights mentioned in Part III are enforceable by the courts. The Directive Principles mentioned in Part IV are non-justiceable, but are fundamental in the governance of the country. Further, the Indian parliament has been empowered by Article 253 of the Constitution to make laws to give effect to the treaties and conventions to which India is a signatory.

The Indian armed forces have been a part of UN peacekeeping efforts since the UN intervention in Korea in 1950. India has so far participated in about 50 UN peacekeeping missions, contributing over 80,000 troops. As of 31 January 2010, India had 8760 troops engaged in peacekeeping operations. They have been lauded for their humane treatment of civilians the world over. In 1971 in particular, the Indian armed forces provided protection to about 20,000 civilians, including women and children, and kept about 95,000 prisoners of war, affording them treatment as per the principles of IHL. During the Kargil conflict in 1999, the armed forces again showed their adherence to IHL in the way they treated captured Pakistani soldiers.

Secessionist groups in India have of late been provoking the armed forces into over-reaction and subsequently mobilizing public opinion against alleged excesses committed by the troops. The militants have used human shields, predominantly women, to escape when confronted by the armed forces. This ruse enables them to allege misconduct on the part of the armed forces through a favourable media. The Indian armed forces, while engaging in counter-insurgency operations, have been maintaining the principles of 'minimum force' and avoidance of collateral damage. Cordon and search operations are being conducted in accordance with the policy guidelines (do's and don'ts) issued by the Army Headquarters on the basis of intelligence, and in association with village elders

AFSPA: Parliamentary Competency

Parliament is competent to enact the AFSPA, in exercise of the legislative power conferred on it under Entry 2 of List I and Article 248 of the Constitution, read with Entry 97 of List I. After the insertion of Entry 2A in List I by the Forty-Second Amendment to the Constitution, the legislative power of Parliament to enact the Central Act flows from Entry 2A of List I. The expression "in aid of civil power" in Entry 2A of List I and in Entry I of List II implies that the deployment of the armed forces shall be for the purpose of enabling the civil power in the state to deal with the situation affecting the maintenance of public order. The word "aid" postulates the continued existence of the authority to be aided. This means that even after the deployment of the armed forces, the civil power continues to function. In the event of the deployment of the armed forces, the said forces operate in the state concerned in cooperation with the civil administration so that the situation which has necessitated the deployment of the armed forces is effectively dealt with and normalcy restored.

Constitutional Provisions

It has been claimed that under Section 4(a) of the AFSPA, which grants armed forces personnel the power to shoot to kill, the constitutional right to life (Article 21) is violated and the AFSPA is not fair, just or reasonable because it allows the armed forces to use an excessive amount of force. The AFSPA came under the scrutiny of the Delhi High Court in the case of *Indrajit Barua* as violative of Articles 14, 19 and 21 of the Constitution. The Delhi High Court held: "If to save hundred lives one life is put in peril or if a law ensures and protects the greater social interest, then such law will be a wholesome and beneficial law although it may infringe the liberty of some individuals: it will ensure the liberty of a greater number at the cost of one and a few. In any organized society claiming to be civilized and governed by the rule of law, social imperatives for the greater good must take precedence over individual rights."

Article 22 of the Constitution states: "(1) No person who is arrested shall be detained in custody without being informed, as soon as may be, of the grounds for such arrest, nor shall he be denied the right to consult, and to be defended by, a legal practitioner of his choice. (2) Every person who is arrested and detained in custody shall be produced before the nearest magistrate within a period of twenty-four hours of such arrest, excluding the time necessary for the journey from the place of arrest to the court of the magistrate, and no such person shall be detained in custody beyond the said period without the authority of a magistrate." The remaining sections of the Article deal with the limits on these first two sections in the case of preventive detention laws. The safeguards under Article 22 are guaranteed to people arrested under Section 5 of the AFSPA. There are hundreds of cases in which captured militants have been handed over to the state police for subsequent trial.

National Human Rights Commission (NHRC)

The NHRC was set up under the provisions of the Protection of Human Rights Act 1993, and came into being on 12 October 1993. Since the Commission was established, a major and reciprocal effort has been made between it and the armed forces to exchange views on human rights, including the training of personnel of all ranks. Sections 17 to 19 of the Protection of Human Rights Act, 1993 relate to the procedure to be followed by the Commission for inquiring into complaints of violation of human rights. Section 17 prescribes the general procedure for inquiring into such complaints, Section 18 specifies the steps (after inquiry) that may be taken by the Commission; and Section 19 prescribes the special procedure with respect to the armed forces while dealing with such complaints. Under Section 19 of the Act, the Commission may seek a report from the Central Government in cases of complaints of violation of human rights by members of the armed forces. It is the responsibility of the Central Government to investigate such complaints in a fair and objective manner. The conclusion reached in the report must be the logical outcome and duly supported by the reasons given in the report. The Commission is empowered to make its recommendations to the Ministry of Defence for compliance.

The NHRC's Annual Report, 2006–07 indicates that the Commission has taken suo-moto cognizance of a newspaper report published in the *Kashmir Times,* dated 17 December 2006, titled "76 army men punished for human rights violations". The newspaper report mentioned that while the higher authorities in the army had given instructions to make the anti-insurgency operations people-friendly and to minimize civilian losses during these operations, 76 army personnel were awarded punishments during the preceding two years after complaints of human rights violations were received against them. The NHRC has asked the Ministry of Defence and the Chief Secretary, Jammu and Kashmir to award ex-gratia to the victims/ next of kin of the human rights violations.

Myths and Realities

In the last few years, enough has been written about the AFSPA. Even those who might never have seen a 'bullet' or ventured out of their home towns have expressed their views on the atrocities being perpetrated by the armed forces under the AFSPA. The views expressed in the media have indoctrinated the general public into believing that armed forces personnel have become 'monsters' under the excessive powers given to them by the AFSPA, and that the rule of law has ended. Certain myths and realities related to the AFSPA are as follows:-

Myth 1. The AFSPA covers the entire North-East and Jammu and Kashmir.

Reality. The AFSPA is applicable in only certain parts of the North-East and Jammu and Kashmir. For example, in Meghalaya, the AFSPA is applicable in only a 20-km range along the Assam border. In Arunachal Pradesh, it is applicable in the two eastern districts of Tirap and Changlang, which have been declared 'disturbed areas'. The same is the case with Jammu and Kashmir.

Myth 2. The armed forces get arbitrary power while functioning under the AFSPA.

Reality. The provisions of the AFSPA and the safeguards that accompany its imposition are intended to prevent the possibility of any arbitrariness in the exercise of power under the Act. The provisions of the AFSPA can be applied only when (i) the Central Government is satisfied that the normal law and order situation has deteriorated to the extent that an area can be considered a disturbed area; and (ii) the state police force is not in a position to stop infiltration or undesirable forces. In the case of *Naga People's Movement of Human Rights v. Union* AIR 1998 SC 431, the Supreme Court held that the powers conferred on the officers and NCOs under the AFSPA are not arbitrary and unreasonable, and are not violative of the provisions of Articles 14, 19 and 21 of the Constitution. Thus, there are ample safeguards to prevent the wanton abuse of power conferred by the AFSPA.

Myth 3. While operating under the AFSPA, the armed forces do not cooperate with the civil authorities.

Reality. The AFSPA also contemplates that in the event of the deployment of the armed forces, the said forces will operate in the state concerned in cooperation with the civil administration, so that the situation which has necessitated the deployment is dealt with more effectively and normalcy is restored faster. Even in a disturbed area, the civil law has to be followed. An order under Section 144 of the Cr PC must be in force before the powers under Section 4 of the AFSPA can be exercised. Before exercising the powers under the Act, a warning is required to be given to those who are violating the law. The military person exercising the powers is answerable for any breach in the policy directives issued by the Army.

Myth 4: Drastic powers have been conferred on low-ranking officials like NCOs.

Reality. In the armed forces, an NCO holds a responsible position. When troops are deployed, the sections/patrols which go for search and patrolling operations are commanded by a trained NCO. In isolated places/ remote areas, while encountering insurgents, the NCO is expected to take a decision as regards the suitable use of force in the particular situation, for which he is trained. We never question his capability in war or during a natural calamity.

Myth 5. The armed forces working under the AFSPA are the biggest human rights violators and not accountable to the NHRC.

Reality. The Indian armed forces have by now established a proud and enviable record of compliance with the dictates of international standards, to which their military manual by and large conforms. The Indian armed forces have participated in more than 50 UN peacekeeping missions. They have been lauded for their humane treatment of civilians the world over. Since 1993, the NHRC has been actively monitoring violations of human rights in the country. There have been a few cases of human rights violations by members of the armed forces, where the commission has directed the payment of compensation/interim relief to the victims/next of kin of the deceased. The NHRC has also taken cognizance of the action taken by the armed forces against its members accused of human rights violations.

Since March 1993, a human rights cell has been functioning in the Army headquarters under the Additional Director General (Discipline and Vigilance). In the last 14 years, it has received 1321 cases from the North-East and Jammu and Kashmir relating to alleged violation of human rights. Only 54 cases have been found true and in these, 115 personnel have been punished. In 17 cases, compensations have been awarded. The Army has also extended all forms of assistance towards the rehabilitation of the victims. The legal machinery in the country has not shirked its responsibility in ensuring suitable action in cases where the law has been violated. The Supreme Court, in *Sebastian M Hongray* AIR 1984 SC 1026, awarded an exemplary fine on the government for failing to produce two persons arrested by the armed forces.

Myth 6. The AFSPA grants total immunity to armed forces personnel.

Reality. Section 6 of the AFSPA does not grant immunity to the members of the armed forces; it only requires that permission be taken from the Central Government before prosecution. This does not amount to the granting of immunity. The question of arbitrariness does not arise as the order of the Central Government refusing or granting sanction under Section 6 is subject to judicial review. In a recent case, *Masooda Parveen v. Union of India* AIR 2007 SC 1840, the Supreme Court refused to grant any compensation as the person killed in the mishap was a trained militant.

Myth 7. The AFSPA is a symbol of oppression, an object of hate and an instrument of high-handedness.

Reality. In 2004, there were allegations that security forces raped and murdered 33-year-old Manorama in Manipur. Following the killing and the outcry by Meira Paibis for repeal of the AFPSA, the Prime Minister, Manmohan Singh, visited Manipur in November 2004. A day before his visit, the Central Government had appointed a five-member committee headed by the Supreme Court judge, B.P. Jeevan Reddy, to examine whether the AFSPA is required. The government neither accepted, nor rejected the committee's report, which was submitted in 2005. The report has not been made public, but various NGOs have selectively quoted a portion of it (which was available on the website of a prominent newspaper): "....for whatever reasons, [AFSPA] has become a symbol of oppression, an object of hate and an instrument of discrimination and high-handedness." However, other portions of the report are never discussed: "...though an overwhelming majority of the citizen groups and individuals pleaded for the repeal of the Act, they were firmly of the view at the same time that the Army should remain to fight the insurgents."

Role of Civil Society

When there is an allegation of the killing of an innocent civilian by the armed forces, the civil society is justified in demanding strict action against the violator. However, not much note is taken of the passage of dirty money (Manipur CM's 'donation' to rebels, *The Times of India*, 17 December 2005) and smuggling of arms to terrorists. Let us remind ourselves: those who kill innocent civilians are terrorists. While the media does not hesitate to give wide coverage to those who demand the removal of the AFSPA, the soldiers who die for the honour of the country are just a statistic. We have no choice but to meet force with force and place barriers in the path of terrorists. We should also not be surprised if there are more deaths of innocent people in the future. This is the price the civil society will have to pay for ignoring its duty towards the nation. We must honestly ask ourselves a few questions. Is it really a free society that wraps layers of security blankets around its own national celebrations for fear of terrorist attacks? Are we really free when we question every unattended piece of luggage on a train or in an airport? What kind of freedom surrounds our citizens when they become innocent prey of terrorists?

Action on Human Rights Allegations

The Indian armed forces take serious note of all human rights allegations against their members. In addition to the Human Rights Cell functioning in the Army headquarters, in each Command headquarters an officer of the rank of Colonel has been specifically designated to monitor and follow up cases of human rights violations reported against army personnel. Every human rights allegation is scrutinized, investigated and answered. On investigation, if an allegation is found to be true, suitable punishment is meted out to the defaulters and redress given to the aggrieved, to the extent possible. Independent bodies like the Press Council of India are invited to investigate the allegations.

The Human Rights Cell of the Western Command has released a detailed report of all allegations of human rights violations against the Army in Jammu and Kashmir during the last two decades. Of a total of 1508 allegations (1990–2008), only 35 (2.3 %) cases were found true, while 1453 cases (96.3 %) were “baseless and without an element of truth”. Strict action was taken in all cases where Army personnel were found guilty of human rights violations. The Army has also extended all forms of assistance for the rehabilitation of the victims. A few highlights of the report are:-

- In several cases, inquiries revealed that the Army had not launched any operation in the area and on the dates mentioned by the complainants.
- In a few cases, persons mentioned as having been killed by the Army surfaced and admitted that they had never been taken into custody by the Army.

- In a large number of cases, the persons who had filed FIRs about a missing person confessed that they were coerced by terrorists to make false complaints.

- In certain cases, charges of torture and illegal detention were made with the sole purpose of receiving compensation from the government.

Training in Human Rights

As part of their obligation to disseminate knowledge of human rights and IHL, the states are required to train officers and other ranks who are likely to be involved in internal or international conflicts. Respect for human rights is an integral part of military training in India. Keeping pace with the law of the land, all training institutions run by the armed forces have introduced the Geneva Conventions and other human rights instruments in their curricula. In addition, training programmes are regularly conducted for the officers and men with the help of the International Committee of Red Cross (ICRC) and NHRC. A Special Army Training Manual has been issued that comprehensively covers all aspects of human rights training. Consequent to the signing of a Memorandum of Understanding between the Government of India and the ICRC in 1995, the ICRC has visited various detention camps in Jammu and Kashmir, including the additional police lock-ups that the army is manning on behalf of the local police. This is a positive step to maintain transparency of operations by the Army and to show the Army's concern for the humane treatment of persons under detention.

Role of the Armed Forces

The decision to take a life should be subject to a clear normative framework and strict scrutiny. However, the right to life is not absolute under Indian or international law. The maintenance of social order necessitates exercising the right to self-defence and acting in defence of others. In most situations under the AFSPA in which a soldier uses

lethal force in order to safeguard innocent lives, his action in shooting to kill does not violate the right to life.

The armed forces are trained to cause death or serious injuries to the designated enemy. However, when they are entrusted with duties which are under normal circumstances the responsibility of the police force, they have to work with their hands tied behind their backs. They are expected to catch a violator and hand him over to the nearest police post for a judicial trial. A system in which a violator of the law of the land can be seized and brought to justice can work as long as the state machinery has physical control over the situation and is backed by a well-developed judicial process. Unfortunately, by the time the armed forces are called in, the state machinery and the judicial process are already influenced by the violators of law and their sympathizers.

Armed forces personnel deployed in disturbed areas suffer casualties every day. Their feelings of impotence, alienation and trauma sometimes translate into acts of revenge against the local population. More often, however, the excesses reported in the media are cases of mistaken identity. The dilemma before a soldier often is whether to use force and risk being accused of violating human rights or wait to make sure and risk his and his comrades' lives. Though under no circumstances should the use of counter-terrorism by the State be justified by the need to quell terrorism, we should perhaps view the instances of excesses by the State machinery in the context of preserving national integrity and stability. We must keep in mind the inhumanity of terrorist acts, like the killing of innocent victims, abduction and political assassinations, and the threat such acts pose to the integrity of the nation.

Conclusion

Being the largest democracy in the world, India is rightly expected to live up to the basic principles of human rights and humanitarian law. The Indian legal and constitutional framework, based on respect for human rights, is extremely conducive, sensitive and responsive to the implementation of international norms. The Indian armed forces have established a proud and enviable record of compliance with the dictates of international standards, to which their military manual by and large conforms. Various engagements across India's borders, as well as those under the aegis of the UN in which India's peacekeeping forces have participated have largely demonstrated India's compliance with international standards. Men in uniform have stood by the nation in its hour of need. They have defended the country against external aggression and assisted civilian powers to quell internal disturbances. Before the government makes any change in the existing law, it must understand the soldier's loyalty to his country. Unprotesting and unsung, he toils on for his country.

The terrorists and insurgents will not only persist but may wreak even greater damage, as the destructive power of their arsenal increases and they continue to get support from the civil society. Commentators point out that many insurgent groups in the North-East are difficult to distinguish from criminal organizations because they are heavily involved in extortion, kidnapping and the cross-border drug trade. The concept of democratic freedom, as we have known it, may need modification to permit strong action against terrorists. We must balance idealism with reality and recognize that terrorism is a national security issue. With terrorist camps operating across the Line of Control and attempting to disturb peace, the security forces need better support from the civil society. The armed forces need special legal protection and powers in the areas where they operate. Special legislation is necessary "from the point of view of morale and operational efficiency to protect the rights of soldiers". The circumstances that necessitated the imposition of the AFSPA in certain parts of the North-East and Jammu and Kashmir still exist. What is missing in these states is an enlightened political leadership which can bridge the gap between the people and the government.

APPENDIX A

List of Do's and Don'ts While Acting Under the Armed Forces Special Powers Act, 1958

Do's

(A) Action Before Operations.

1. Act only in the area declared "Disturbed Area" under Section 3 of the Act.

2. Power to open fire, use of force or arrest is to be exercised under this Act only by an officer/JCO/WO and NCO.

3. Before launching any raid/search, obtain definite information about the activity from the local civil authority.

4. As far as possible, representative of local civil administration must accompany during the raid.

(B) Action During Operations.

5. In case of necessity of opening operation and using any force against the suspect or any person acting in contravention to law and order, ascertain first that it is essential for maintenance of public order. Open fire only after due warning.

6. Arrest only those who have committed a cognizable offence or who are about to commit a cognizable offence or against whom a reasonable ground exists to prove that they have committed or are about to commit a cognizable offence.

7. Ensure that troops under command do not harass innocent people, destroy the property of the public or unnecessarily enter the house/dwelling of people not connected with any unlawful activity.

8. Ensure that women are not searched/arrested without the presence of female police. In fact, women should be searched by female police only.

(C) Action After Operations.

9. After arrest, prepare a list of the persons so arrested.

10. Hand over the arrested persons to the nearest police station with the least possible delay.

11. While handing over to the police, send along a report mentioning the detailed circumstances occasioning the arrest.

12. Every delay in handing over the suspects to the police must be justified and should be reasonable, depending upon the place, time of arrest and terrain in which such person has been arrested. The least possible delay may be 2–3 hours, extendable to 24 hours or so, depending upon a particular case.

13. After a raid, make out a list of all arms, ammunition or any other incriminating material/ document taken into possession.

14. All such arms, ammunition, stores, etc. should be handed over to the police station, along with a seizure memorandum.

15. Obtain a receipt of the persons and arms/ammunition, stores, etc. handed over to the police.

16. Make a record of the area where the operation is launched, including the date and time and the persons participating in the raid.

17. Make a list of the commander and other officers/JCOs/ NCOs forming part of such force.

18. Ensure medical relief to any person injured during the encounter. If any person dies in the encounter his dead body should be handed over immediately to the police,

along with the details leading to the death.

(D) Dealing with Civil Court.

19. The directions of the high courts/Supreme Court should be promptly attended to.

20. Whenever summoned by the courts, the decorum of the court must be maintained and proper respect paid.

21. Answer questions of the court politely and with dignity.

22. Maintain a detailed record of the entire operation. The record must be correct and explicit.

Don'ts

1. Do not keep a person in custody for any period longer than what is strictly necessary for handing him over to the nearest police station.

2. Do not use any force after having arrested a person, except when he is trying to escape.

3. Do not use third-degree methods to extract information, confessions, etc. about involvement in unlawful activity.

4. After the armed forces have arrested a person, their members shall not interrogate him.

5. Do not release the person directly, on your own, after apprehending him. If any person is to be released, he must be released through the civil authorities.

6. Do not tamper with official records

7. The armed forces shall not take back a person after he has been handed over to the civil police.

LIST OF DO'S AND DON'TS WHILE PROVIDING AID TO CIVIL AUTHORITY

Do's

1. Act in closest possible communication with the civil authorities throughout.

2. Maintain inter-communication, if possible, by telephone/radio.

3. Get the permission /requisition from the magistrate, when present.

4. Use the minimum force and do as little injury to person and property as may be consistent with the attainment of the objective in view.

5. In case you decide to open fire:-

   (a) Give warning in the local language that fire will be effective.

   (b) Before firing, attract attention by bugle or other means.

   (c) Distribute your men in fire units with specified commanders.

   (d) Control fire by issuing personal orders.

   (e) Note the number of rounds fired.

   (f) Aim at the front crowd actually rioting or inciting to riot, or at the conspicuous ring leaders, i.e., do not fire into the thick of the crowd at the back.

   (g) Aim low and shoot for the effect.

   (h) Keep light machine guns and medium guns in reserve.

   (i) Cease firing immediately once the object has been attained.

   (j) Take immediate steps to secure the wounded.

6. Maintain cordial relations with the civilian authorities and paramilitary forces.

7. Ensure a high standard of discipline.

Don'ts

8. Do not use excessive force.

9. Do not get involved in a hand-to-hand struggle with the mob.

10. Do not ill-treat anyone, in particular women and children.

11. Do not harass to civilians.

12. Do not torture anyone.

13. Steer clear of criminal bias while dealing with civilians.

14. Do not meddle in the civilian administration's affairs.

15. Avoid military disgrace by loss/ surrender of weapons.

16. Do not accept presents, donations and rewards.

17. Avoid indiscriminate firing.

CHAPTER 12

STRESS MANAGEMENT IN THE ARMED FORCES[1]

Introduction

The armed forces operate in a dynamic environment, which presents several challenges to its personnel. As the armed forces are becoming more and more complex in terms of technology and operations, the amount of stress faced by the personnel is also increasing. Stress manifests itself in various ways in peacetime and wartime, and can affect anyone serving at any level. In general, the failure to achieve one's goal, the search for personal fulfilment, any real or perceived grievance, and dissatisfaction at work are some reasons for stress. Each person has a profile of needs related to his or her job. The job—often by its very nature and sometimes because of the organizational structure—may satisfy only certain of these needs and not others. When the job needs of an individual and the need-fulfilling properties of the job are closely related, stress is less likely to occur. Stress is a result of a misfit between a person's skills and abilities, on the one hand, and the demands of the job, on the other; as well as a misfit between a person's needs and the extent to which these are satisfied by the job environment. The stress faced by the personnel is likely to affect an organization in terms of grievances, low performance and low morale.

The challenging environment of operations, the handling of emergencies, threat to personal safety and night guards in militancy-prone areas are some factors which contribute to stress in the armed forces. For air force personnel, in particular, one must consider factors such as the

---

1 The text of this chapter is based on the presentation given to the Parliamentary Standing Committee on Defence on 19 May 2008.

greenhouse effect, engine heat, aircrew clothing and helmets, which cause thermal stress inside the aircraft cockpit. Working on the tarmac in the summer months could be a source of stress for technicians and could increase errors in performance. Noise is one of the most extensively studied stressors in aviation and military situations. An individual is often unaware of the progressive decline in his / her accuracy while working in a noisy environment. In addition, there is stress caused by irregular working cycles, long working hours and monotonous duties. Over and above all this is the stress caused by the pyramidal structure of the armed forces, i.e., stress related to promotions and peer competition.

The Effects of Stress

Stress has been recognized as a cause for a variety of illnesses and behavioural problems. It can lead to suicide, fratricidal killing and early mortality. The direct cost of stress for the Indian armed forces could be several hundred crores of rupees per year due to the man-days of work lost, cost of treatment and deaths. The indirect costs are very difficult to estimate, and include such things as impaired motivation, prolonged un-serviceability of equipment, poor decision-making, poor quality of work, loss of creativity and accidents.

Stress threatens the integrity of an individual. It affects a person physiologically and psychologically. The following data highlights the effect of stress on the armed forces:-

- During the period 2003 to 2006, there were 501 cases of suicide in the armed forces.
- Over 250 soldiers die battling terrorists, while over 350 soldiers, sailors and airmen die in road accidents every year.
- Over 550 armed forces personnel were discharged from service in 2006 due to mental disorder and alcohol dependency.
- The Indian Air Force lost more than 210 personnel in accidents and suicides in 1999 and 2000.

- Over 1700 officers applied for premature retirement in the armed forces in 2007.

Human Rights Approach

Though the rising instances of suicide and fratricidal killing in the armed forces started a nationwide debate, the Army chief was initially reluctant to attribute these to operational stress. He claimed that these incidents were due to marital, financial and medical problems and issues related to children's education. His statement was, however, not supported by any empirical study. In a subsequent submission to Parliament, the Ministry of Defence stated that various remedial measures had been taken to tackle the problem. These included appointing junior commissioned officers as counsellors, introducing relaxation techniques such as yoga, liberalizing leave policy and improving man management. These measures are just a knee-jerk reaction and may not offer any permanent solution. The problem needs to be examined holistically, in the context of human rights.

The armed forces were looked upon as a body of men whose sole purpose was to fight during an armed conflict; the needs of the individual were treated as subservient to this supreme purpose. The hierarchical structure of the armed forces, based on rank, placed an obligation on the men to obey the orders of superiors. The officers had formal education, while the soldiers were generally uneducated, and military organizations usually considered it inappropriate to treat all ranks equally in relation to certain aspects of military life. However, all this has changed in the last 50 years, due largely to the international human rights laws.

It is now held that members of the armed forces must be granted the same rights as civilians, except in certain select matters. While the protection and promotion of certain civil and political rights, such as freedom of expression and freedom of thought, conscience, and religion or belief, may be qualified in the light of military duties, all members of the armed forces, whatever their status, must enjoy certain inalienable fundamental freedoms and rights, in an absolute manner and without restriction. In particular, no derogation is possible from the right to life, bearing in mind, however, the inherent dangers of the military profession (Article 6, ICCPR). Members of the armed forces have the right to protection against inhuman or degrading treatment. This means that they must not suffer humiliating or degrading treatment, for instance during particularly harsh or rigorous training. Nor must they be subjected to ill-treatment, brutality or other practices that may be deemed to be inhuman or degrading. These rights are reaffirmed in the United Nations Convention against Torture and Other Cruel, Inhuman or Degrading Treatment or Punishment. The Convention on Elimination of Discrimination against Women (CEDAW), ratified by India in June 1993, requires the signatories to legitimize women's claims for rights and equality. This is another human rights instrument that is relevant in the context of the armed forces. The universal human rights cannot be restricted, even by military requirements.

This chapter examines certain specific issues related to the armed forces in the light of universal human rights. The proper handling of these issues may, in the long run, offer a solution to the effective management of stress in the armed forces.

A. Leave

Members of the armed forces are entitled to 60 days of annual leave in a calendar year. This is non-cumulative. In addition to this, officers are entitled to 20 days and personnel below the officer rank (PBORs) to 30 days of casual leave every year. Officers are also entitled to a furlough of 60 days (half-pay) in a cycle of three calendar years.

After joining the armed forces, an individual soon comes to terms with phrases like "leave is a matter of privilege and not a right". Due to the shortage of officers/PBORs in most of the units, an individual may not get his authorized leave and also may not be able to choose the time when he is sanctioned his leave. Various formation commanders have issued letters for curtailing leave. The commanding officers at the unit level generally follow these instructions blindly as any violation may go against them. Shortages in the officer's cadre not only creates problems related to leave, but also places an increased workload on the existing staff, a load for which they do not get any compensation. The issue of leave is more serious in the case of PBOR. In order to meet their family obligations, most of them plan visits to their native place during leave. Failure to meet these family obligations due to denial of leave leads to a great deal of frustration and stress among them.

B. Ill-treatment

Non-derogable human rights should be granted to all members of the armed forces, without any restriction. The prohibition of inhuman or degrading treatment, servitude, and forced or compulsory labour falls under this category of rights. Sections 45, 46 and 47 of the Army Act, 1950 make unbecoming, cruel and indecent conduct and ill-treatment of a subordinate an offence. Certain practices in the armed forces must be examined in the light of the human rights of military personnel. In this context, it would be relevant to refer to a reader's response to an article, "Suicides in the Armed Forces", which appeared in *The Hindu* (22 December 2006):-

> *"Officers should be sensitized to be receptive and to empathize with the emotional trauma a subordinate is subjected to or goes through. Lending an ear to a subordinate does not in any way affect operational effectiveness. In this context, it may be worthwhile to suggest that the army should dispense with the anachronous and colonial post of batman—soldier assigned to an officer as a personal servant who is often used for domestic work."*

Psychological and physical violence against members of the armed forces remains one of the main issues facing the armed forces of many countries. Training in peacetime attempts to simulate battle conditions; hence, fatigue and hardship are an essential part of military training. Soldiers are supposed to "train as you fight" and have to undergo many hardships in order to achieve combat readiness. The dualism between peacetime training and wartime practice may create difficulties in distinguishing between legitimate methods of training and harassment. In many cases, the investigation of alleged mistreatment remains in the hands of the commanding officers, who may themselves be the source of grievance or may have an interest in covering up such cases. To counter mistreatment, it is imperative that military personnel be informed of their rights at the time of recruitment and illegal punishment be outlawed. Collective punishment and punishment resulting in demeaning treatment or humiliation should, in particular, be banned.

C. Service Accommodation and Family Life

In publicity campaigns and advertisements calling the youth to join the armed forces, the provision of service accommodation takes a front seat. Armed forces personnel, whether single or married, are entitled to accommodation in accordance with the Scales of Accommodation for the Defence Service. Unfortunately, in reality, an individual may not get his entitled accommodation for even half of the period served in the armed forces. The non-availability of service accommodation forces an individual to live away from his family as financial constraints do not allow him to hire private accommodation.

The Ministry of Defence, in a reply to a Starred Question (No. 63, answered on 27.07.2006) in the Lok Sabha, stated that the analysis of the findings of the courts/board of inquiry relating to cases of suicide reveals that a majority of individuals took this extreme step due to personal and family problems, like marital discord, extra-marital affairs, medical problems and financial or property issues, and not because of professional or organizational reasons.

It is well known that family support is an important de-stressor. The non-availability of service accommodation is, therefore, an organizational failure which can result in marital discord and extra-marital affairs. Alcohol dependence and psychological problems may also arise in lonely places where both officers and men are already under stress. Thus the ministry's stand that suicides among service members are "due to personal and family problems" and not "service reasons" is incorrect.

The specific nature of military life, including international deployment and frequent shifting, has an impact on the family members of armed forces personnel and, therefore, on the members themselves. There is a need to create authorized accommodation suitable for married military personnel at every station. The government must take measures to help the members of the armed forces to achieve a good balance between their private and military life, and to accept the constraints inherent in military life. There is a need to evolve special programmes to offer support to personnel and relatives who are threatened by, or suffer from, the psychological after-effects of traumatic incidents experienced in the service. The target group should include both discharged and serving personnel.

D. Just and Favourable Conditions of Work

The "enjoyment of just and favourable conditions of work" forms a part of a broad set of social and economic rights that include the rights to work, to form or join unions, to an adequate standard of living, to equal opportunities and to the highest attainable standards of physical and mental health. Just and favourable working conditions should not to be perceived as a legal minimum standard; rather, the government should ensure that such conditions are provided. For example, the International Covenant on Economic, Social and Cultural Rights (ICESCR) requires states to give effect to the rights "by all appropriate means". It adopts a broad and flexible approach that takes into account the specific characteristics of the legal and administrative systems of states that are party to the Covenant.

This is necessary because the military profession is subject to specific risks and demands that have an impact on the health and safety of servicemen. A number of military tasks, e.g., working in counter-insurgency operations, flying aircraft, specific naval duties, minesweeping and intelligence assignments, involve health and safety risks. Just and favourable conditions of work, including effective safety and health policies, are necessary not only to reduce stress, but also to prevent accidents in the workplace. In this context, it would be worthwhile to recall that during OP PARAKRAM, a total of 60 army personnel lost their lives and 142 were wounded while laying mines (Lok Sabha Starred Question 466 for 28 April 2005).

Except for the right to join or form a union (Article 8), the ICECSR does not limit the enjoyment of the rights related to just and favourable working conditions by armed forces personnel in the interest of national security. Since the government has ratified the ICESCR, it has a legal obligation to implement just and favourable work conditions "by all appropriate means". Just and favourable conditions of work have a positive impact on the work and life of personnel. They also help to improve team cohesiveness and operational effectiveness. Finally, ensuring that soldiers enjoy a broad range of social rights can foster a positive public image of the armed forces and make it easier to recruit new personnel.

E. Working Hours and Compensation for Overtime

In India, the armed forces do not follow any specific rules on work hours due to the premise that military personnel should always be available. A research carried out by Georg Nolte and Heike Krieger (2003) shows that in Europe, the average period of work for armed forces personnel is between 36 and 50 hours per week. According to the same research, some countries take an approach comparable to that of the civil service. In Belgium, armed forces personnel generally work 38 hours per week. In Denmark, the working hours of armed forces personnel follow those of other civil servants, with modifications to ensure the effectiveness of the armed forces. For instance, it is normally required in Denmark to grant employees 11 hours of free time within each 24-hour period. Since military exercises sometimes last for several days and it is not possible to comply with this provision, compensation is granted. In Italy, the regular working time is 36 hours per week. Overtime compensation can be provided in money or in time.

In some countries, the organization of working time is still based on the principle of the permanent availability of soldiers. This is true in the case of France, for example, where a soldier can be requested to be on duty at all times in accordance with Article 12 of the General Statute on Military Personnel. Recently, however, the French Ministry of Defence adopted a system of compensation for overtime for armed forces personnel. On the basis of this regulation, armed forces personnel were granted 15 extra days of annual leave, in addition to the existing 60 days.

Restrictions on the exercise and enjoyment of social and economic rights by armed forces personnel need to be specific. General restrictions should be avoided. The ministry of defence should take all possible measures to ensure that provisions related to working conditions are implemented in accordance with national law and international obligations.

F. Health Care

The military profession is subject to specific risks and demands that have an impact on the health and safety of servicemen. In accordance with Article 12 of the ICESCR, military personnel are entitled to the right to the highest attainable standard of physical and mental health. It is true that Indian military personnel are entitled to full health care. However, referral to psychiatric treatment is considered a 'stigma'. The commanding officer fills up a document called Medical Form 10 for psychiatric evaluation. The fact that Form 10 has been raised for an individual makes him an outcaste. When an individual is referred for psychiatric evaluation and treatment, he is kept under escort till his psychiatrist clears him. This 'stigma' may adversely affect an individual's service career, thus prompting him to conceal his mental problems.

For example, it has been reported in a study conducted by Harris Interactive for the American Psychiatric Association (APA) that a majority of US soldiers who have done tours of duty in Iraq or Afghanistan suffer from stress-related troubles linked to their deployments. However, most keep their psychological problems to themselves for fear of being stigmatized or seeing their careers take a nose-dive. The study further revealed that nearly six in 10 US military members said their deployment in a war zone had caused them to suffer from "negative experiences" associated with stress. But a mere 10 per cent have sought treatment for mental health. Over 60 per cent said they avoided seeking help for mental health problems because they feared that doing so would impact negatively on their career. Fifty-three per cent said they felt others would think less of them if they were to seek help for psychological troubles resulting from their deployment. Two-thirds of military members said they rarely, if ever, talked about their mental health with family and friends. Nearly half (48 per cent) of the soldiers said they had difficulty sleeping, half reported feeling depressed, and one-third reported a lack of interest in daily activities. The RAND Corporation study estimated the cost of treating soldiers diagnosed with depression in the first two years following their return from Iraq or Afghanistan at up to 6.2 billion dollars.

In case of death, disability or injury, financial benefits, disability compensation or pension, pension rights and payment of compensation also apply to the family members and relatives of deceased, injured or incapacitated armed forces personnel. However, the family health care offered to PBORs needs more attention.

G. Discrimination against Women Officers

The role of women in the armed forces is a subject of debate in most democracies. Although the opportunities for women in the armed forces have expanded in recent years, even in a country like the USA, where women have among the highest levels of participation in the military services, women account for only 15 per cent of military personnel. Women are still exposed to discriminatory policies and actions. For example, in many countries they are excluded from combat positions (Bangladesh, France, India, Nepal, Pakistan, Portugal, Sri Lanka, Ukraine, the United Kingdom). The countries where they are allowed to fulfil combat positions are Austria, Belarus, Belgium, Bosnia and Herzegovina, Canada, Croatia, the Czech Republic, Denmark, Estonia, Finland, Georgia, Germany, Ireland, Latvia, Lithuania, Luxembourg, Norway, Poland, the Russian Federation, Serbia, Slovakia, Slovenia, Spain, Sweden, Switzerland and Turkey.

Taking part in the nation's defence is an integral part of the rights and duties associated with citizenship. If women are excluded from participation in such an important national institution as the armed forces, they are in an unequal position vis-a-vis men. The UN Security Council Resolution 1325 on Women, Peace and Security (2000) upholds "the important role of women in the prevention and resolution of conflicts and in peace-building. [It urges states] to ensure increased representation of women at all decision-making levels in national, regional and international institutions and mechanisms for the prevention, management, and resolution of conflict".

Article 15 of the CEDAW, adopted in 1979 by the UN General Assembly, states that all state parties "shall accord to women equality with men before the law". Article 7 prescribes that state parties take "all appropriate measures to eliminate discrimination against women in the political and public life of the country". Article 8 stipulates: "States Parties shall take all appropriate measures to ensure to women, on equal terms with men and without any discrimination, the opportunity to represent their Governments at the international level and to participate in the work of international organizations."

Sexual harassment and sexual violence against women in military establishments is also a widespread problem. Sexual harassment and sexual violence not only damage the emotional or psychological well-being of the victim, but also harm her work performance and damage the public image of the armed forces. Preventing sexual offences in the armed forces is essential for ensuring a non-discriminatory and safe work environment. Many abuses remain unpunished because very few women use the military's formal or informal grievance process as they lack confidence in the military system for redress. Many women do not tell anyone if they have been a victim of abuse because they fear that their complaint could have a negative effect on their career or because they feel they would not be believed.

CEDAW mandates states to ensure (a) equality of opportunity through law, policy, programmes and institutional arrangements; (b) equality of access by (i) eliminating all obstacles that prevent access to the opportunities, as well as (ii) institution of positive measures/enabling conditions, including temporary special measures, to level the playing field between men and women; and (iii) equality of results that entitles women to outcomes and social goods (education, employment etc) on an equal basis with men. The government should, therefore, improve the military's ability to recruit, retain and advance women. During training, armed forces personnel should be made aware of what behaviour constitutes sexual harassment. There should be no tolerance of sexual harassment or sexual violence. An adequate complaints mechanism should be available for women to report harassment or violence, and an effective system of sanctions should be provided for cases reported.

H. Redress of Grievance

The processing of grievance petitions is also faulty. The officials who may be the root cause of the grievance process the complaint. The complainant is not informed about the comments of his superiors and there is no independent judicial forum to review the executive decision. There is a need to create an independent body outside the normal military chain of command for managing all complaints and grievances. There is no fixed time-frame within which the service headquarters are bound to give the final order in grievance cases. Delay in the finalization of such cases causes undue stress, hardship and misery to the aggrieved soldier.

In this direction, the Australian Department of Defence took an important step in streamlining the redress of grievances (ROG) process by establishing the Fairness and Resolution Branch. The branch was formed in January 2006, outside the military chain of command, by amalgamating a number of complaint agencies. There has been a significant improvement in the department's handling of ROGs over the past year, with a reduction both in the number of cases awaiting allocation to a case officer and the time taken to finalize ROGs. There has also been a reduction in the number of complaints to the Ombudsman about ROG processes.

The Armed Forces Tribunal created under the Act of 2007 also does not have any jurisdiction in matters relating to leave, postings, transfers, summary disposals and trials. Ironically, these are the core issues leading to grievances and stress in the armed forces. The denial of the right to approach the Tribunal in these matters, when viewed from a different perspective, would lead the military chain of command to have the perception that their decisions, even if arbitrary, cannot be questioned. The issue of the Tribunal's jurisdiction, therefore, needs re-examination.

I. Military Justice System

The members of the armed forces serve within a system of discipline that regulates their lives more pervasively than the systems regulating other professions. They spend a major part of their life in military bases and, when on active service, most of their time and efforts are devoted to military tasks under the command of a superior. In situations involving potential conflict, the urgent and overriding importance of the military task and the risk to life justify the need for consistent obedience. The division that exists in other professions between work and private life virtually disappears under these circumstances. The constant need to train servicemen to be ready for active military deployment means that discipline must be maintained even under peacetime conditions, although it can be argued that a more nuanced approach to discipline should be taken, bearing in mind the actual circumstances.

The pervasive nature of military discipline gives superior officers a very high degree of control over the life of servicemen. Disciplinary matters may need to be dealt with under extreme conditions of service, where full procedural safeguards are not attainable and where there is an urgent and paramount need to restore discipline if the effectiveness of a mission is not to be compromised. Equally, however, a miscarriage of justice may lead to the imposition of severe punishments that may have far-reaching consequences that could, for example, affect an individual's safety, health and family life.

The military justice system plays an important role in the protection of the human rights of armed forces personnel. In order to have credibility and legitimacy in the eyes of both the armed forces and the public, military justice must be detached from the immediate chain of command. Defendants in military trials should have access to legal advice and representation of their choice, and if unable to pay, should be granted legal aid. Any variations in procedure (as compared to the civilian system) should be fully justified by military exigencies and be in keeping with the restrictions on procedural rights contained in the relevant human rights conventions. There is an urgent need to abolish the arbitrary system of trial followed in summary court-martial, carried over from the era of colonial rule. The incorporation of constitutional or human rights guarantees into the military justice system will lead to significant improvement in the morale and well-being of the armed forces.

Morale and discipline are enhanced when the troops understand that they are being treated with dignity, fairness and equality under the law. Thus, there is a need for review and modernization of the military justice system, which should be administered fairly, effectively and promptly to improve transparency.

J. The Responsibility of Commander as a Leader

The power to command and the duty to obey are of central importance in the armed forces. Commanders play a crucial role in guiding the military, social and moral behaviour of their units. The overriding operational imperative of the armed forces is to sustain team cohesion, as well as the maintenance of trust and loyalty between commanders and those they command. This imposes a need for values and standards which are more demanding than those required by society at large. As part of their responsibility of ensuring operational effectiveness, commanders build up effective team relationships within their units, thus fostering team spirit and a climate of mutual trust and respect. Their leadership is crucial for fostering respect for human rights within the barracks and they have an obligation to take all measures necessary to prevent their subordinates from committing unlawful acts.

A former senior army officer attributes stress-related acts of indiscipline to poor man-management or "weak leadership". In the light of the prominent role of commanders in ensuring that human rights are respected among the troops, it is crucial that officers and JCOs be provided with adequate training. There must also be a clear framework that defines the responsibility and individual accountability of commanders. Officers and JCOs need to be trained not only in the exercise of leadership, but also in military law, human rights and international humanitarian law. This would help them acquire a thorough knowledge of their duties, to develop a sense of justice and to learn how to be a model for their subordinates. It would also reduce the number of cases of human rights violations against the armed forces.

Parliamentary Standing Committees' Report

Concerned over as many as 635 cases of suicide and 67 cases of fratricidal killing in the armed forces during the years 2003 to 2007, the Parliamentary Standing Committee on Defence examined the issue of stress management in the armed forces. In its 31st report submitted to Parliament on 21 October 2008, the Committee observed:-

> To the utter dismay of the Committee, the Ministry of Defence have made an attempt to downplay the magnitude of the problem by putting forth the plea that "the overall psychiatric morbidity in the Armed Forces has been less than the national figures". Equally specious is the plea advanced by the Ministry of Defence that there is a rising trend of psychiatric illnesses in our country over the last few decades and Armed Force personnel being drawn from the same society are not immune to these influences. The Committee consider it lamentable that the Ministry of Defence, rather than making an earnest attempt to identify the precise reasons for untimely loss of such a large number of precious lives of trained soldiers, have taken recourse to drawing satisfaction from the facts that such cases are on the rise in the society and the psychiatric morbidity in Armed Forces is less than the national averages. In the opinion of the Committee, this attitude of the Ministry not only displays insensitivity towards the problem but also highlights their inaction to improve conditions in Armed Forces where soldiers are trained enough to fight under adverse situations.

The report highlighted the following issues:-

1. **Welfare.** While armed forces personnel have to strike a balance between their personal and military life within the constraints inherent in military service, the government, too, must look after the welfare of the personnel engaged in meeting the diverse challenges before the nation. The Committee recommended that

(i) the government should provide family accommodation at the station of choice for personnel deployed in counter-insurgency operations and border areas; (ii) the children of armed forces personnel should be helped in getting admission to schools and institutions for higher professional and technical studies; and (iii) the welfare organizations of the three services should be financially strengthened to enable them to extend the necessary help to distressed families. Since the denial of leave was seen to be an important factor causing stress amongst armed forces personnel, the Committee recommended that the issue of liberalized leave policy be examined by the Ministry of Defence (MoD) with an open mind so that its benefits may percolate down to the lower ranks.

2. **Shortage in Officer Cadre.** A major problem being faced by the armed forces is the existing shortage of over 12,500 officers, together with the fact that 1700 applications for premature retirement are under consideration. The shortage of personnel in the officer cadre is causing a lot of stress among junior and middle-level officers, who have to perform multiple functions and hence, do not have adequate time and opportunity for the effective administration of personnel under their command. The Committee has recommended that the shortage of personnel at the unit level be kept at the barest minimum, particularly in the border areas and areas where counter-insurgency operations are under way. However, it may not be easy to find a solution to this problem, considering that the Sixth Pay Commission's recommendations with regard to the armed forces are yet to be finalized. The government and the armed forces may have to work out alternative strategies to fill the vacancies in the officer cadre.

3. **Interpersonal Relations.** On the issue of interpersonal relationships in the armed forces, the Committee felt that appropriate training is needed to change the mindset of the senior officers. The officers have to be sensitized towards the needs of the soldiers, both as individuals and as a group. This assumes

greater importance because the soldiers who are now being inducted possess a higher level of education. The Committee was highly critical of the practice of utilizing the services of Jawans as 'sahayak' in one form or another. It was of the opinion that the use of a combatant person for household work was demeaning and humiliating. It urged the Ministry of Defence to issue instructions to put a stop to this practice, which lowers the self-esteem of Jawans. The Committee also desired that similar action be taken by the Ministry of Home Affairs in respect of paramilitary organizations.

4. **Health.** Another daunting issue faced by the armed forces is the mental health of its members. Over 550 armed forces personnel were discharged from service in 2006 due to mental disorders and alcohol dependency. In the armed forces, referral to psychiatric treatment is considered a 'stigma' and may have an adverse impact on an individual's career. Thus, personnel suffering from mental health problems fight shy of seeking help. The Committee felt that the system of referring a person specifically for psychiatric evaluation should be suitably modified and that personnel of all ranks should undergo such evaluation during routine medical examinations at fixed intervals of time. While the modified system would allow the distressed person to get appropriate and timely treatment, he would be saved from being branded as an outcaste in the eyes of his colleagues.

5. **Research Work.** The armed forces have also conducted as many as nine in-house studies, including one by the Defence Institute of Psychological Research (DIPR), on stress-related issues. However, these reports are classified and not available for scrutiny and analysis. These studies have identified certain causative factors for stress. The causes can be classified as socio-economic, organizational and psychological. The Committee was critical that the MoD has not contemplated multi-pronged strategies to address the problem of negative stress behaviour among different ranks in

the armed forces. The Committee was also concerned that no effective follow-up action was taken on crucial areas such as sensitizing the officers or improving basic facilities in the field. Since such studies can yield the desired results only if they are made public, the Committee suggested that the veil of secrecy be removed and the studies be placed in the public domain.

6. **Complaint Monitoring.** With a view to mitigating the hardships of military personnel, state government officials need to be more pro-active about giving a prompt response to the grievances and problems of serving personnel and their families. The Committee also wanted the MoD to make institutionalized arrangements, in close coordination with the state governments, and put in place a central computerized mechanism to monitor the progress of complaints received from defence service personnel or their family members. It urged the MoD to make a realistic assessment of the problems plaguing defence service personnel and identify the areas needing urgent reform.

Recommendations

Stress is a normal part of human existence — a double-edged sword, which can help us mobilize and achieve, or physically and psychologically incapacitate us. In order to raise awareness among armed forces personnel, all new entrants must be given a handbook, which may contain the following information: (i) details of the conditions of employment; (ii) responsibilities and obligations; (iii) entitlements and rights as a member of the defence forces; (iv) promotion prospects; (v) health and safety policies; (vi) interpersonal relationships; (vii) unacceptable behaviour and harassment; (viii) how to seek redress and make a complaint; and (ix) honours and awards.

There is a need to establish an ombudsman's office common to the three services to help the military chain of command and the military justice system ensure that the rule of law is respected in the armed forces. It would promote transparency and accountability in defence structures and focus attention on problems in the armed forces requiring corrective action. The independence of the ombudsman's office is crucial for ensuring robust accountability of the military. In order to be independent, the ombudsman should be granted statutory authority, operational independence and adequate legal staff.

The MoD should also cooperate with NGOs and the media and "open the doors" of military units to enhance transparency. External institutions, e.g., ombudsmen, the human rights commission and NGOs, should be allowed to monitor how human rights are being upheld in the armed forces and their recommendations should be examined for better adherence to human rights norms. In this context, a letter published in *The Hindu* (Letters to Editor, 1 August 2007) is reproduced:-

> "As one whose immediate family members are all serving in the armed forces, I would like to say that the Indian armed forces, particularly the jawans, are among the most disciplined in the world. The jawans toil day and night and draw very low salaries. They leave their families alone and unprotected at home. They do not get the leave due to them as the army is almost always understaffed. On top of all this, they come under an authoritative and non-transparent administrative system with no proper grievance redress mechanism in place. They are tried by the army court and not given the freedom of an independent and transparent justice system. The Indian jawans certainly do not get any misplaced sympathy. In fact, it is official apathy that they face every day."

The standing committees and representative associations of retired armed forces personnel should be involved in determining the working conditions, including salaries, allowances and pensions; working time; leave and compensation for leave; health; safety at work; and issues related to achieving a balance between private/family life and working life. Independent arbiters (armed forces tribunal, ombudsmen or committees) should have full powers to investigate or mediate cases, including access to military premises, opportunities to question armed forces personnel, and access to classified information, and they should have the authority to make recommendations wherever necessary.

Conclusion

The armed forces are an integral part of a democratic state and society. Their role is not merely to defend the state and its citizens against internal and external threats, but also to protect and uphold the human rights and fundamental freedoms on which democratic societies are based. As representatives of the state, armed forces personnel are bound to respect human rights and international humanitarian law in the exercise of their duties. It follows that they must be entitled to the same rights and protections as all other persons, subject to certain limitations imposed by military life. When the human rights and fundamental freedoms of members of the armed forces are protected within their institution, they will be more likely to uphold these while carrying out their duties.

BIBLIOGRAPHY

1. *A Guide to the Legal Review of New Weapons, Means and Methods of Warfare; Measures to Implement Article 36 of Additional Protocol I of 1977*, International Committee of the Red Cross, Geneva, January 2006.

2. Advisory Opinion on *Legality of the Threat or Use of Nuclear Weapons*, (1996) *Reports of the International Court of Justice (ICJ Report),* p. 262-266.

3. Alexander Orakhelashvili. The Legal Basis of the United Nations Peacekeeping Operations, *Virginia Journal of International Law*, (2003), Vol. 43 p. 485-524.

4. Allenby, BE. Environmental Security: Concept and Implementation, *International Political Science Review*, (2000), 21 (1), p. 5-21.

5. Andrews, J.A.1982. *Human Rights in Criminal Procedure: A Comparative Study*, The Hague: Nijhoff.

6. Arnold Roberta, Military Criminal Procedures and Judicial Guarantees: The Example of Switz erland, *Journal of International Criminal Justice*, (2005), Vol. 3, No. 3, p. 749-777.

7. Asthana Vandana & Dr AC Shukla. Environmental Consequences of Armed Conflict in South Asia, *South Asian Journal*, (Oct-Dec 2008), p. 79-91.

8. Bekou Olympia and Rober t Cryer. The International Criminal Court and Universal Jurisdiction: A Close Encounter, *International and Comparative Law Quarterly*, Vol. 56, (January 2007), pp. 49-68.

9. Bellamy Alex J. No Pain, No Gain? Torture and ethics in the w ar on terror, *International Affairs*, Vol. 82, No. 1, (2006), p. 121-148.

10. Brownlie, Ian. & Guy, S Goodwin-Gill.2000. *Basic Documents on Human Right.* New York: Oxford University Press.

11. Caforio, G. (ed.). 2003. *Handbook of the Sociology of the Military*, New York: Kluwer Academic/Plenum Publishers.

12. Careiras, H.2006. *Gender and the Military: Women in the Armed Forces of Western Democracies*, London: Routledge.

13. Carnduff, H.W.C. 1904. *Military and Cantonment law in India.* Calcutta:

Lahiri & Company.

14. Cleary Laura R. and McConvilee Teri. 2006. *Managing Defence in a Democracy*, London: Routledge.

15. Clode, C.M. 1869. *Military Forces of the Crown, Vol. I and II.* London: John Murray.

16. Conte Alex. 2004. *Defining Civil and Political Rights: The Jurisprudence of the United Nations Human Rights Committee*, UK: Ashgate.

17. Dahl, Arne Willy. Environmental Destruction in War, *Disarmament* Vol. 15, No. 2, (1992), p. 113-127.

18. Damgaard Ciara. 2008. *Individual Criminal responsibility for Core International Crimes*, Berlin: Springer-Verlag.

19. Daphna Shraga. UN Peacekeeping Operations: Applicability of IHL and Responsibility for Operation-Related Damage, *American Journal of International Law*, Vol. 94, (2000), p. 406-12.

20. Davidson Michael J . 1999. *A Guide to Military Criminal Law: A Practical Guide for all the Services*, USA: Naval Institute Press, Annapolis.

21. Deka, A.K. ULFA and the Peace Process in Assam, *IPCS Special Report* 21, New Delhi: Institute of Peace and Conflict Studies, 2006.

22. Detter, I. 2000. *The Law of War*, Cambridge: Cambridge University Press.

23. Dinstein Yoram. 2004. *The Conduct of Hostilities under the Law of International Armed Conflict,* Cambridge: Cambridge University Press.

24. Dolgopol Ustinia and J udith Gardam. 2006. *The Challenges of Conflict: International Law Responds*, Leiden: Martinus Nijhoff Publishers.

25. Donohue Laura K. 2008. *The Cost of Counterterrorism: Power, Politics and Liberty*, Cambridge: Cambridge University Press.

26. Downey JCT. 1987. *Management in the Armed Forces: An Anatomy of the Military Profession*, Dehradun: EBD Educational Pvt. Ltd.

27. Falk, R.A. The Shimoda Case: A Legal Appr aisal of the Atomic Attacks Upon Hiroshima and Nagasaki, Vol. 59, *American Journal of International Law*, (1965) p. 759.

28. Fenrich W.J. The Conventional Weapons Convention: A Modest but Useful Treaty', Vol. 30, *International Review of the Red Cross,* (1990), No.

279, p. 498.

29. Finer, S.E. 1962. *The Man on Horseback: The Role of the Military in Politics*. London: Pall Mall Press.

30. Fleck Dieter. 2009. *The Handbook of International Humanitarian Law*, Oxford: Oxford University Press.

31. Foot Rosemary. Human Rights in Conflict, *Survival*, Vol. 48 No. 3, (Autumn 2006), p. 109-126.

32. Frederick Rawski. To Waive or Not to Waive: Imm unity and Accountability in UN P eacekeeping Oper ations, *Connecticut Journal of International Law*, Vol. 18, (2002), p. 103-32.

33. Gabriel Rachard A.1981. *Crisis in Command*, New Delhi: Himalayan Books.

34. Ganguly Sumit and Da vid P. Fidler. 2009. *India and Counterinsurgency: Lessons Learned*, New York: Routledge.

35. Garrett Laur ie. The Nightmare of Bioterror ism, *Foreign Affairs*, (January/February 2001), p. 76-89.

36. Gray Christine. 2004. *International Law and the Use of Force*, New York: Oxford University Press.

37. Greenberg Karen J. (ed.). 2005. *The Torture Papers: The Road to Abu Ghraib*, USA: Cambridge University Press.

38. Handbook on Human Rights and Fundamental Freedoms of Armed Forces Personnel. 2008. Published by the OSCE Office f or Democratic Institutions and Human Rights (ODIHR).

39. Haskell John D. The Complicity and Limits of Inter national Law in Armed Conflict Rape, *Boston College Third World Law Journal,* Vol. XXIX, (Winter 2009), No. 1, p. 78.

40. Haye E ve La. 2008. *War Crimes in Internal Armed Conflicts*, Cambridge: Cambridge University Press.

41. House John M. 2008. *Why War? Why an Army?* London: Praeger Security International.

42. Hoyt Timothy D. 2007. *Military Industry and Regional Defence Policy: India, Iraq and Israel*, London: Routledge.

43. Jain M.P. 2005. *Indian Constitutional Law*, Nagpur: Wadhwa and Company.

44. Jha U. C. 2009. *The Military Justice System in India: An Analysis*, New Delhi: LexisNexis.

45. ——————. 2010. *Armed Forces Tribunal*, New Delhi: Manas Publications.

46. Jia Bing Bing. The Doctrine of Command Responsibility: Current Problems, *Yearbook of International Humanitarian Law*, Vol. 3, (2000), p. 132.

47. Joseph, Sarah. & Schultz, Jenny. 2000. *The International Covenant on Civil and Political Rights.* New York: Oxford University Press.

48. Justin McClelland. The Review of Weapons in Accordance with Article 36 of Additional Protocol I,Vol. 85, *International Review of the Red Cross*, (June 2003), No. 850, p. 410.

49. Katherine E Cox. Beyond Self-Defence: UN Peacekeeping Operations and the Use of Force, *Denver Journal of International Law and Policy*, Vol. 27, (1999), p. 239-273.

50. Keir Starmer. Responsibility for Troops Abroad: UN Mandated Forces and Issues of Human Rights AccountabilityVol. 3 *European Human Rights Law Review* (2008). p. 318.

51. Kondoch Boris (ed). 2007. *International Peacekeeping*, UK: Ashgate.

52. Krishna Rao, General V.K. 1997. *The Genesis of the Insurgency in Jammu and Kashmir, and in the Northeast, and Future Prospects*, New Delhi: United Service Institution of India.

53. Kumar Brig. Nilendra. 2000. *Court-Martial and Military Matters*, New Delhi: Manas Publications.

54. Lanier-Graham, Susan D. 1993. *The Ecology of War: Environmental Impacts of Weaponry and Warfare*. New York: Walker and Company.

55. Leck, Christopher, International Responsibility in UN Peacekeeping Operations: Command and Control Arrangements and the Attribution of Conduct, Vol. 10, *Melbourne Journal of International Law*, (2009).

56. MacQueen Norrie. 2006. *Peacekeeping and the International System*, USA: Routledge.

57. Maresca Louis and Stuart Maslen. 2000. *The Banning of Anti-Personnel Landmines*, Cambridge: Cambridge University Press.

58. McCoubrey H. & White ND. 1996. *The Blue Helmets: Legal regulation of UN Military Operations*, Dartmouth Publishing Co Ltd, Aldershot.

59. Mertus Julie A. 2009. *The United Nations and Human Rights: A Guide for a New Era*, UK: Routledge.

60. Moir Lindsay. 2002. *The Law of Internal Armed Conflict*, Cambridge: Cambridge University Press.

61. Moskos, C., J.A. Williams, and D. Segal (eds.). 2000. *The Post-modern Military: Armed Forces after the Cold War*, Oxford: Oxford University Press.

62. Muray, J. Who will Police the Peace-Builders? The Failure to Establish Accountability for the Participation of United Nations Civilian Police in the Trafficking of Women in Post-Conflict Bosnia and Herzegovina, 34 *Columbia Human Rights Law Review*, (2003), p. 475-527.

63. Murphy, Ray. 2005. *UN Peacekeeping in Lebanon, Somalia and Kosovo*, UK: Cambridge University Press.

64. Navlakha Gautam. A Force Stretched and Stressed, *Economic and Political Weekly*, (November 18, 2006), p. 4722-24.

65. Nair Pavan. The Siachin War: Twenty-Five Years On, *Economic & Political Weekly*, Vol. XLIV, No. 11, p. 35.

66. Nigel D. White. The United Nations Char ter and Peacekeeping Forces: Constitutional Issues, *International Peacekeeping*, Vol. 3, (1996), p. 43-63.

67. Nolte, G. (ed.), 2003. *European Military Law Systems*, Berlin: De Gruyter Recht.

68. Ola Engdahl. Protection of Personnel in Peace Operations, *International Peacekeeping: The Yearbook of International peace Operations*, Vol. 10, (2006), p. 53-69.

69. Paulsson Jan. 2005. *Denial of Justice in International Law*, UK: Cambridge University Press.

70. Protection of the environment in times of armed conflict: Report of the Secretary General, UN Doc. A/47/328 (July 31, 1992).

71. Rant Judge J.W. 2003. *Court-Martial, Discipline, and the Criminal Process in the Armed Services*, New York: Oxford University Press.

72. Rauch, E. The Protection of the Civilian Population in International Armed Conflicts and the Use of Landmines, Vol. 24, *GYIL*, (1981), p. 262-283.

73. Ray Murphy. United Nations Militar y Operations and Inter national

Humanitarian Law: What Rules Apply to P eacekeepers? *Criminal Law Forum*, Vol. 14, (2003), p. 153-94.

74. Richardson, Mervyn. 1995. *The Effects of War on the Environment: Croatia*. London: E & FN Spon.

75. Roberts Adam. Transformative Military Occupation: Applying the Laws of War and Human Rights, *American Journal of International Law*, Vol. 100, July 2006, No 3. p. 580-622.

76. Roskill, Capt S.W. 1964. *The Art of Leadership*, London: Collins.

77. Rowe P. Maintaining Discipline in UN Peace Support Operations: The Legal Quagmire for Military Contingents, *Journal of Conflict and Security Law*, Vol. 5, (2000), p. 45-62.

78. ————. 2004. *The Impact of Human Rights Law on Armed Forces*, Cambridge: Cambridge University Press.

79. ————. Maintaining Discipline in UN Peace Support Operations: The Legal Quagmire for Military Contingents, *Journal of Conflict and Security Law*, Vol. 5, (2000), p. 45-62.

80. Sands, Philippe. 2004. *Principles of International Environmental Law*, UK: Cambridge University Press.

81. Sandoz, Y. Commentary on the Additional Protocols of 8 June 1977 to the Geneva Conventions of 12 August 1949, Geneva: ICRC.

82. Schabas William A. 2004. *An Introduction to the International Criminal Court*, Cambridge: Cambridge University Press.

83. Schlueter, D.A. 2004. *Military Criminal Justice: Practice and Procedure*, Virginia: LexisNexis.

84. Schmitt, M.N. Green War: An Assessment of the Environmental Law of International Armed Conflict', Vol. 22 *Yale JIL,* (1997), p. 1-109.

85. Schmitt Paul. The Future of Genocide suits at the ICJ France's Role in Rwanda and Implication of the *Bosnia v. Serbia* Decision, *Georgetown Journal of International Law*, Vol. 40 No. 2, (Winter 2009), p. 586.

86. Sepinwall Amy J. Failure to Punish: Command Responsibility in Domestic and Inter national Law, *Michigan Journal of International Law*, Vol. 30, No. 2, (2009), p. 255-56.

87. Shankar Shylashri. 2009. *Scaling Justice: India's Supreme Court, Anti-Terror Law, and Social Rights*, New Delhi: OUP.

88. Sharma, O.P. Rear Admiral. 1990. *Military Law in India*, Bombay: N.M. Tripathi Pvt. Ltd.

89. Shelton, D. 2005. *Remedies in International Human Rights Law*, Oxford: Oxford University Press.

90. Singh, Brig. K. Kuldip. 1998. *Overcoming Crisis in Leadership: Indian Army,* New Delhi: Manas Publications.

91. Sinha Lieutenant General S.K. 2008.Terrorism in South Asia and its Impact on India's Security, Proceedings of Seminar held at United Service Institution of India, New Delhi on 15 September 2008, USI Publication S-48, p. 6-7.

92. Sinha Manoj Kumar. 2010. *International Criminal Law and Human Rights*, New Delhi: Manak Publications Pvt. Ltd.

93. Tabak Shana. Article 24, War Crimes, and the Development of the Rome Statute, *Georgetown Journal of International Law*, Vol. 40, 2009, p. 1069-1099.

94. Thakur Ramesh. 2006. 'Chemical Weapons and the Challenge of Weapons of Mass Destruction', in Thakur Ramesh and Ere Haru (ed.), *The Chemical Weapons Convention: Implementation, Challenges and Opportunities*, Tokyo: United Nations University Press.

95. The Parliamentary Standing Committee on Defence, 31st Report submitted to Parliament on 21 Oct 2008. Report available at: <http://164.100.47.132/committeereports/Defence/31st%20Report-stress%20Management.pdf>

96. Thomas, William. 1995. *Scorched Earth: The Military's Assault on the Environment.* Philadelphia, PA: New Society Publishers.

97. Tonry Michael. The Functions of Sentencing and Sentencing Reform, Vol. 58 (1) *Stanford Law Review*, (2005), p. 37-66.

98. Trechsel Stefan. 2005. *Human Rights in Criminal Proceedings*, New York: Oxford University Press.

99. UN Doc. E/CN.4/2005/L.10/Add.11 (19 April 2005). *The UN Basic Principles and guidelines on the right to a remedy and reparation for victims of gross violations of international human rights laws and serious violations of international humanitarian law.*

100. UN Department of Peace-Keeping Operations, General Guidelines for Peacekeeping Operations, October, 1995.

101. UN DPKO, Handbook on United Nations Multidimensional Peacekeeping Operations, 2003.

102. UN Peacekeeping Operations: Principles and Guidelines, "Capstone Doctrine", 2008.

103. Weinberg, Bill. 1991. *War on the Land: Ecology and Politics in Central America*. London: Zed Books.

104. Westing, Arthur H. The Environmental Aftermath of Warfare in Viet Nam. *Natural Resources Journal*, Vol. 23, (April 1983), p. 365-389.

105. Williams, Jody. Land Mines: Dealing with the Environmental Impact, *Environment and Security*, Vol. 1, No. 2 (1997), p. 107-124.

106. Y Sandoz, Commentary on the Additional Protocols of 8 June 1977 to the Geneva Conventions of 12 August 1949, Geneva: ICRC.

107. Zappala, Salvatore, 2008, *Human Rights in Criminal Proceedings*, New York: Oxford University Press.